THE
WRITTEN
W**ORLD**
ESSAYS
&
REVIEWS

To Jamie, with all my love

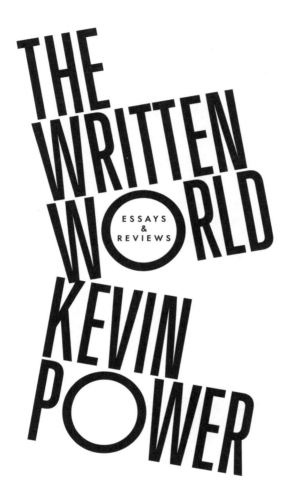

THE
WRITTEN
WORLD

ESSAYS
&
REVIEWS

KEVIN
POWER

THE LILLIPUT PRESS
DUBLIN

First published 2022 by
THE LILLIPUT PRESS
62–63 Sitric Road, Arbour Hill
Dublin 7, Ireland
www.lilliputpress.ie

Paperback ISBN 9781843518327

A CIP record for this title is available
from The British Library.

10 9 8 7 6 5 4 3 2 1

The Lilliput Press gratefully acknowledges
the financial support of the Arts Council/
An Chomhairle Ealaíon.

Set by Iota Books (www.iota-books.ie) in
11pt on 14.8pt Minion with Dunbar titling

Printed in Poland by Drukarnia Skleniarz

Contents

Short Takes

Envoi

Note & Acknowledgments

Herein, you will find ten years' worth of thinking about books, offered as a partial account of how I spent my time in the decade-plus gap between my first novel and my second (a more specific account of these years can be found in the first piece collected here). All of these pieces were written quickly, and the collection is therefore offered with all due modesty, not to say humility. In my defence, I would suggest that thinking about books is one way of thinking about life, and that thinking on the fly can be as useful in its way as the slower kind of thinking – but then, I would say that, wouldn't I? I'll take this opportunity to pay homage to some wonderful editors. To Nadine O'Regan, Thomas Morris, Jon Smith, Martin Doyle, and Tom Fleming: all my gratitude. And a particular thank you to Enda O'Doherty at the *Dublin Review of Books*, where most of the longer essays first appeared; in the most literal sense, this book would not exist without him. One last note: 'Apocalypse No' was delivered as the 2020 Nora Niland Lecture for the Yeats Society of Ireland; thanks to Susan O'Keefe for thinking of me.

Briefly Personal

THE LOST DECADE

I published my first novel in October 2008. At the time I was on the dole, trying and failing to get various jobs. I had spent three years studying for a PhD in American Literature that was nowhere near being finished. I owed money to my parents and to my landlord. My book had earned me precisely €4,000 – this was the advance paid by my Irish publisher.

A month after the book was published in Ireland, my agent sold the reprint rights in a two-book deal to a UK publisher for more money than I had ever made in my life. (Given that I had never earned more than €16,000 a year, this should not be taken for a particularly startling metric.) Then she sold the film rights. Then she sold foreign rights, to Spain, Italy, Germany, Slovenia, Brazil.

The success of *Bad Day in Blackrock* allowed me to become that superficially glamourous thing, a full-time professional writer. I moved into an apartment in the centre of Dublin with bookshelves lining the hallway. The apartment overlooked the courtyard of a busy hotel, which meant that every morning at 6 am I was awoken by the sound of glass bottles crashing into the recycling bin directly below my window.

On any given day, I did not have to write, if I didn't want to. And, more often than not, I found that I didn't. Instead I engaged in what I thought of as writing-adjacent (and therefore justifiable) activities: reading, writing book reviews, re-watching all seven seasons of *The Sopranos* on DVD, keeping a journal, rearranging my books, watching the 24-hour news channels (since a writer needed to keep up with the news), scrolling through my Facebook newsfeed, smoking, entering into various ill-advised romantic relationships whose ups and downs could plausibly be rationalised as the sort of 'experiences' a novelist might draw on when he did, at last, sit down to write, drinking in immodest quantities, taking drugs in modest quantities, and so on.

What I found, when I did at last sit back down to write, was that I was not a professional writer at all. I was still an apprentice – despite the fact that I had published a first novel, despite the fact that I was contributing regularly to various newspapers, despite the fact that people occasionally called me up and asked me to read at literary festivals, or to travel on promotional junkets to Italy, Serbia, Paris (where I smoked too much and drank too much and viewed other writers with a mixture of curiosity and scorn: who *were* these frauds, anyway?). It dawned on me only belatedly, but it was a devastating realization when it finally struck. My apprenticeship had not ended with the publication of *Bad Day in Blackrock*. It had barely begun. This was my peculiar fate: to find myself 'a writer' while I was still unformed, unknown to myself, and lacking utterly in the kind of discipline that a sustained career in writing requires.

Perhaps a version of the crisis that followed happens to every writer who publishes a first novel in their twenties – and years later, I was to come across Virginia Woolf's epistolary advice to a young poet, and nod savagely in assent: 'For heaven's sake, publish nothing before you are thirty.' Or perhaps it was mine uniquely. Dazzled by the sheer unlikelihood of what I had accomplished – by the fact that, as Nathan Zuckerman puts it in Philip Roth's *The Ghost Writer* (1979), 'I had miraculously made it from my unliterary origins to here,' to *being a writer* – I had blithely assumed that my apprentice years were over, that I would now simply write more books, in a kind of foreordained pattern of achievement that would lead me inevitably to the sense of repose that accompanies, or so I imagined, a serene and established literary middle age.

In fact, I was condemned to serve out those arduous years with a published novel already behind me. It is an open question whether those years were made easier by the fact of *Bad Day*'s existence – no, scratch that: they certainly *were* made easier, in some respects. I was freer than I might otherwise have been. I could get jobs teaching creative writing, an activity about which I quickly became passionate. I was invited to write short stories for anthologies, articles for newspapers. Not every apprentice enjoys such advantages, and I was very lucky to have them. Even so, those were the years I spent failing where, I imagined, it counted most: at the desk, on the page.

For years I had shaped my inner world around a single project (learn to be a writer), and I regarded anything that was not directly related to, or could not be rhetorically aligned with, this project as an imposition, a burden, an error. As defence mechanisms go, this is a luxury model. It keeps you safe from a thousand natural shocks, at least for a while.

I've never really suffered from 'writer's block', as that predicament is generally conceived. I have never opened up a Word document and found that I had no words to type. The problem, during my years of crisis, was that the words I *did* type, whenever I tried to write fiction, were worthless – what an avalanche of dismal prose I produced, during those years – and, more to the point, that I couldn't finish anything.

If my problem *had* been as simple as writer's block, I might, after a while, have abandoned my desk altogether. I might have gone off and done something else. And as it happened, I did, for a year, go off and do something else: in 2012, operating under stern instructions from various mentors, I finished my PhD thesis, working in terror right up to the deadline, writing all night, drinking cup after cup of coffee and chain-smoking Marlboro Lights, producing twenty or thirty pages a day in a state of reckless agitation indistinguishable from despair. I was able to write my thesis, I see now, because it wasn't fiction, and therefore I did not expect it to redeem my sufferings. I had not, after all, staked my entire sense of self-worth on writing academic literary criticism. And no publisher was waiting (that accursed two-book deal!) for my in-depth analysis of politics in the fiction and non-fiction of Norman Mailer. There was no pressure from the world; merely from myself. Why had I not finished my thesis in the first place? Because I didn't think I needed to bother. I was in the process of *becoming a writer*. We make the same mistakes over and over, until we see them for what they are.

2010: I wrote most of a play about the Irish financial crisis. (It ended, or was supposed to end, with Brian Cowen and Enda Kenny dancing a waltz across the stage to the tune of 'The Offaly Rover'. Oh, dear.) 2011: I tried to write a novel about the family of a disgraced banker. 2012: I cranked out two hundred crazed pages about a South Dublin rugby schoolboy on a business junket to Serbia (where I had spent a weird week promoting my book a few years previously). 2013: I wrote most of a novel loosely based on the murder of Meredith Kercher (an attempt, hideously misguided, to recapture whatever magic had animated *Bad Day*).

All of these projects consumed endless hours of my time and remained unfinished, unreadable, hopeless, dead.

Now, of course, I can see what all of these projects had in common, which is that they were impersonal, written not out of an honest attempt to understand my own experiences and to communicate that understanding to others, but out of ambition, undiluted: the ambition to *be a writer*. I was unable to write about the things that had happened to me (growing up; falling in love; flailing around in college and after: all the stuff that is usually taken by young novelists as their material) because I never thought about the things that had happened to me. I was too busy trying to *be a writer*.

Late in 2013, my confidence collapsed. There was no single cause. Rather, there were many causes. My agent had politely returned fifty pages of my Meredith Kercher manuscript along with a note, the unmistakable implication of which was that my novel was not good and that I should write something else. But I had no further ideas for novels. My contractual deadline was three years past. Examining my progress, I could no longer sustain the illusion that 'a writer' was what I was. Writers wrote books. I did not know how to write books. Ergo, I was not a writer. Worse, I was a fraud. A loser. A fool. I was also broke. I had been watching the not-that-large-in-the-first-place amount of money that *Bad Day* had produced dwindle steadily away for four years, consumed by rent, food, booze, books – and I had done nothing to arrest its outward flow, nor to procure another source of income. I had been operating on the assumption that I would somehow get my second novel written just in time to shore up the looming hole in my finances. Now this assumption stood revealed as the delusion it had always been. I had no second novel and no money.

I was prescribed Xanax for anxiety. I was prescribed Lexapro for depression. I took jobs in call centres, staffing the phones. My chief memory of this period – late 2013 – involves cycling along the Dodder (I was then living with my future wife in Ringsend), pushing the pedals as if against lead weights, and feeling as if my whole life was an overcast day: low grey cloud, empty streets, a dull, even pressure flattening everything, and no particular joy or hope to be found anywhere.

It took me a long time to climb out of my despair. Astonishingly (at least, it astonishes me now), I did not stop writing, even when things were at their bleakest – even during those long periods when I would feel the twist of rancour in my heart whenever I heard about another writer's success, or on those afternoons when my sense of despair and hopelessness was such that I could not bestir myself to get up from the couch. Failure forces you to see clearly – this is the one thing that can be said in its favour. Slowly, I came to see that, in trying to 'be a writer', I had been trying not to be a human being, that bleeding, undefended thing. I had been trying to avoid making what I saw, in my stupidity, as the various boring or distressing compromises that, properly understood, make up the substance of an actual life.

Stripped of its function as the thing that held my personality upright, writing gradually became a way of making objects to put in the world – a process that required the acquisition of certain skills, and therefore (what a thought!) a certain humility. The first step was to admit that I knew nothing – that I was still an apprentice, and that I should therefore act like one.

I started small. Doggedly, I completed the exercises prescribed in John Gardner's instructional handbook *The Art of Fiction* (1983). Then I tried a short story, salvaged from the ruins of my banker novel. I took my time. I wrote each paragraph carefully, walking a high wire of tension until the thing was, after two weeks, finished. It seemed good. It had its own integrity, I thought. I had made it, but that fact said nothing particular about me, beyond the fact that I was a man who had written a story.

I tried another story. It gave out. I tried another. I joined a writer's group, and submitted work. I began to write literary essays – long book reviews, really, but satisfying to do, and people seemed to like them. I came off Xanax, I came off Lexapro (I didn't miss the trembling legs, the nightmares, the overcast interior weather). I had no hopes of writing a novel. I began to think about my past, and about the ways in which I had used the idea of being a writer to cushion myself against uncertainty, and doubt, and fear. I began to admit to myself that I was angry, and that the source of my anger was, in large part, the success of *Bad Day in Blackrock* and its bewildering aftermath.

Publishing that book, I had been foolish, and young, and inexperienced. I had been completely unprepared for any kind of success – for the collision with a world that I did not understand and couldn't control. I was angry at myself for my failure to cope. And I was angry at the world for not being softer, kinder, less mercenary. (Naivety dies hard.) One day – this was in late 2015 – my wife and I went Christmas shopping in Blackrock. I was thinking about my anger. Half-quoting Dostoevsky's *Notes from Underground*, I thought to myself: *I am a sick man, I am an angry man.* I wondered if this might become the opening sentence of something: a short story, or a novel. A novel, perhaps, that might serve as an analogue for some of the things that had happened to me. And just a novel. Not a means of redeeming my life. More like: something to work on, while I lived.

An analogue for some of the things that had happened to me. A gallingly simple insight. But there it is.

Two years later, I finished the first full draft of *White City.* It was 2017. Things had changed. When I sat down at my desk and opened my laptop, I no longer imagined that the meaning of life was at stake. In fact, I began to feel that when I sat down at my desk, nothing much was really at stake at all. Just this sentence. And the next one. And the next one after that.

In my late thirties, I had started to grow up a bit, at last.

The Irish Times, 28 April 2021

Books/Life

A PERISHABLE ART

Okay, we're going to try an informal experiment here. This piece was originally intended as a more or less straightforward review of Megan Nolan's debut novel *Acts of Desperation* – the usual 1500-odd words on the book's merits and demerits (mainly merits, in this case), its contexts, its nature. I would locate the book, I airily told my editor, in the context of the Female Millennial Novel: Sally Rooney, Louise O'Neill, Louise Nealon, Lauren Oyler, Ottessa Moshfegh, Naoise Dolan, Ling Ma et al. But things went awry. Delays occurred. Suddenly it was June. *Acts of Desperation* was three months old. It had already been assessed – summarized, dissected, praised – in almost every possible venue. A straightforward review, my editor agreed, now seemed sort of pointless.

Hence, our experiment: not merely to review the novel, but to review, in a sense, both the novel and its reviews – to widen the context of our reflections, if possible. What are reviews of novels for? What is the state of contemporary book reviewing?

These are largish questions, which I hope to answer in suggestive, rather than definitive, ways. Let's not wade out into unmanageably deep waters here. This is not so much a review, then, as a metareview: a review of reviews. A review of reviewing itself.

Credentials: I've been a working book reviewer for thirteen years, during which time I have assessed in print, at a rough count, 350 books. Like Orwell's hack – Orwell did not approve of vocational book reviewing – I have been pouring my immortal spirit down the drain, half a pint at a time, since 2008. I've also been on the other side of this particular transaction, having published two novels that were reasonably widely reviewed. I have reviewed and I have been reviewed. One you have control over. One you do not. Guess which I prefer?

Context: perennial worry about the decline of the book review. Its latest incarnation: a widely circulated article by the Canadian critic Steven Beattie called 'What We Lose When Literary Criticism Ends' (*The Walrus*, 21 May 2021). 'These days,' according to Beattie, 'the status of the professional critic – that is, someone who can earn a living writing criticism for the general public – has largely been subordinated to enthusiastic amateurs giving thumbnail reactions.' In Canada, Beattie says, there is now 'hardly any' mainstream books coverage. No longer is it possible to make a living through criticism. This is a disaster, because, Beattie insists, 'serious works of literature require a response that is more nuanced, calculated, and considered than the rapid-fire rating system offered on user-generated sites such as Goodreads'.

An old complaint revisited, in part (it is possible, actually, to find nuanced responses on Goodreads, in amongst the rapid-fire ratings and the amusing misinterpretations of literary classics). For the apocalypse-minded, mainstream books coverage, like the novel itself, is always on the brink of death. But it is, I think, idle to assert that there is no longer a thriving literary-critical culture in the West. That culture exists: it has merely been, as the businesspeople say, 'siloed'.

You are interested in books. You find your way to certain online venues; you subscribe to certain journals (let's say, those occupying the *London Review of Books*-to-*New Left Review* spectrum). You read excellent criticism – in fact, you have a hard time keeping up with all the excellent criticism. It is clear to you as you read, however, that what you are doing is pursuing a niche interest. It is also clear that this niche interest is largely insulated from other niche interests and from whatever may be said to constitute 'mainstream culture'.

It is also clear to you that the critics whose work you are reading are not critics *tout court*. They do not earn their living exclusively from writing criticism. They have day jobs, side gigs, private incomes. They are often novelists themselves. In fact, book reviewing is pretty much the only sphere of cultural endeavour in which practitioners assess one another's work in public. Directors do not review each other's films. Billie Eilish does not rate albums for Pitchfork. The effect is often to alienate the general audience even further. Novelist-reviewers, people say, cannot be trusted, especially if they have a new book out. Allow me to say, in defence of novelist-reviewers, that we are generally scrupulous about not reviewing books by our friends. The blurb economy, of course, is another story.

Bearing all of this in mind: what we are looking at, just now, is a literary-critical culture practised as a vocation by a largely self-selecting but nonetheless hermetic elite. Or, as Zadie Smith remarked in a recent interview, 'Bottom line? Most people don't read.'

But this has always been the case. Complaints about the decline of book reviewing resemble other persistent narratives of cultural decay. Once there was a Golden Age, now everything is tarnished. This narrative is as true as you want it to be. At a guess, I'd say book reviewing right now is about as healthy – or unhealthy – as it ever was. Most reviews are bland: blandly written, offering bland appraisals. Some are memorably caustic. A small handful qualify as genuine criticism, reflecting on values. Lauren Oyler on Jia Tolentino, Leo Robson on Joyce Carol Oates, James Wood on almost anyone. I scroll through the book's pages hurriedly, looking for evidence of decline, finding the usual hopeless mixture. On the other hand, I may have a partial view.

When you do something professionally for thirteen years, you sooner or later stop asking theoretical questions about it. Rushing to meet this week's deadline, you seldom stop to ponder the nature and purpose of book reviewing. You file the piece, and crack open the next Advance Reading Copy (*BOUND PROOF – NOT FOR QUOTATION OR RESALE*). You are a conveyor belt of opinions. Good! Bad! Could be better! Could be worse! A certain deadening of the responsive faculties must inevitably occur. Most of the time, you have 800 words or fewer in which to say what, if anything, you think. For some books, 800 words is far too little. For most books, 800 words is far too much.

This is because most books are bad. We all know this, but we seldom say it. We could certainly stand to say it more. On the other hand, perhaps only the professional book reviewer, grimly digesting each season's fresh crop, really *knows* how bad most books are. Renata Adler, in her great 1980 essay on Pauline Kael: 'Normally, no art can support for long the play of a major intelligence, working flat out, on a quotidian basis. No serious critic can devote himself, frequently, exclusively, and indefinitely, to reviewing works most of which inevitably cannot bear, would even be misrepresented by, review in depth.'

Adler knew whereof she spoke. In 1968–9 she spent a year as the daily movie critic for *The New York Times*. The book that collects her reviews (*A Year in the Dark*, 1969) provokes, as it was surely intended to, the reflection that in any given year, most movies (most books, most TV shows, most operas or ballets or plays) are trash. The flattening of the faculties, across a lengthy stint of quotidian reviewing, is partly a consequence of exposure to instance after instance of subpar art.

Most art sucks. This is why critics get grumpy, develop crotchets, become impossible to please. Certainly I went through a crotchety phase – one suspiciously co-synchronous, I now see, with the prolonged struggle to finish my second novel. On the other hand, a bad review is hardly ever written out of mere spite. In most cases, the motivation for a hatchet job is disappointed idealism. Real critics are people who love art, and who hate to see it traduced. Hence the critic's sempiternal cry: *You're doing it wrong!* What the critic wants is for you to do it better.

Yes – oh dear me, yes: most art sucks. On the other hand, most art gets pretty good reviews. You can choose your own preferred recent literary example – I am not about to invoke the online Furies by naming Last Year's Most Overrated Novel According to Me. (Hint: it was shortlisted for the Booker Prize.) Has nothing changed since 1959, when Elizabeth Hardwick observed that 'sweet, bland commendations fall everywhere upon the scene; a universal if somewhat lobotomized accommodation reigns'?

Of course, it's generally true that, no matter how bad the art, *somebody somewhere* will like it. I like the music of Styx, for example, even though I know that by any reasonable standard of taste, Styx suck. We have observed this phenomenon recently on a large scale: lots of people liked *Game of Thrones*, even though, by any reasonable standard, etc.

However, the whole point of a professional reviewer is that he or she is supposed to speak *on behalf of* a reasonable standard of taste – not merely to express an ill-argued subjective preference, and not merely to go with the crowd (though as Norman Mailer noted years ago, 'very few people in the literary world have any taste – they are much too tense with fashion'). When we turn to professional reviewers, we do so in the expectation that they will do more than simply vent their hatred or their joy.

This brings us to what is, by tacit consensus, one of the main functions of book reviewing. In the same way that news reporting is supposed to be the first draft of history, periodical book reviewing is supposed to be the first draft of 'the canon', that evolving constellation of acknowledged achievement that exists not just for purely ideological reasons but because we seem to need it as a cultural heuristic (this is who/what we are). In practical terms, what this means is that the professional book reviewer should ideally demonstrate: 1) an awareness of technical considerations: prose style, focalization, structure, etc; 2) some sense of the history of the art form in question: is this new novel in dialogue with previous novels?; 3) some knowledge of the history of taste: people used to value certain books; now they value different ones, for different reasons, et cetera; 4) a high degree of emotional sophistication, aka sanity; 5) wide-ranging general knowledge.

It's a lot to ask of someone bound by the 800-word limit. But deprived of this equipment, the periodical book reviewer is reduced to providing a consumer information report. Thumbs up. Thumbs down. Five stars. None. If you liked that, try this. We have algorithms that can do this for us, now. The book review operates in the cash nexus, like any other piece of commercial copy. But unlike most pieces of commercial copy, the book review offers an opportunity to talk about questions of value. Most book reviewers fail to take this opportunity. We honour the ones who do take it by calling them critics.

The critic is engaged in the analysis of values, using this week's work of art as his or her pretext. If art, and particularly literature, is a kind of ongoing conversation, then criticism is the arena in which much of that conversation takes place; the critic, in offering his or her response to the work of art, is an answering voice, provoking, ideally, yet more questions, yet more answers, in the form of another work of art, another critical piece. Criticism needs art: this is obvious to say. Less obvious: art needs criticism. Writers learn from their reviews, especially from the bad ones. And readers glean access to elements of the artwork that they might otherwise have overlooked. Something like this, I think, is what we mean when we say that literary criticism is, or has the potential to be, an art unto itself.

A perishable art. But this is the point. The critic speaks to his or her contemporaries, not to posterity. Most reviewers are conscious that they are operating on a provisional basis. They are ready to be wrong about the book at hand. I gave Marilynne Robinson's *Lila* a stinker of a review ten years ago. Then I read more Marilynne Robinson, and then I read more criticism of Marilynne Robinson's work, and I learned that the critical tools I had brought to bear on her work (a snooty preference for the high style in prose; a putatively urbane condescension to novels that are unapologetically about religious belief) were risibly insufficient. But reviewers must be ready to look foolish. The reviewer for the *London Athenaeum* in 1851 called *Moby-Dick* 'so much trash belonging to the worst school of Bedlam literature'. Oh, dear.

Book reviewing – the front line of evaluative criticism – deals in superlatives. An instant classic! The worst novel ever written! Superlatives lose their cogency quickly; hence book reviews age quickly, especially if they consist of nothing but superlatives. Perishability is built into the form. Criticism is a form of journalism: day-writing. You have a deadline, a word limit. What you hope to produce is a stylish, accurate, informed report on a book that you have read. There is a remote hope that you will be able to articulate an *idea* – that is, give your readers a new thought. Of course this presupposes that you are capable of having a new thought in the first place. And you aren't, always. A happy consonance of novel and reviewer will tend to produce ideas; an unhappy consonance, quite the reverse. The empty mind reaches for clichés. A tour de force. Unreadable. Lyrical.

Reading reviews of your own work – tracking the clichés – you try to bear all of this in mind. The reviews of my own work that I find most valuable are those that have shown me a fault in that work that I couldn't have figured out on my own. But such reviews are rare – as rare, I like to think, as faults in my work. I try also to bear in mind the advice of Edmund Wilson, who, in 'The Literary Worker's Polonius', a now largely forgotten essay published in *The Atlantic* in June 1935, explained that

> for an author, the reading of his reviews, whether favorable or unfavorable, is one of the most disappointing experiences in life. He has been laboring for months or for years to focus some comprehensive vision or to make out some compelling case, and then finds his book discussed by persons who not only have not understood it, but do not even in some instances appear to have read it.

Wilson advised the writer to understand his or her reviews as 'a collection of opinions by persons of various degrees of intelligence who have happened to have some contact with his book'. What a sane thing to say. On the other hand, what you look for, in a review of your own work, is some engagement with technique, and some engagement with values. A rave is nice, but it teaches you nothing. A critique just might help you grow.

Keeping this experiment vaguely in mind, I avoided reading reviews of *Acts of Desperation*, so that, when I began the novel, all I knew was that it was about a toxic relationship. What would I make of it? How would it be reviewed? Would anyone articulate a useful idea? Reflect on values? Would the usual clichés appear? Compulsive. A page-turner. Taut. Relevant. Would it be called, as all novels by young women are now called, 'whip-smart'? (Yep: Sarah Gilmartin in the *Irish Times*.) We complain about book-reviewing clichés. But reviewing books is an adjectival business. Try reviewing a book without adjectives, and see how far you get. The trick is to find less careworn adjectives – to expunge cliché, to the extent that this is possible. What's a synonym for 'compulsive'? *Uncontrollable*, says Google. This uncontrollable novel …

Actually, *uncontrollable* wouldn't be the worst adjective to apply to *Acts of Desperation*. Frame it like this: *Acts of Desperation* is a tightly controlled novel about uncontrollable compulsions and desires. It's harrowing, brutal, unblinking. Adjectives! But it *is*. Setting: bourgeois-bohemian Dublin, 2012–14. Our unnamed narrator, age twenty-five, meets Ciaran, an art critic. They fuck. They move in together. Chapters are short. Paragraphs are short. The narrator and Ciaran: two emotionally maimed people who try desperately (see title) to extract from one another the meaning that their own lives seem to them so signally to lack. The narrator is profoundly self-knowing; also profoundly self-hating. The point is intensity. The relationship is intense, so the book is intense. All those short chapters and short paragraphs mean that the crushing weight of the book's intensity is evenly distributed. The principle is the same one that allows the mystic to lie down on a bed of nails. Interchapters, headed 'Athens 2019', offer perspective; these, too, are short, diaristic, intense.

This is yet another novel – why not say it? – by a millennial woman about having a horrible relationship with a complete bastard. Often I find the bastards in these books rather spectral – not fully realized. Possible PhD thesis: 'Spectral Bastards: Representations of Men in the Millennial Novel'. Examples, from two excellent books: Julian, the banker in Naoise Dolan's *Exciting Times*; Trevor, the banker in Ottessa Moshfegh's *My Year of Rest and Relaxation*. (Not all bankers? Maybe all bankers.) This is a neat reversal, I assume, of how women feel, reading novels by men about the bad relationships they have had with women. In other words: fair enough, although I might gently suggest that two aesthetic wrongs don't make an aesthetic right. In any event, I did not have this feeling as I read *Acts of Desperation*. Ciaran is extremely well-rendered, extremely believable. A visit to his grotesque father is one of many small points that explicate his unconscious misogyny. I *know* bastards like Ciaran. He feels real, as many of his counterparts do not, quite.

So. The largest context for this book is the fundamental crisis of modernity: what Max Weber called 'the disenchantment of the world', the supposed loss of wholeness or security engendered by the displacement of religion by secular science and industry. The unnamed narrator of *Acts of Desperation* recognizes that her addiction to obsessive love – her belief in the potential of obsessive love to abnegate the self in the name of something larger and more sacred – is essentially religious in nature. 'There was no religion in my life after early childhood,' she tells us, 'and a great faith in love was what I had cultivated instead.' Viewed from this angle, *Acts of Desperation* – note the echo of *Acts of the Apostles* – is a kind of parable about the void of meaning that faith leaves behind it when it goes. It's a serious book. Humour does not really feature. But my sense of it is that Nolan is trying to tunnel her way beneath irony, beneath humour, beneath wit. The medieval penitent did not pause between self-imposed lashes of the scourge to make quips.

Nina Renata Aron, reviewing the novel for the *Los Angeles Times* (3 March 2021), noted the religious language: 'Our narrator is lost to a devotion that borders on the religious. Here, Nolan often slips into cliché, drawing analogies to redemption or purification through love. Ciaran's body is a "site of prayer" and love a "force which would clean me".' Calling attention to clichés is one of the most devastating weapons in the reviewer's arsenal. But it often misfires. Nolan *knows* that her narrator's religious language is clichéd. Her narrator knows it, too. She says: 'Oh, don't laugh at me for this, for being a woman who says this to you. I hear myself speak.' Chapter 4 ends with a quotation from Romans (7:15-25): 'I do not understand what I do; for I don't do what I would like to, but instead do what I hate.' It is, as Marxists say, no accident that a quotation from St Paul, that great self-scourger in prose (and that exemplary misogynist) appears in this novel about a contemporary penitent (and a contemporary misogynist).

Immediately following the quotation from Romans is this: 'That night after meeting Ciaran I drank until I vomited and blood vessels beneath and above my eyes burst, and I traced them gently in the mirror, knowing they would be markers of a beginning.' The shift in registers tells us what this book is doing. The intensity is religious; the mode is contemporary-confessional, with an emphasis on the body. In other words, the mode of the book is that of the personal essay.

Nolan made her reputation with personal essays. What distinguishes her from the average personal essayist is not just her intensity of focus but the depth of her self-knowledge. Most confessions confess more than they mean to; most personal essays contain revelations that their authors did not intend.

It is difficult to imagine Megan Nolan confessing anything accidentally. One of the best reviews of *Acts of Desperation* took the form of a longish piece by Lamorna Ash for Sidecar, the blog of the *New Left Review*. Ash describes Nolan's 'writerly procedure': 'An event [...] prompts her to focus in on an aspect of her life she considers shameful.' This is, we reflect, also the method of *Acts of Desperation*. It anatomizes shame – its erotic power, its capacity to change us, and to change us back, afterwards.

Ash's review is one of the very few that express reservations about Nolan's novel. Most of the shorter pieces, published in newspapers, were raves: 'fierce', 'brave', 'fearless', 'real', 'poignant', 'extremely strong'. Adjectives! But the work of criticism, as opposed to the mere consumer notice, seeks the values beneath the adjectives, and lays them bare. Ash notes that *Acts of Desperation* can be read as occupying the same aesthetic continuum as Nolan's personal essays; however, for Ash, Nolan hasn't made the leap to novelistic expansiveness. Calling our attention to the 'Athens 2019' chapters, Ash points out that 'tonally, despite the intervening years there is no shift from the voice of the Dublin chapters, nor a convincing change in psychological distance from the relationship. This is a novelistic requirement, different in kind to that demanded by the essay.'

This is sharp, and tells us something about why the sort of intensity that animates personal essays may not necessarily work in a mixed form like the novel – tells us, in fact, that novels do not really work by intensity alone. For the novelist, modulation is all. And the problem with intensity, as an aesthetic principle, is that it doesn't do modulation; it makes something last that perhaps shouldn't. Life, after all, is *nothing but* modulation. Intensity, in life, doesn't last. Is it a worthwhile experiment, to write novels in the mode of the personal essay? Isn't that sometimes what we mean by *autofiction*? Often, in autofictional novels, the lack of modulation becomes wearying. Too much self and not enough other. Not enough world. It makes you – it makes me – nostalgic for the traditional social novel.

Also sharp is Philippa Snow in *The New Republic*. Her review of *Acts* begins thusly:

> The film critic Nicole Brenez once described Philippe Grand-rieux's 2002 film *La Vie Nouvelle*, with its raw style and frightening plot and reddish-purple, bruise-like palette, as having the air of something made 'inside the human body, not only physiologically, but also in the sense of showing everything that dwells within us'. The same might be said of *Acts of Desperation*, which is tonally and thematically bodily and alive – hot as viscera, inward-looking, dark and soft.

This struck me, because the textural word I had found myself applying to *Acts of Desperation* was not *soft* but *hard*. This is what led me to that bed-of-nails formulation above. The difference in responses might make us wonder about the utility of these textural words, applied to something textual. They are metaphors, of course, referring to style, and therefore to ideas about human character: some people are 'hard', some are 'soft'. What did I mean by 'hard'? Perhaps I meant that in my view it took hardness to write such a novel – to stare unblinkingly at mess, squalor, degradation, need, and to write it all down in crisp epigrammatic prose. But Snow's description of the novel as 'soft' is, I think, equally applicable: it *is* a novel about softness – the softness of bodies, but also the softness of selves, their porousness, their violability by the world, by other people; the softness that love both requires and provides.

This might be as good a point as any to note that all of the reviews I have been quoting from so far were written by women – meaning that the piece you are reading right now is a sort of *rara avis*, the only review of *Acts of Desperation* written by a man. No, wait: a review did appear in the Boston journal *ArtsFuse*, by a chap named Drew Hart. He refers to the narrator of *Acts of Desperation* as 'our lass'. I seem to have avoided doing anything quite this crass. Hooray for me? And wait again: Tadhg Hoey reviewed *Acts* for the *Dublin Review of Books*. His approach – an honourable one – is to proceed by careful description of what the novel is doing, step by step, while keeping critical commentary (on values, say) to a minimum. This kind of careful paraphrase is designed to render the book's subjects and methods transparent to us, and works, here, extremely well, though some ideas might have been more fruitfully developed. When Hoey writes, 'While this is undoubtedly a book about a uniquely female kind of suffering, Nolan has sublimated it so that it is neither cheap nor generic', we might legitimately ask for a bit more rumination on the idea of 'a uniquely female kind of suffering', especially as seen through the eyes of a male reviewer.

There has, I think, lately been a certain overcorrection at work, in the assigning of reviews. Literary editors have been giving novels by women almost exclusively to female reviewers. In an actuarial sense, at least, this is a near-necessity. As Anne Enright observed in her 2017 Fiction Laureate lecture, the vast majority of book reviews have historically been written by and about men, and even recent efforts to redress the balance have tended to see women writers writing about women writers, while the men keep reviewing each other – a practice that merely reinforces 'the old authoritarian style which liked to keep men and women separate'.

This is true. Replacing one monoculture with two – men reviewing men; women reviewing women – may redress the actuarial balance. But it impoverishes our conversation about books, and forecloses one of literature's utopian possibilities. Gender may be a social construct, but it has, of course, extremely real effects, and one of those effects is that men and women end up experiencing the world differently. If one of our hopes for literary fiction is that it might critique that difference and finally even, perhaps, transcend it, then the school-discoing of the book's pages – boys on one side of the dance floor, girls on the other, with occasional awkward clinches in the middle – will tend to undermine that hope.

There is no doubt that *Acts of Desperation* is a novel written self-consciously in response to recent feminist arguments about female agency and female victimhood. Hephzibah Anderson, writing in the *Guardian*, noted that 'this is a book with plenty to say about victimhood and sexual violence, about the way women censor their own needs and ironise or eroticise their abasement'. This is true. Nolan's narrator: 'Female suffering is cheap and is used cheaply by dishonest women who are looking only for attention – and of all our cardinal sins, seeking attention must surely be up there.' Aesthetically, the effect is to introduce a new and agonizing wrinkle into the narrator's self-consciousness: in telling her story of suffering, is she merely contributing to a long-established and corrupt tradition of female attention-seeking? Is it permissible, in 2021, to call attention to this corrupt tradition? Can the narrator be ironic about it? Can she be both ironic about her suffering, and earnest about it, too? Can she legitimately ask for attention for her pain, knowing that to do so risks confirming a poisonous stereotype?

A majority of the better reviews of *Acts of Desperation* makes a point of saying that Nolan has negotiated this labyrinth honestly and well. Philippa Snow, for instance, suggests that Nolan's narrator is 'cognizant enough of the absurdity of caring as much as she does about her body to lament it, and aware in equal measure of the gendered inevitability of her obsession'.

On the other hand, the book's invariant tone, and the limitations of its chosen confessional mode, might lead us to wonder whether *Acts of Desperation* poses its specifically contemporary feminist dilemma only to answer it with that old Derridian standby, the *aporia,* aka irresolvable ambiguity. As Lamorna Ash points out, the narrator of *Acts* does not really appear to have grown or changed much, at the end of the book. She has asked for attention. She has been earnest. Has the corrupt tradition of attention-seeking been altered, or escaped? Does the novel helplessly replicate an insoluble cultural paradox in which contemporary Western women have found themselves trapped?

My own answer to this question might go something like this: *Acts of Desperation* is a first novel by an author who turns thirty-one this year. In other words, Megan Nolan has just begun to do what she wants to do. I imagine that these questions will continue to preoccupy her, as she continues to think and to write; that she will find new answers, and new questions, as she goes. You don't, in other words, have to solve every problem first time out. I hope she has read some of the more incisive reviews; good criticism (in this case, the pieces by Philippa Snow and Lamorna Ash) is capable of suggesting to artists where they might need to look next.

If I were to venture into prescriptive territory myself, I might note that the tendency towards intellectual stalemate or *aporia* might actually be built into the confessional mode that Nolan has deployed so powerfully in *Acts of Desperation.* The confessional mode exalts not dialogue but soliloquy. How to escape the soliloquy? You might start with the dialectic – the heart of drama. Look for the antithesis, and go from there.

Well. What are the results of our informal experiment? Taking a broad if shallow view, I would suggest that book reviewing still serves, as it always has, too many masters. Sitting down to compose your 800 words, or, if you're lucky, your 4000 words, you must reckon with various obligations, some of which might just be mutually exclusive. You want, if you are human, to show off. You also want, if you are human, to make people like you – not quite the same thing. Your editor wants a snappy piece: not too academic, if you're writing for a newspaper; not too journalistic, if you're writing for a more upmarket journal. Your readers want to know if they should shell out for the book in question. The publisher wants you to write a rave – to serve, essentially, as a pliable adjunct of the publicity department. The author wants a rave that also teaches her something about her work. Your deadline looms. Integrity is at stake – not just your own integrity, but the integrity of criticism as a cultural and artistic practice.

Fairly regularly – regularly enough, anyway – the miracle occurs. Good criticism gets written. The critic negotiates her way through the clash of contending forces, and teaches us something about art, about values. Often, of course, the contending forces succeed in warping or deforming the final piece. The result is something that satisfies no one, and is, in general quickly forgotten (mere journalism). The collected reviews of *Acts of Desperation* do, I think, bear out this broad if shallow view. A festival of heavily adjectival raves, which we can safely ignore; two or three pieces of genuine criticism, for which we should all be grateful.

So, on balance, it's a wash. It always is. In the end, what we have is *Acts of Desperation*, a novel by a gifted writer; and, accompanying it, a handful of reviews that, read judiciously, might just help both its author and its readers to begin to do some thinking about what it is, what it means, and where we go from here.

The Stinging Fly, June 2021

DIFFERENT CLASS
On Ross O'Carroll-Kelly

1.

Like most non-rich people who are also not definitively poor, I first encountered the realities of class in college. To move from community-school three-bedroom semi-detached suburbia, where I grew up, to fee-paying-school six-or-seven-bedroom detached-house-with-atrium suburbia, where I went to university, isn't quite to enact the vertiginous class dislocation described by Mark Fisher in his 2014 essay 'Good for Nothing', in which he suggests that 'someone who moves out of the social sphere they are "supposed" to occupy is always in danger of being overcome by feelings of vertigo, panic and horror'. But a dislocation is what it was; and the revelation of privilege evidently struck me with such force that I have now written two books about it. And here I am, writing about it again.

I arrived at University College Dublin in September 1999: the very apogee of the Celtic Tiger. Traffic jams in general all over Ireland. Fianna Fáil and the Progressive Democrats in minority coalition government. Mary Harney's 'between Boston and Berlin' speech – defining Ireland's position in a boom-time neo-liberal world – just under a year away. Cocaine (invisibly) and Nokias (visibly) everywhere. People kept asking me where I'd gone to school. I didn't understand the question. 'Just school,' I would say. 'As in, the school up the road from my house.'

I am a slow learner. It took me three undergraduate years to work out what this oddly persistent line of questioning portended. One evening in the arts block, in September 2001, I ran into a recently made friend. He was scanning the results of a Maiden Speakers competition, posted on a noticeboard. 'A good night for Gonzaga,' he said. 'What's Gonzaga?' I said. (We betray our class by the things we say.) 'It's, ah …' My new friend wrung his hands and frowned. Just possibly, he had never been asked this question before. 'It's a school,' he said. 'It's my school.'

A school. But *Gonzaga*, evidently, was not like my school. For one thing, it came with you, when you went to college. For another, it appeared to command something like loyalty, or *esprit de corps*: to me, a mystifying notion. Gonzaga, it appeared, partook of a network of inter-school collaborations and rivalries. You could be *for* Gonzaga and *against* some other school, whereas in my experience, what you were, if you were anything, was against the whole concept of school itself. And one more thing. Your parents paid money so you could go to Gonzaga. Ergo, if you went there, your parents were rich. (Current per annum fee for attendance at Gonzaga College: €6,605.)

My curiosity was aroused. In tutorials, in the drama club, in the English Literary Society, in the offices of the college broadsheet, I started to ask people where they'd gone to school. 'Michael's,' they said, or 'Blackrock,' or 'Holy Child,' or 'Alex,' or 'Muckross.' They were everywhere! And they all knew each other! Class, when you first become aware of it, presents the aspect of a conspiracy in a pulp novel. *It's all connected!* I had stumbled, or so it felt, upon a closed and coded world: the world of the children of the rich. It was, in its way, an erotic discovery. By which I mean to say that my curiosity was aroused in both senses of the word. The revelation of the hidden structures of social class (if I may strike a Marxist-Freudian note) often evokes in us a feeling of erotic submission, though it is surely transgressing a taboo to say so. Not coincidentally – it may, in fact, be the same feeling – the discovery of social class also often evokes in us a desire for erotic conquest. Think of Julien Sorel in Stendhal's great novel *Le Rouge et le Noir*: the archetypal striver from the provinces, who determines that the swiftest way to advance in life is simply to sleep his way to the top; or of Becky Sharp, his female counterpart, in Thackeray's *Vanity Fair*.

And then there was the world of the rich themselves, which it turned out was more or less coterminous with 'the world', i.e. the public and professional world that presented itself to your attention when you read the newspapers or listened to the radio. Judges, barristers, academics, architects, property developers (lots of these), businessmen, bankers, TDs, GPs, consultants, writers, editors, journalists … And then there were the houses. Georgian, or Edwardian, or simply bespoke McMansion, with pianos, pool tables, conservatories, plum-coloured carpets, imported rugs, Eames chairs, wood-burning stoves, Sabatier knives in the kitchen, framed art on the walls …

Operating (so I felt) as an interloper or spy, I attended parties in houses with built-in steam rooms, or landscaped gardens, or libraries. At these parties, people frowned when I told them the name of the village in south-west Dublin where I'd grown up. 'Rathcoole,' one girl said. 'Oh, yeah. I think we drive past there on the way to the stables.' One of my college girlfriends (Loreto Foxrock) referred casually to growing up in 'a normal six-bedroom family house'. A Gonzaga grad I knew referred casually to his school's tennis courts and theatre. A female friend (Alexandra College) once complained: 'Our school had no money. We had to fix our hockey sticks with gaffer tape.' We betray our class by the things we say.

To another college girlfriend (Holy Child), I explained that hanging out with all these private-school kids had afforded me the stupidest, and also the most indispensable, of political epiphanies: *These people are rich and they'll grow up to run the country.* 'I have to write about this,' I said. 'Oh,' she said. 'You should read Ross O'Carroll-Kelly.'

2.

Because someone was already writing about it: the *Sunday Tribune* sports journalist Paul Howard. By his own account (in a preface to the reissued and rewritten 2004 O'Brien Press edition of the first Ross book, *The Miseducation Years*), Howard first encountered the world of South Dublin fee-paying schools when the *Irish Independent* asked him to cover a schools rugby match in Skerries in 1989. Howard grew up in Ballybrack and describes his own background as 'working class'. He didn't even know the rules of rugby at the time. 'I must have done okay,' he writes, 'because shortly afterwards I was asked to cover a match involving Blackrock College. [...] My first Rock match was when my eyes were truly opened to the extraordinary social phenomenon that was schools rugby.'

Howard notes that Ross O'Carroll-Kelly, the Senior Cup Team goon whose initials ostensibly encode the name of his fictional school, Castlerock, but which actually, as everyone knows, encode the name of Blackrock College, cohered in his imagination when he watched 'a young buck with the confident bearing of a five-star general' stride off the pitch and say to his father, 'I don't give a fock how you think I played – just crack open the wallet.' We betray our class by the things we say.

The Ross O'Carroll-Kelly column – 'The Diary of a Schools Rugby Player' – began running in the now-defunct *Sunday Tribune* in 1998. The first book, *The Miseducation of Ross O'Carroll-Kelly*, was turned down by mainstream publishers and printed by Howard himself under the *Tribune* banner in 2000. In interviews, Howard has recalled having to pulp half of the first print run. A sequel, *Roysh Here, Roysh Now: Ross O'Carroll-Kelly – The Teenage Dirtbag Years*, in which Ross goes to UCD, appeared, again under the *Tribune* aegis, in 2001. These first two books were successful enough to be picked up and repackaged by the O'Brien Press between 2004 and 2005; since 2007, Ross has been published by Penguin Ireland, at the rate of at least a book a year. According to the *Irish Independent*, Ross hit 1 million sales in 2014. There have been four successful plays, most recently *Postcards from the Ledge* (2017). A plaque commemorating RO'CK adorns (or adorned, at one point – I have not been able to check if it is still there) the bathroom wall of Kiely's in Donnybrook: Ross's favourite pub. We might also mention the statue of Ross erected in Eason's on O'Connell Street. *Normal Sheeple*, the twenty-third Ross book, debuted at number one on the *Irish Times* bestseller list in August of this year.

We love RO'CK!

Should we?

3.

Then again, this raises a question: who do I mean when I say *we*? Who reads Ross O'Carroll-Kelly? His subjects – the targets of his satire? Partly, yes. Here's Howard, talking to *The Journal* in 2017: "'Oddly with Ross, people tended to recognise their friends rather than themselves,' he says. Friends in bookshops would tell him about sailing jacket-wearing teens reading the book and exclaiming "that is SO loike Tiernan'". On the other hand, Tiernan's mates, chortling in bookshops, simply aren't numerous enough to make up a readership that buys 1 million copies. Who else reads Ross? Statistics on the actual readership of a given book are impossible to come by. We can only speculate. My own guess: the majority of Ross's readership is made up of people who are not themselves members of the South Dublin ruling class, but who have nonetheless found themselves professionally adjacent to it, via the various routes of class mobility available to Irish people in the twenty-first century (chiefly free university education, which was introduced by the Rainbow Coalition government in 1996).

In other words, Ross's fans tend to be members of the Professional Managerial Class: university educated, corporate but not C-suite (you find them in HR), working for NGOs, or in tech, or in academia, or in journalism, or in medicine (though not as consultants) … Well-paid but financially insecure – vulnerable, that is, to large-scale economic shocks. Socially liberal (voted Yes in 2015 and 2018). Anxious about manners (crusaders for the 'appropriate'). Anxious about status (to be in the middle is to sit in the Status Hot Seat). Most of Ross's fans, I would hazard, grew up somewhere that is not South Dublin. But they know South Dublin well. Most likely, they went to college there. These are the people who love RO'CK. These are the people I mean when I say *we*.

4.

Here's a quick and dirty theory. Up until the mid-nineties, Ireland had a well-demarcated class system: small elite, small lower-middle class, big underclass. Then neo-liberal policies of global deregulation sparked a boom in foreign direct investment, leading to various social transformations: free university education, net immigration, more and better jobs, cheap air travel … If the history of Ireland over the last thirty years tells a story not so much of increasing liberalization as of large-scale class mobility, then one of the lessons of this story is that the demarcations of our class system have become during this time simultaneously more permeable and more visible.

As the tide of neo-liberalism waxed and waned (and waxed again), people who had grown up working class looked around to find themselves occupying a spot somewhere in the lower-middle class. People who had grown up lower-middle class now found themselves hanging out with the really rich – or at least watching them from unwontedly close quarters. As of the mid-2000s, you have something new in Ireland: a large PMC underwritten by cheap credit and deeply anxious about its status, colliding socially with the established ruling class. This is the context in which Paul Howard begins to write the first RO'CK columns. And it's still, I would argue, the context in which the Ross books are written and read.

When class barriers become visible, you get a crisis of manners. How should the PMC comport itself, when, in this unstable new order, it encounters its rulers, or its subalterns? What constitutes rudeness, in a given interaction? What constitutes politeness? Can you express your envy and fear aloud, or should you sublimate them? Make anxious jokes? In *The Politics of Magic*, his 1987 study of the work of Tom Murphy, Fintan O'Toole writes about manners in an industrial society: 'Discipline, self-control, deferring to others, keeping one's impulses in check – these are the things which the lower orders had to be taught for them to be useful in industry.' As our PMC learned new manners, becoming useful in the new neo-liberal industries, what happened to their impulses – all that envy, all that ambition, all that ressentiment?

5.

One answer: we began to use Ross O'Carroll-Kelly as a kind of psychological safety valve. The PMC is the sole constituent Irish social group who do not appear in Howard's pages. Still unformed, and still unstable, they (we) are not yet fully valid subjects for sharp-eyed social satire. But we are interested – as who is not? – in seeing ourselves on the page. In our project of collective self-fashioning, we seek encouragement and help. Works of non-fiction that describe us using the blunt instruments of pop sociology have prospered: for instance, *The Pope's Children: Ireland's New Elite* (2005) and *Renaissance Nation: How the Pope's Children Rewrote the Rules for Ireland* (2018), both by David McWilliams. In the latter of these books, the PMC is described as 'Ireland's radical centre' – 'the common people who, through their tolerance, respect those around them. They can be found in the background, beavering away, and are driven by the expectation that tomorrow will be a little bit better than today'. They are therefore the real, if unacknowledged, 'heroes of the great Irish economic transformation'. Isn't it pretty to think so?

If McWilliams flatters the Irish PMC directly, the Ross books perform the same service obliquely. The Ross books tell us that our social betters are venal, idiotic, boorish – objects of mockery. They also tell us that those below us are endearing chancers, or operators, or gangsters – objects of a more nervous kind of mockery. In *Normal Sheeple*, Ross's granddaughter, Rihanna-Brogan, takes part in a 'jiddum kada' (gymkhana) in 'the cor pork of The Broken Orms Pub in Finglas'. Like Rihanna-Brogan, the other working-class girls who compete in the car park gymkhana own horses: 'The first rider out ends up being eight-year-old Shania Madden from Con Colbert Terrace in Coolock, on her albino pony, Henrik Lorsson,' et cetera. This is funny. But if it wasn't so obviously a caricature, and if Howard had not lavished substantial care and attention on making his characters feel likeable and real, it might read uncomfortably like a satirist punching down.

As it is, the jiddum kada scene offers food for cogitation. Halfway through the event, Ross observes Kennet, Rihanna-Brogan's grandfather, injecting Rihanna-Brogan's pony, Moxy, with a stimulant, at the direction of Hennessy Coghlan-O'Hara (the unstoppable Charles O'Carroll-Kelly's equally unstoppable partner in evil). The upper classes and the lower classes, working together for nefarious ends: isn't this the political eventuality that, in its darkest moments, the PMC most fears? An unholy alliance of rich and poor was the very conjunction decried by the larger Western Professional Managerial Class in the aftermath of Donald J. Trump's victory in the US Presidential election of 2016 (all those rednecks, voting Republican) and in the aftermath of the 2016 UK Brexit vote (all those shopkeepers, voting Tory). There is a sense in which Ross uncovering a doping scandal at the gymkhana channels the deepest terrors of the Irish PMC and, in the same moment, flatters them implicitly: after all, the jiddum kada in the cor pork of The Broken Arms is for the corrupt rich and the vulgar poor. It's certainly not for members of the PMC: custodians of the appropriate, hard-working backbone of 'the radical centre'. Beneath its surface comedy, the scene at once awakens our fears and flatters our self-conceptions: we are neither vulgar nor corrupt; we are the people of the decent middle.

Heavy stuff to tease out of a jokey scene in a popular novel, perhaps. Grant me a point worth making. Beneath their explicit satirical focus on the South Dublin ruling elite, the Ross books have an implicit subject, and this implicit subject is, I would suggest, identical with the implied readership of the books. The books are in this sense 'really' about the new Irish Professional Managerial Class: its fears, its ambitions, its uncertainty about manners. The one social class whom Howard does *not* satirize – how can the PMC be anything other than the great absent presence of his books? The satirist – the comedian of manners – holds up bad behaviour to ridicule: so goes the cliché. But the question must always be asked: to *whom* is the satirist showing this bad behaviour? And to what end? We members of the PMC love Ross, in part, because he behaves so badly and thus teaches us, in our uncertainty and self-regard, to behave well. By being 'inappropriate', Ross affirms the rightness of our own 'appropriate' behaviour, about which we live in constant doubt.

Aiding in the self-definition of Ireland's new PMC: this is one function that the Ross books serve. Another is this: they offer us a means of articulating our ambivalence about the ruling class – our covetousness, our envy, and our hatred (emotions that often derive from a sublimated eroticism). The books tell us, repeatedly, that our elites will always act to protect their own material interests, and that we should not be charmed by them, no matter how sexy or funny or morally inconsequential we find them. In *Normal Sheeple*, a late aside reveals that J.P. and Christian have been working with Charles O'Carroll-Kelly all along to sell Ireland to the Russians for profit. The effect is shocking, because for the previous four hundred pages, we've watched J.P. and Christian take part in trivial sex-farce subplots. Our rulers serve themselves: the books remind us of this fact repeatedly. They gratify overtly our secret contempt for the powerful. On the other hand, Ross is a 'beloved character'. There he sits, at the heart of our popular culture, reminding us that our society is unjust; that our elites are shallow and self-serving; and that materialist greed is a hollow pursuit. We love him. We think he's great. And his family and friends, that nest of vipers: we love them, too. Should we? Of course we should. That's how class works. The Ross books enable us safely both to love and to fear our rulers; to envy their wealth and to disapprove of their behaviour; to experience naked capitalist ambition and sheer class hatred at one and the same time and without contradiction; to map the shifting landscapes of an increasingly unstable world.

6.

This is to make a socio-psychological claim for the value of the Ross books. What about literary value? Are the books any good *as books*? Paul Howard's name doesn't appear on the cover of any of them; only on the title page: 'As told to Paul Howard.' This is a conceit, of course. Howard, we are invited to assume, is simply transcribing what Ross, a real person, tells him (the conceit was made explicit, not entirely successfully, in one of the more peculiar Ross books, *We Need to Talk About Ross* [2009], in which Paul Howard, appearing as himself, interviews his own creations). But those words – *As told to* – have, I've always thought, another meaning, having to do with language, accent and class, and with the places, literary and otherwise, where these things intersect. State it plainly: Paul Howard's great literary gift is his ear; and the central aesthetic assumption underlying the Ross books is, *We betray our class by the things we say.*

Think, for a moment, about how little visual imagery there is in the Ross books – how utterly dependent they are on voice. Not just Ross's voice: a Babel of other voices. Ronan, Ross's working-class son, who says, 'Ine Arthur fookin' it up, Rosser. Enda bleedin' stordee.' The Northern Irish guy Ross meets at a wedding, who asks him: 'Did yeh drave op?' The Nigerian woman who calls Ross 'Rosockeral Kelly'. We don't really read these books. We hear them. And we hear them because Howard hears them first. His books are heard. In fact, they're overheard.

In the acknowledgments of *The Miseducation of Ross O'Carroll-Kelly*, Howard offers 'MAJOR gratitude to Dublin Bus. Thank you for the 46a, a rich source of material'. In 2001, the 46a was the bus that went from the city centre to Dún Laoghaire, stopping at or near Trinity College, Leeson Street, Donnybrook, UCD, Stillorgan, Foxrock, and Monkstown. To travel on the 46a was therefore to travel through the heart, not just of South Dublin (the geographical location) but of 'South Dublin' (a place located both in the mind and in the bank account).

Taking notes on the 46a: a local version of the sort of reportorial work praised in Tom Wolfe's perennially unpopular 1989 essay 'Stalking the Billion-Footed Beast'. Here Wolfe argued that novelists should eschew postmodernist involution and stare reality (the Billion-Footed Beast) in the face; that they should operate in emulation of Zola, with his 'documenting expeditions to the slums, the coal mines, the races, the *folies*, department stores, wholesale food markets, newspaper offices, barnyards, railroad yards, and engine decks, notebook and pen in hand'. For those of us who feel that a novelist's job is to speak to his or her contemporaries, and not to some notional literary or academic posterity, and to those of us who think that social satire is and always has been the heart of the novel, Wolfe's essentially populist argument still carries a furtive appeal. And it seems safe to suggest that people who feel this way are often also people who, beginning somewhere on the lower end of the social scale, have been forcibly struck at some point in their lives by the reality of class, and have been thereby aroused to outrage, sceptical curiosity and erotic desire: the Holy Trinity, if you ask me, of writerly impulsions.

In any event, the 46a clearly did Paul Howard a lot of good. His dialogue is sublime, and it has been sublime since the first chapter of the first Ross book ('Don't get too drunk now, Ross,' says Ross's father in *The Miseducation of Ross O'Carroll-Kelly*, to which Ross replies, 'Yeh roysh! I'm HORDLY likely to on forty focking quid now, am I?') As of *Normal Sheeple*, this dialogic sublimity remains unadulterated. Examples: 'Vanessa Orlean? She did German and Neuroscience in UCD. She pulled me off around the back of the Wicked Wolf the night Ireland lost to Scotland in the Foot and Mouth Six Nations' – Ross speaking. 'Would anyone be interested in sponsoring my cleaner, who's doing a ten-day virtual walk of either the Pennines or the Apennines in aid of fibrodysplasia?' – Ross joins a Mount Anville mums' WhatsApp group. 'Thank you. Even though the priority for me isn't to win TV debates, Mallorie – it's a net-zero corbon emission rate in the medium term' – Sorcha O'C-K becomes Minister for Climate in Charles O'C-K's new government.

Language is where the considerable literary worth of the Ross books lives. Take Ross's narrative voice, which, after twenty-three books, remains tuned to an exquisite pitch of comic surprise. 'Yeah, no, the old pair invited us around to the Áras for, like, an intimate family dinner – we're talking me and Sorcha, we're talking Ronan and Shadden, and we're talking Hennessy and a prostitute named Davina, who comes from Russia and looks like Emmy Rossum.' Or this:

> Sorcha is wearing her famous Stella McCortney trouser suit – the one that says she is not a woman to be focked with. I once saw her reduce a clamper to tears while wearing it, after she porked her Nissan Leaf in a bus lane to run into Donnybrook Fair for a tub of sweet pea saffron hummus and possibly pitta pockets.

That *possibly*: superb. Or take the virtuoso run of pages, in the middle of the book, in which Ross accompanies his daughter Honor to the Gaeltacht, where he meets a teacher named Marianne, who is, naturally, a Sally Rooney character (although she's less Marianne from the novel *Normal People* and more Daisy Edgar-Jones as Marianne in the TV version); at the same time, Ross is invited to join the local over-50s Gaelic football team. In these pages, Howard's comic ear is operating with maximum brilliance across a range of registers. The Kerry footballers all talk like characters from J.M. Synge (a running joke, whenever Ross visits rural Ireland, and perhaps an intimation that the Ross books and their readers half-share Ross's Dublin-centric sense of things): 'And isn't it my blood that shivers whenever I think of that cursed town! You see, there is great spite between our two peoples. 'Tis a bitterness as old as Brandon itself!' When Ross and Marianne flirt, it sounds like this:

'So how *are* you?'
'Grand.'
'Good to hear.'
'And you?'
'Cracking form.'
'I'm sorry I—'
'It's cool.'
'—just forgot something.'
'It happens.'
'The man had already started putting my messages through—'
'Hey, it's not my first time in a supermarket.'
'And I remembered I didn't get—'
'Toilet roll.'
'Yes.'
'So I see.'

Meanwhile, Ross's father – now head of the New Republic party and Taoiseach – is tweeting Trumpishly: 'For too long, farmers have had it all their own way with their EU grants and their FFG friends bending over backwards to please them!' (CO'CK is never without his exclamation marks – as in, *never*.) And mediating, as always, is Ross's narration: 'I literally haven't set eyes on the woman since that scene on the beach in Ballydavid a week ago and it's as awks for me as it is for obviously *her*?' Howard's prose, like the world, is polyphonic. He vanishes into the way his characters speak. What do you call this, if not art?

Closely allied with Howard's ear for language is his eye for the markers of social class. Sorcha's Nissan Leaf (electric, of course). The sweet pea saffron hummus. The Stella McCartney trouser suit. 'Do you know where my Molton Brown is?' Sorcha asks, in *Should Have Got Off at Sydney Parade* (2006). 'Just grab my Skinfresh Facial Wash, my Skinfresh Toning Lotion, my Active Defence City-Day Hydrator, my Skinboost …' In fact, Sorcha – the emptily liberal fashion victim – is a fount of material specificity. 'You even agreed it'd go amazing with my Thierry Mugler white chiffon dress,' she says, in *Rhino What You Did Last Summer* (2009). We betray our class by the things we buy.

Among their other virtues, the Ross books are master-pieces of denotative realism. A century from now, an interested cultural historian will be able to reconstruct a near-total catalogue of contemporary upper-middle-class lifestyle accoutrements from Howard's pages: the clothes, drinks, food, make-up, coffee machines, music, movies, actors and actresses … Denotative realism is out of fashion in the academy and in the upper-echelon mainstream literary journals, and has been for a long time. Mere denotation, the argument goes, is de-universalizing, hence unaesthetic. Following Barthes, we are meant to dismiss itemized catalogues of stuff in fiction as mere 'reality effects', evoking a specious verisimilitude. Obeying an ancient writing-class nostrum, we are meant to believe that brand names date fiction unacceptably. The hell with this. So what if fiction dates? The Ross books are ours, not posterity's. We can use them however we like.

7.

So how do we use them? As mirrors, partly. *Pace* Stendhal, who said that a novel must be like 'a mirror carried down the high street', reflecting impartially what it sees: mirrors are not neutral messengers. We bring to them our moods, our pasts, our immediate contexts, and we interpret carefully what we behold (some days you hate how you look; some days you like what you see). When I read Ross O'Carroll-Kelly, I can see Ireland in the mirror. I don't always see the same thing, of course. The country I tend to see most often, however, closely resembles the England described by George Orwell in 1941: 'a family with the wrong members in control'. How do they rule, these people who shouldn't rule at all? Can we unseat them? Should we? Don't we admire them, sneakily, in our darkest moments? Don't we fancy them, hate them, covet their expensive lives? Ross allows us to think these things with a clear conscience, even if we aren't quite ready to utter them aloud.

It follows that we should also use Ross as a kind of counsellor. In his company we find ourselves auditioning our hidden impulses, fashioning ourselves in the image of our various taboo desires. Our rulers might see themselves clearly in Howard's pages, should they choose to look. The rest of us can see ourselves indirectly. Thus we examine ourselves in Paul Howard's ambiguous light. The popularity of Ross O'Carroll-Kelly, as a cultural phenomenon, occupies a highly unstable fault line: the place where the self-interest of our ruling elite meets the sublimated ressentiment of everyone else. Ross began as a joke. Now he's something like our therapist: a place to put all of the vertigo, panic and horror that attends any genuine confrontation with the realities of class in the twenty-first century.

As a bonus – as more than a bonus – there's the language. We betray our class by the things we say. On every page of every book, Paul Howard betrays his membership of the highest class of popular writer. In *Normal Sheeple*, Christian winds up dating the much younger Lychee Greenhalgh, daughter of one of CO'CK's ministers and (in Ross's words) a 'gorgeous idiot'. In Kiely's:

> Christian's like, 'Drink, Lychee?'
>   And she goes, 'I'm going to have a Cab Sav, but I'll get it because I want to film myself pouring it!'

> Ross comments: 'That's, like, word for word.'
> But then, it always is.

The Stinging Fly, October 2021

PRETENTIOUSLY OPAQUE

What the hell *was* Literary Theory, anyway? *Jouissance.* The death of the author. Phallogocentrism. The metaphysics of presence. Binary oppositions. Hegemonic discourses. Subaltern narratives. Necropolitics. Biopower. Bentham's (or is it Foucault's?) panopticon. The male gaze. The cultural logic of late capitalism. The unconscious is structured like a language. There is nothing outside the text. Are any of these ideas useful, or true?

There exists a whole alphabet of textual warriors, from Althusser to Žižek, to tell you that they might be both. There also exists a whole panoply of university departments to tell you the same thing. On the other hand, the twenty-first century has already brought us books with titles like *After Theory* (Terry Eagleton, 2003), and *Criticism After Critique* (ed. Jeffrey R. Di Leo, 2014), and *The Limits of Critique* (Rita Felski, 2015). Are we finished with Theory? Is Theory finished with us? Did Theory change the world, while it had the chance? Did it even manage to change literature?

Novelists of a certain vintage have tended to endorse a rather florid scepticism about Theory. In A.S. Byatt's *Possession* (1990), Roland Michell – a humble Romanticist and devotee of old-fashioned archival research – misses out on a job that goes instead to Fergus Wolff (note the surname) who is 'in the right field, which was literary theory'. (Later in the novel, we find ourselves privy to Fergus Wolff's idea of a love letter: 'Did you read Lacan on flying fish and vesicle persecution?') Delphine Roux, the prying, puritanical villain in Philip Roth's *The Human Stain* (2000), is a Literary Theorist who graduated from the École normale supérieure. 'Isn't he a structuralist?' asks Sefton Goldberg, the protagonist of Howard Jacobson's *Coming from Behind* (1983), of one of his academic rivals; the insinuation is that such a man exhibits a slavish vulnerability to intellectual fashion, and is therefore not to be trusted.

Chip Lambert, the 'well-published' Theorist in Jonathan Franzen's *The Corrections* (2001), exhibits a similar vulnerability, and pays for it heavily. Contemplating his volumes of Theory, Chip (the author of a PhD thesis entitled 'Doubtful It Stood: Anxieties of the Phallus in Tudor Drama') remembers 'how each of them had called out in a bookstore with a promise of a radical critique of late-capitalist society, and how happy he had been to take them home'. The problem is that all of these critiques of late-capitalist society have availed Chip nothing; fired from his tenure-track job for sleeping with a student, he is forced to sell 'his feminists, his formalists, his structuralists, his poststructuralists, his Freudians, and his queers' in the Strand bookshop for $115 (having already 'purged the Marxists from his bookshelves' for $65 – and that word, *purged*, is superbly chosen). Thereafter, Chip buys dinner in the Nightmare of Consumption, a high-end supermarket that has co-opted Theory's critique of late capitalism and ironically tracks its own projected quarterly dividends via an in-store digital banner.

This sequence neatly dramatizes what we might think of as the liberal-pragmatic objection to Theory: that it has failed to change the world, and that its various revolutionary insights have been swallowed so effortlessly by the omnivorous jaws of capitalist modernity that the whole project of critique boils down to nothing more than an embarrassing form of arm-chair radicalism (Chip is scandalized when his petit-bourgeois father confesses that he 'can't see the point' of Literary Theory – but it is Alfred's view, not Chip's, that is borne out by the novel). So: according to a certain kind of novelist, Literary Theorists are (or were) wolfishly predatory, villainous and hopelessly trendy (if they operated in bad faith); or (if they operated in good faith) politically impotent; devoted to a radical critique that has no hope of effecting radical societal change.

According to another kind of novelist – let's just say it: a younger kind of novelist – Literary Theory is less a source of reactionary agitation than it is simply a part of the air that bright young people breathe, particularly if they have been, or are currently going, to university. Frances, the protagonist of Sally Rooney's *Conversations with Friends* (2017), chills out with Gayatri Spivak's *A Critique of Postcolonial Reason* (1999), though she admits that she doesn't really understand much of what she reads in its pages; more to the point, her conversations with her friend and former lover Bobbi tend to deploy Theoretical tropes in a way that is both ironic and serious, a habit that carries over into Frances's inner life: 'Have I sometimes exploited a reductive iteration of gender theory to avoid serious moral engagement ... yes.'

Ava, the 22-year-old narrator of Naoise Dolan's *Exciting Times* (2020), is fresh from her BA, and hyperalert to any suggestions of racism or misogyny underlying the attitudes of people she encounters in the wider world. She notes that the TEFL school she works for in Hong Kong has a 'racist' recruitment policy but that her employers approve of her coldness towards the children she teaches: 'I found this an invigorating respite from how people usually assessed women.' Later, she remarks to her lover Edith that 'not like nice guys' is 'such a misogynist trope'.

Unlike Frances, Ava does not speak the language of Theory (no 'reductive iterations' here). Nonetheless, she is transparently proceeding from various assumptions inculcated by a Theoretical education. Outside of their novels, both Rooney and Dolan have made statements that draw on a hinterland of Theoretical axioms. 'Ethically I felt opposed to individualism, never mind market liberalism,' Rooney wrote in the *Irish Times* in 2017. And Dolan, in her own *Irish Times* appearance last month, remarked that 'it is strange to me that anyone wants to know about my life just because I write novels [...] I consider political, historical, social context; but I do not care about personal minutiae.'

Behind these statements lurk the ghosts of Marx (the great philosopher of anti-individualism, or, if you will, of 'political, historical, social context') and of Barthes and Foucault (the thinkers who hoped to sever once and for all the umbilical connection between author and text). These are thinkers that Rooney and Dolan certainly encountered during their years studying English at Trinity – because they are thinkers encountered by anyone who undertakes an English degree in the Age of Theory (1966 – present [?]). All those radical critiques: have they made a difference, after all? If only to the ways in which intelligent young people think about themselves, their art, and the world? Is that enough? Is this what Literary Theory wanted, or promised?

The short answer to this latter question is No. But the long answer might begin with another question: why would you expect literary criticism to change the world? Why *literary criticism*, of all things? Especially, when you get right down to it, a literary criticism that sounds like this:

> Literature as well as criticism – the difference between them being delusive – is condemned (or privileged) to be forever the most rigorous and, consequently, the most unreliable language in terms of which man names and transforms himself.
>
> (Paul de Man, *Allegories of Reading*, 1979)

Or like this:

> If, for a while, the ruse of desire is calculable for the uses of discipline soon the repetition of guilt, justification, pseudo-scientific theories, superstition, spurious authorities, and classifications can be seen as the desperate effort to 'normalize' *formally* the disturbance of a discourse of splitting that violates the rational, enlightened claims of its enunciatory modality.
>
> (Homi K. Bhabha, *The Location of Culture*, 1994)

Or like this:

> The move from a structuralist account in which capital is understood to structure social relations in relatively homologous ways to a view of hegemony in which power relations are subject to repetition, convergence, and rearticulation brought the question of temporality into the thinking of structure, and marked a shift from a form of Althusserian theory that takes structural totalities as theoretical objects to one in which the insights into the contingent possibility of structure inaugurate a renewed conception of hegemony as bound up with the contingent sites and strategies of the rearticulation of power.
>
> (Judith Butler, 'Further Reflections on the Conversations of Our Time', 1997)

These last two examples – the Bhabha and the Butler – took prizes in the annual Bad Writing Contest, run by the journal

Philosophy and Literature between 1995 and 1998, which aimed to celebrate 'the most stylistically lamentable passages found in scholarly books and articles'. Certainly these bits of phrase-making are obdurately undecodable, and not just to the lay reader. Tackling them gives rise to that characteristic feeling, the one we have when we read pure Theory: of swimming in a dark sea, from which elusive fish of meaning periodically emerge, displaying their marvellous, glittering scales, only to vanish once more in the murk.

This is the one thing that everybody knows about Literary Theory: it is difficult to read. The difficulty of Theory has always been intrinsic both to its prestige and to its notoriety, a binary not-quite-opposition neatly dramatized in the scene from *Conversations with Friends* in which Frances reads, or at least holds, *A Critique of Postcolonial Reason*. Terry Eagleton, reviewing that very volume for the *London Review of Books* in 1999, spoke for many when he said:

> Post-colonial theorists are often to be found agonising about the gap between their own intellectual discourse and the natives of whom they speak; but the gap might look rather less awesome if they did not speak a discourse which most intellectuals, too, find unintelligible. You do not need to hail from a shanty town to find a Spivakian metaphorical muddle like 'many of us are trying to carve out positive negotiations with the epistemic graphing of imperialism' pretentiously opaque.

Pretentiously Opaque would perhaps have made a good alternative title for *The Meaninglessness of Meaning*, a slim volume collecting some of the *LRB*'s best writing on 'the Theory Wars', ranging from Brigid Brophy's review of Colin MacCabe's *James Joyce and the Revolution of the Word* (1979) to Adam Shatz's essay-portrait of Claude Levi-Strauss (2011), and touching, via essays on various gurus, on most of the key Theoretical points in between: Pierre Bourdieu on Jean-Paul Sartre; Richard Rorty on Foucault; Michael Wood on Roland Barthes; Frank Kermode on Paul de Man; Judith Butler on Jacques Derrida; and Lorna Sage on Toril Moi, among others. Pretentious opacity is not, of course, the sort of thing you tend to find in the *LRB* – as Adam Shatz notes in an elegant introduction, 'you'll never see a piece of "pure" theory in the *LRB*', because the paper is committed to 'the kind of lucid exposition of ideas that theorists have rejected in favour of a more Baroque, circuitous, self-consciously rarefied style'. *The Meaninglessness of Meaning* is therefore a partial (and inevitably lopsided) record of how Theory fared once it ventured past the campus gates and found itself wandering the streets of the metropolis. More or less useless, I would imagine, to anyone who doesn't already know something about Theory, it nonetheless provokes some interesting reflections on the world that Theory made – which is our world, whether we like it or not.

In its early, more combative, years, the *LRB* perhaps overdid its hostility to Theory. Karl Miller, the paper's first editor, announced in the inaugural issue: 'We are not in favour of the current fashion for the "deconstruction" of literary texts, for the elimination of the author from his work.' So speaks the old guard of liberal humanism, in 1979. We might note that Miller himself could have used a tincture of Theory – just enough, perhaps, to stop him from assuming that all authors must be male. But this is to write with Theory in the rear-view mirror. In 1979, the *LRB* looked as if it would offer aid and shelter to those among the literati whom Theory made tetchy. Thus Brigid Brophy, reviewing Colin MacCabe's *James Joyce and the Revolution of the Word* for the paper, has a high old time demolishing MacCabe's pretentious opacity, wielding the wrecking-ball of common sense.

MacCabe, Brophy writes, has 'no discernible literary talent'. His Theoretical musings laboriously reinvent the wheel: 'One type of discourse, he says, consists of "the object-language (the marks held in inverted commas)". By this, it presently proves, he means dialogue.' And MacCabe frequently perpetrates his own version of the higher nonsense:

> My own favourite among the theories Mr. MacCabe redacts and reports on is one that originated with a French critic and maintains that in an epic the readers 'know that the hero is good and the villain is bad', whereas a novel 'suspends these disjuncts for the course of the narrative – is the hero good or bad? – only to affirm a final identity and with this affirmation to retroactively deny the suspense produced by the narrative'.
>
> [This is] a theory according to which not only is *Vanity Fair* (that 'novel without a hero') not a novel but the *Iliad* and the *Odyssey* cannot be epics, since the one has no hero and other has a hero whom the reader doesn't always know to be good.

Match point: Brophy. Of course, mocking cherry-picked gobbets of fatuous prose is one of the cheapest tactics available to the enemy of Theory (or to the advocate of one particular Theory over another – Terry Eagleton, in his review of Gayatri Spivak, assumes the stance of hard-headed dialectician, scolding the woollier postcolonial school for its refusal to face Marxist facts). Plenty of Theoretical writing is pretentiously opaque (or, might, like MacCabe's book on Joyce, best be described as supererogatory). But to dismiss all of Theory on the grounds of fatuousness or pretentious opacity – we might call this the bluff-empiricist objection to Theory – is to shirk the responsibility of discovering what might be interesting or useful in the Theoretical canon.

Of course, this raises the question of just what we might mean by 'interesting' or 'useful'. Interesting to whom? Useful for what? 'Radical academics,' Terry Eagleton writes in his review of Spivak, 'one might have naively imagined, have a certain political responsibility to ensure that their ideas win an audience outside senior common rooms.' For Eagleton, the point of Theory is clear: not to interpret the world, but to change it. And if that's what you think Theory is for, then it is sensible to propose that your Theoretical analyses err on the side of intelligibility. (Although to anyone familiar with Eagleton's own efforts in the Theoretical field, his criticism of Spivak on grounds of unintelligibility has an inescapable tinge of irony: on finishing *The Function of Criticism* (1983), Eagleton's book about the eighteenth century, a few years ago, I found it hard to dismiss the suspicion that I now knew less about the eighteenth century than I had when I started.)

Most Theorists would probably accept the suggestion that their work is intended to be 'radical', and to have 'radical' effects on its readers, and, through them, on the world at large. Radical: of the root. If academics don't think about the roots of things, who will? On the other hand, the phrase 'an academic question' is not just a piece of casual slander, and much of the comedy of the Age of Theory has arisen from the disparity between what Theorists talk about (destroying late capitalism, reordering gender hierarchies, queering the future and so on) and what they actually do all day (look at documents; read books and talk about them). Twenty years ago, as an undergraduate studying English – fresh from the Leaving Certificate English curriculum, which was, in those days, still vestigially Leavisite – I used to wonder why so many of my lecturers appeared to be more interested in overturning bourgeois liberalism than they were in reading novels. *If you wanted to be a revolutionary*, I used to think, *why did you become a professor of English?*

This is, of course, both a naive question and an extremely sophisticated one (though I was certainly being naive and not sophisticated when I asked it). Nobody told me this at the time, but I had begun my study of English just as the discipline was negotiating its way out of a forty-year-long identity crisis – the Theory Wars, as the *LRB* would have it. On one side of the Wars stood the Theorists, who sought, having been defeated by the forces of the bourgeois state in the late 1960s, to transform the English department from a redoubt of dilettantish connoisseurship into a hotbed of revolutionary agitation. (They called it 'the long march through the institutions'.) On the other were people who felt that Theory constituted an onslaught on both common sense and basic morality and that there was absolutely nothing wrong with a little bit of dilettantish connoisseurship: wasn't that the essence of civilization, after all?

This is the conflict dramatized in the best novel about the Theory Wars, Malcolm Bradbury's *The History Man* (1975). Howard Kirk, the History Man of the title, is a lecturer in sociology at the fictional University of Watermouth, and a Theorist *avant la lettre*. The History Howard embodies, or wishes to embody, is Marx's History: the unstoppable march of the communist revolution. To bring about the end of bourgeois capitalism, Howard will stop at nothing. He lies, cheats, schemes, compels his doubting wife to swing, abuses his students, sleeps with everyone. Opposing Howard, in the novel's moral scheme, is Annie Callendar, an introverted and self-doubting lecturer in English. Howard seduces her, of course. One of the lines he uses is from Blake's *Proverbs of Hell*: 'Sooner murder an infant in its cradle than nurse unacted desires.' Annie points out that the proverb is a trap – that the 'unacted desires' *are* the infant we should murder in its cradle. 'So that's what you do over there in the English department,' Howard muses. Thus Bradbury very neatly suggests that what Annie does (spot the moral nuances in a text before they trip us up) represents a serious improvement on what Howard does (harangue his students on charges of 'bourgeois individualism'; write a book calling for 'the death of privacy'). That Howard seduces Annie is a nice bit of allegory: Howard, here, is radical left-wing Theory, and Annie is poor old insecure untheorized literary criticism, helpless before the swaggering charm of History.

In 1975 the History Man was a sociologist. If the novel had been written a decade later, he would have been a Literary Theorist – and he would have stayed a Literary Theorist, if Bradbury had thought to update his book at ten-year intervals. The answer to the question, Who won the Theory Wars? is, of course, Theory. Not Annie Callendar's reticence but Howard Kirk's radicalism has become the dominant style in university departments of English. But *The History Man* raises an interesting question: what is Howard Kirk, the enemy of bourgeois privilege, doing in a university in the first place? Why isn't he out storming the barricades, or organizing cadres of workers? Bradbury's answer is sly: teaching in a university allows Howard to indulge his bourgeois-individualist desires for comfort and freedom while permitting him to remain politically right-on. This is the satirist's answer, of course: Theorists are hypocrites. And this is also the satirist's answer to the question, Why would you expect literary criticism to change the world? You wouldn't; but if you act as if you do, you might just get to have your cake and eat it.

A more charitable answer to this question might point out that you would only expect literary criticism to change the world if you had already exhausted all the other options. If Theory has appealed strongly to people who happen to be non-rich, non-male, non-white, non-cis, or non-straight (or all of the above), this may be because it has helped them to create powerful accounts of their lives, and because it is easier to change minds in the seminar room than it is on the hustings, or on the factory floor. Not every Theorist is Howard Kirk (just as not every liberal humanist is Annie Callendar). One of the recurrent objections to Theory has taken the form of a complaint that it promotes moral and epistemic relativism. This objection has been voiced by highbrows (Allan Bloom, *The Closing of the American Mind* [1987]), middlebrows (Michiko Kakutani, *The Death of Truth* [2018]), and nobrows (Jordan Peterson, *12 Rules for Life* [2018]). Bloom blames Theory (he calls it nihilism) for the incuriosity and apathy of kids today. Kakutani blames Theory (she calls it postmodernism) partly for the rise of Trump. Peterson blames Theory (he also calls it postmodernism) for eroding traditional masculine ideals. As objections to Theory go, this is among the more foolish, but it is also among the more sinister. The alternatives to moral and epistemic relativism are, of course, moral and epistemic absolutism; and when they argue for a universe of non-relative values, these thinkers are often expressing, whether they know it or not, a barely disguised hunger for a world in which minorities knew their place and stuck to it. To the extent that Theory has helped to drag us at least partway out of this world, it has been an unmixed good.

A version of this point was made by John Sturrock when he reviewed Alan Sokal and Jean Bricmont's *Intellectual Impostures: Postmodern Philosophers' Abuse of Science* for the *LRB* in 1998. Sokal is a physics professor at NYU, who in 1996 submitted a hoax article to *Social Text*, then as now a prominent Theoretical journal. Sokal's article was called 'Transgressing the Boundaries: Towards a Transformative Hermeneutics of Quantum Gravity', and it was, as Sokal put it, 'liberally salted with nonsense', including the claim that quantum gravity was socially constructed. The editors of *Social Text* published the article, Sokal maintained, because it 'flattered [their] ideological preconceptions'. The point of the hoax was that Theorists were borrowing scientific ideas without grasping what they actually meant and using them to give their radical politics a patina of legitimacy; according to Sokal, if you couldn't trust

Jacques Lacan when he talked about topography, you would be an idiot to trust him when he talked about psychoanalysis. (It hadn't occurred to him that the people who went to Lacan for his reflections on psychoanalysis were capable of understanding his topographical language as a metaphor.)

Sokal restated his argument in *Intellectual Impostures*, written in collaboration with another physicist, Jean Bricmont. *Intellectual Impostures* is fun to read for a chapter or two, but, as Sturrock notes, its critique of Theory is based on a series of misprisions, and in place of imaginative thinking and writing, it argues for a narrow scientism as the only legitimate way of understanding the world. Sokal and Bricmont complained that the Theorists (to call them 'postmodern philosophers', as per their subtitle, is to suggest that you do not know very much about either postmodernism or philosophy) preferred a tricksy 'verbal veneer' to clear language expressing hard facts. Sturrock counters with the example of Jean Baudrillard, a writer for whom 'the "verbal veneer" is the very thing; so that to read it as a disguise rather than a display is to misread it in a particularly philistine and irrelevant way'. Sturrock's larger point is that there is no imaginative writing without moral and epistemic relativism. Art is a free country, and so is thought; and the essence of that freedom lies in the recognition that there is always another point of view. You could call this recognition '*différance*', if you happen to be a Theorist; or, if you're of a more liberal-humanist persuasion, you could simply call it irony, or play. It is hardly surprising that an intellectual movement founded on this recognition was taken up by women, people of colour, queer activists and so on; nor is it surprising that this should have caused some blowback from the more privileged parts of society. A more recent hoax, in which three right-leaning scholars submitted bogus articles on what they called 'grievance studies' to various journals, ended up saying more about the flaws in academic publishing than it did about Theory, but, once again, the unspoken message was reactionary in import – one of the hoaxers, Helen Pluckrose, is the author of a book complaining that Theory has 'made everything about race, gender, and identity'. *Quelle horreur.*

If *l'affaire* Sokal constituted a major skirmish in the Theory Wars, then the case of Paul de Man probably counts as a small war unto itself. Probably the best piece collected in *The Meaninglessness of Meaning* is Frank Kermode's extended rumination on the posthumous disclosure of de Man's wartime journalism. Writing in 1942 for the Belgian newspaper *Le Soir*, de Man – then in his twenties – published an article on 'the Jews in modern literature', which included sentences along the lines of this one: 'It is sufficient to discover a few Jewish writers under Latinized pseudonyms for all contemporary production to be considered polluted and evil.' At the time of his death in 1983, de Man was the most celebrated of the Yale Deconstructionists – the author of *Blindness and Insight* (1971) and *The Resistance to Theory* (1986), works distinguished, in Kermode's words, by an 'ever-increasing density and strangeness'. When de Man's collaborationist journalism came to light in 1987, the Theory-resisters pounced: here at last was irrefutable evidence that Theory was rotten to the core; that its antipathy to bourgeois liberalism was fascism in a new dress; and that its expositors in the academy were not to be trusted. (It may have been the de Man affair that led the bestselling right-wing horror writer Dean Koontz to create, in his 2003 thriller *The Face*, a serial murderer whose day job is teaching Deconstruction to university students.)

Kermode is properly severe about de Man's anti-Semitic journalism, observing that the wartime writing is 'odious, that of a clever young man corrupted by ideas, and corrupted by war (for in wartime the intellect grows as sordid as the conflict), or merely opportunist, or a mixture of all of these'. But he is not so intellectually gauche as to imagine that it easily or simply discredits de Man's later thought, or Theory itself. Louis Menand, writing for *The New Yorker* in 2014, observed that Theory 'has never really recovered its reputation' in the aftermath of the de Man case. But the fact that Theory has faded from public view may be less a function of specific scandals and more a function of Theory's inescapable absorption into the cultural mainstream – its gradual but undeniable de-radicalization, as its language and concepts migrate from the graduate seminar and the peer-reviewed journal to the Twitter feed and the op-ed column. When online ironists refer to 'the discourse', they are telling us that Theoretical ideas are now part of our everyday armature of concepts; and as Louis Menand points out in his essay on de Man, the hostility to Theory was always strange, because to express a preference for one text over another is already to hold a Literary Theory – the point being that Theory, taken *in toto*, merely made visible certain things that we had in a sense been looking at all along.

The Meaninglessness of Meaning charts the gradual transformation of Theory from exotic financial instrument to the pocket change of the intellectual economy, a process coextensive with the years during which the Theorists themselves died and become the stuff of respectful obituaries. Thus the gender theorist Judith Butler, memorializing Jacques Derrida for the *LRB* in 2004, writes:

> Derrida kept us alive to the practice of criticism, understanding that social and political transformation was an incessant project [...] How is justice done? What justice do we owe others? And what does it mean to act in the name of justice? These were questions that had to be asked regardless of the consequences, and this meant that they were often questions asked when established authorities wished that they were not.

This is as eloquent a defence of Theory as you could hope to find: a moving claim for its continued relevance in a world shaped, in constantly changing ways, by power and by those who resist it. But it's worth noting that the terms in which Butler makes her appeal channel a radicalism that any liberal might approve of. We had come a long way, by 2004.

There are certainly problems with the world that Theory has helped to create – it does sometimes feel as if we are stuck with an intellectual culture that, at its worst, devotes itself to finding misogyny, racism and capitalist greed in texts like prizes in boxes of breakfast cereal, and that in teaching us to see the politics in every text, Theory has left us unable to see anything *but* the politics in every text. In her 2015 book *The Limits of Critique*, Rita Felski observes that in the contemporary academy, 'rigorous thinking is equated with, and often reduced to, the mentality of critique [i.e. Theory]. The result can be a regrettable arrogance of intellect, where the smartest thing you can do is to see through the deep-seated convictions and heartfelt attachments of others'. Or, as Susan Sontag noted, back in pre-Theoretical 1963, 'Interpretation is the revenge of the intellect upon art.' On campus, at least, things seem to be changing: Felski herself is an influential advocate of 'post-critique', a school of criticism that seeks to add ideas about emotion, affect, aesthetics and form to the Theoretical menu. Which sounds oddly like liberal humanism to me – but there you go. As John Sturrock notes here, *pace* Sokal and Bricmont, 'The more styles of intellectual discourse cultures find the room and time for, the healthier.' This should go without saying. But if Theory has taught us anything, it's that nothing – literally nothing at all – ever goes without saying. Or, to put it another way: *La théorie est morte, vive la théorie!*

The Dublin Review of Books, June 2020

Contemporaries and Otherwise

MARTIN AMIS
Wilde at Heart

Novelists are great makers of personal pantheons – although very few novelists have been as consistently frank about their fetishes as Martin Amis. Reading Amis's literary criticism – the essays and reviews collected in *The Moronic Inferno* (1986), *Visiting Mrs. Nabokov* (1993), *The War Against Cliché* (2001) and now *The Rub of Time* (Jonathan Cape, 2017) – you quickly discover that the Amis Canon shakes down to an austerely cultivated handful of Approved Writers. Shakespeare, John Updike, J.G. Ballard, William S. Burroughs (once upon a time), Anthony Burgess (sort of), Philip Roth, Iris Murdoch (maybe), Joseph Heller (the early stuff), James Joyce (ditto), Philip Larkin, Don DeLillo (with reservations), Jane Austen … Oh, and don't forget Saul Bellow and Vladimir Nabokov, whom Amis describes, in the new book, as his 'Twin Peaks'.

These are the writers about whom Amis has written most feelingly and most often, and a good number of them duly shuffle onstage in the course of *The Rub of Time* to be bigged up or shot down, according to the iron laws of the Amisian aesthetic standard. Updike is briefly praised ('Updike's prose, that fantastic engine of euphony, of first-echelon perception'), before his final volume of short stories, *My Father's Tears* (2009), is dissected and found to consist of 'a blizzard of false quantities'. DeLillo is admired ('this luminous talent') but then there are those pesky reservations ('The great writers can take us anywhere; but half the time they're taking us where we don't want to go'). Bellow, of course, is fulsomely lauded ('His was and is a pre-eminence that rests not on sales figures and honorary degrees, not on rosettes and sashes, but on incontestable legitimacy') and escapes censure. So too does Nabokov ('the words detach themselves from the everyday and streak off like flares in a night sky') – although upon revisiting the darker precincts of the master's oeuvre, Amis finds himself no longer quite so keen to defend or excuse V.N.'s lifelong fascination with the sexual despoliation of prepubescent girls ('You will, I hope, admit that the hellish problem is at least Nabokovian in its complexity and ticklishness').

So, as of 2017, the Amis Canon is still in order, with only some mild fluctuations in market value to trouble us (Updike, down ten at close; invest heavily in Bellow futures). With remarkable consistency, Amis has been praising more or less the same small group of (mostly male, definitely straight, definitely white) writers for four decades now. He even uses them to critique one another: 'Bellow is quite unlike, say, Vladimir Nabokov and John Updike, to take two artist-critics of high distinction.' Amis's critical insights are drawn from deep familiarity with a rigorously winnowed corpus. There have been no lately discovered enthusiasms; no essays in praise of younger novelists; certainly none in praise of writers from non-Anglophone countries (with the obvious, and meaningless, exception of

Nabokov); and, increasingly, no full-length pieces about women writers of whatever vintage. (An essay in *The Rub of Time* on how Jane Austen's novels have fared at the hands of filmmakers was originally published in *The New Yorker* in 1995.) In much the same way, Amis's critical principles, across forty years of reviewing, have remained intransigently firm. 'Only connect the prose and the passion,' instructed E.M. Forster, at the crux of *Howards End* (1910). For Martin Amis, of course, the prose *is* the passion – or perhaps I should say, the passion is the prose.

To make Team Amis, you must be a writer, not necessarily of brilliant novels, or even of brilliant chapters, but of brilliant sentences and brilliant paragraphs. Amis's critical method is to quote the bits he likes – the brilliant bits – and to point out why he likes them; or, conversely, to quote the bits he doesn't like, and to point out that they are clichés. He is up front about this: 'When I dispraise,' he explains, in the Foreword to *The War Against Cliché*, 'I am usually quoting clichés. When I praise, I am usually quoting the opposed qualities of freshness, energy, and reverberation of voice.' Nobody is better than Amis at filleting a text for good bits. In his memoir, *Experience* (2000), Amis quotes a passage from Nabokov's short novel *The Eye* (1930), in which the narrator, contemplating suicide, reflects that

> to sit down and write his will would be, at that moment, an act just as absurd as winding up one's watch, since, together with the man, the whole world is destroyed; the last letter is instantly reduced to dust and, with it, all the postmen; and like smoke, vanishes the estate bequeathed to a non-existent progeny.

'All the postmen,' Amis comments: 'that is genius.' And, of course, he's absolutely right: it *is* genius. Amis has identified the precise moment at which this passage moves beyond the merely literary and becomes instead something terrible and strange. As a cicerone, Amis has few equals. He greets you at the gates of the garden, and, with exquisite tact, escorts you to the flowers that bloom most beautifully – and just in case you're curious, he has all the taxonomic and botanical information at his fingertips, too.

But the obverse of a keen eye for the good bits is, of course, a sharp eye for the bad bits, and Amis the gardener is also an unsparing rooter-up of literary weeds. Look again at his review of Updike's *My Father's Tears*, in which he offers this example of 'a sentence that audibly whimpers for a return to the drawing board': 'He was taller than I, though I was not short, and I realized, his hand warm in mine while he tried to smile, that he had a different perspective than I.' Ouch. Or, from the same review, this 'quatrain' of clunkers:

> ants make mounds like coffee grounds …
> polished bright by sliding anthracite …
> my bride became allied in my mind …
> except for her bust, abruptly outthrust …

For four decades, Amis has been a redoubtable antagonist of this sort of thing: of 'internal rhymes and chimes' in prose. He will unfailingly pounce on 'sentences that resemble train wrecks – "the cook took a look at the book" etc'. These last two phrases are taken from Amis's 1980 essay on V.S. Pritchett, who is, according to Amis, guilty of perpetrating such 'jangles' as 'Sitting behind the screen of the machine.' Amis forgives Pritchett, on the grounds that 'the effect is entirely appropriate to his way of looking at life', but his tone ('This is surely a feminine style of apprehension') leaves you in no doubt that his personal preference is for the stringently masculine exertions of (say) J.G. Ballard, whose prose he commends for its 'glazed and melodious precision' (*The War Against Cliché*) and its 'hypnotically varied vowel sounds' (*The Rub of Time*).

Slovenliness in prose is Amis's version of Original Sin – the snake in the literary garden. Suggestively, the author's note at the beginning of *The Rub of Time* carries a subtitle, borrowed (via John Updike) from T.S. Eliot: 'The Natural Sin of Language':

> By 'the natural sin' of language I take it that Eliot is referring a) to its indocility (how it constantly and writhingly resists even the most practised hands), and b) to its promiscuity: in nearly all of its dealings language is as indiscriminate as currency, and gathers many deposits of silt and grit and sweat.

Amis's heroes are writers who have redeemed language from its fallen state – who have successfully wrestled language into docility, and who have purified it, as thoroughly as they could manage, of its encrusted deposits of cliché. 'All writing,' Amis suggests, in what has become his most famous critical epigram, 'is a campaign against cliché. Not just clichés of the pen but clichés of the mind and clichés of the heart.' Thus, the members of the Amis Canon are measured by two contiguous metrics: care with language and sensitivity to cliché. So, D.H. Lawrence (for instance) is demoted on the grounds that he is perhaps 'the most extravagantly slapdash exponent of language' (*Experience*) among twentieth-century greats; whereas Bellow is praised (and praised again) for writing 'prose of [...] tremulous and crystallised beauty' (*The War Against Cliché*), which exhibits 'a dynamic responsiveness to character, place, and time' (*The Rub of Time*).

Carefully fashioned sentences embodying a dynamic responsiveness: these are what Amis values – and he values them to the exclusion of almost everything else. Assessing a work of fiction, Amis wastes no time unpicking ethical imponderables or ruminating on the oddities of human psychology. In fact, Amis the critic has almost no interest in psychology at all – which perhaps explains why there is a whole essay in *The*

Rub of Time called 'Saul Bellow, as Opposed to Henry James', which arraigns the master for using too much elegant variation ('this repast', 'this receptacle'). There isn't a whole lot, it turns out, that a critic of Amis's persuasion can *do* with Henry James, a writer for whom psychology was all and sentences something else again. Amis's canon is therefore self-limiting: too many elegant variations (or too many rhymes), and you're out, no matter how profound your psychological insights, no matter how dexterous your structural architectonics. In his 1998 *Paris Review* interview, Amis lays it on the line:

> If the prose isn't there, then you're reduced to what are merely secondary interests, like story, plot, characterisation, psychological insight and form [...] What is important is to write freely and passionately and with all the resources that the language provides.

It follows from this sentence-fetishism that Amis should be an implacable foe of the extra-literary response. He is caustic about the sort of reviewer who tuts and clucks and calls a book 'scandalous' or 'immoral' or (the more sophisticated version) 'depressing'. Reviewing *The Wild Boys* by William S. Burroughs for the *Observer* in 1972 (the piece appears in *The War Against Cliché*), Amis wrote: 'The only time an educated and well-balanced person has any business being depressed by a book is when its author is simply a bore. (One wearily instances the possibility represented by *King Lear*, at once the most harrowing and uplifting work in the language.)' And tackling J.G. Ballard's *Crash* upon its first publication in 1973, a resolutely unshocked Amis insisted that 'the tone of the book is neither gloating nor priapic; the glazed monotony of its descriptions and the deadpan singlemindedness of its attitudes aren't designed to convert or excite the reader, merely to transmit the chilling isolation of the psychopath' (*The War Against Cliché*).

What matters is to avoid being 'a bore'; if you are scandalized, then you are guilty (unpardonable *gaucherie!*) of misreading the 'tone'. Art is the thing; life, merely material for more 'dynamic responsiveness'.

All of which is to say that Amis the critic is a capital-A Aesthete. He is guided almost entirely by the pleasure principle, and he dismisses moral, psychological and ethical questions as footling. Such concerns are, for Amis, irrelevant to the true business of literature, which is the giving of pleasure via sentences. In the Author's Note to *Einstein's Monsters* (1987), Amis explains that his short stories about the nuclear terror were written 'with the usual purpose in mind: that is to say, with no purpose at all – except, I suppose, to give pleasure, various kinds of complicated pleasure'. That *I suppose* is disingenuous – as, of course, is that *complicated*. Amis's work, he coyly insists, is centrally about pleasure – and only incidentally about the myriad other varieties of human experience that we might imagine to have been subsumed under that slippery word *complicated*. We are led, I think, to feel that Amis would prefer to do without the *complicated* part of *complicated pleasure*. 'The artist is the creator of beautiful things,' Amis insists. And: 'There is no such thing as a moral or an immoral book. Books are well written or badly written. That is all.'

Ah, but of course you've spotted that those last two epigrams are not Amisisms at all, but in fact come from Oscar Wilde's Preface to *The Picture of Dorian Gray* (1890). That they might just as easily have been taken from (say) *The War Against Cliché* or *Visiting Mrs. Nabokov* tells us something important about the roots of Amis's aesthetic philosophy – and about his own complicated relationship with those roots. To observe, as I did above, that Amis is a capital-A Aesthete is to notice at once that there is someone missing from his roster of Great Names – a significant precursor whom Amis has declined to elect. Bellow? Oh, sure. Nabokov? Makes sense. But Amis has discreetly scrubbed from the record any trace of his true onlie begetter: the author of 'The Critic as Artist' and 'The Decay of Lying' (both 1891), the writer who raised the banner for *ars gratia artis* at a time when to do so constituted a truly radical gesture. To put it at its simplest: Amis's criticism, *in toto*, updates Wilde's Aestheticism for the twentieth and twenty-first centuries – with many a telling deformation, to be sure, but also with considerable fealty to the original. That Amis has never acknowledged Wilde as one of his 'inspirers' (no entry for 'Wilde, Oscar' appears in the indices of *Experience*, *The War Against Cliché* or *The Rub of Time*) is also significant – because the influence is there, and once you start to look for it in Amis's work, you begin to see it everywhere.

This is more than a case of Wilde's work having had its moderate effect. Behind every word of Amis's corpus, Wilde lurks – unacknowledged, but indisputably central. Look again at Amis on Burroughs; at his 'weary instancing' of *King Lear* as a reproof to those who imagine that a work of art can be depressing. This is Wilde, in 'The Soul of Man Under Socialism' (1891): 'To call an artist morbid because he deals with morbidity as his subject-matter is as silly as if one called Shakespeare mad because he wrote *King Lear*.' Similarly, when Amis says, 'Only in art will the lion lie down with the lamb, and the rose grow without thorn' (*Koba the Dread*, 2002), it is a contemporary edition of Wilde's 'It is through Art, and Art only, that we can realise our perfection' ('The Critic as Artist'). Further examples proliferate. Included in *The Rub of Time* is Amis's report from the Republican Party convention of 2012, held in Tampa, Florida. Amis offers this assessment of Mitt Romney:

> He is a crystallised and not an accidental believer. You can see it in his lineless face. Awareness of mortality is in itself ageing – it creases the orbits of the eyes, it torments the

brow; and Romney has the look of someone who seriously thinks that he will live forever.

In *The Picture of Dorian Gray*, the remorselessly epigrammatic Lord Henry Wotton gives us this observation on the senior clerics of the Church of England: 'But then in the Church they don't think. A bishop keeps on saying at the age of eighty what he was told to say when he was a boy of eighteen, and as a natural consequence he always looks absolutely delightful.'

At the beginning of *Experience*, Amis complains that the trouble with life

> is its amorphousness, its ridiculous fluidity. Look at it: thinly plotted, largely themeless, sentimental and ineluctably trite. The dialogue is poor, or at least violently uneven. The twists are either predictable or sensationalist. And it's always the same beginning; and the same ending.

And here is Gilbert, one half of the duologue in 'The Critic as Artist', complaining of life in eerily similar terms:

> Life! Life! Don't let us go to life for our fulfilment or our experience. It is a thing narrowed by circumstances, incoherent in its utterance, and without that fine correspondence of form and spirit which is the only thing that can satisfy the artistic and critical temperament. It makes us pay too high a price for its wares.

The Wildean debt is evident even in Amis's fiction – particularly in the early stuff. In *Dead Babies* (1975), we find the Honourable Quentin Villiers and his girlfriend Celia preparing to greet their American guests:

> 'I think I'll make them a cooked breakfast,' said Celia.
> 'A cooked breakfast? [says Quentin.] A "cooked" *breakfast*? My sweet, sometimes you are too deliciously *outré*.

Eating a cooked breakfast – it would be like going to bed in
pyjamas or reading an English novel.'

In *The Picture of Dorian Gray*, Basil Hallward and Lord Henry
arrange to go to the theatre to see the doomed Sybil Vane play
Juliet:

'Not eight, Harry, please. Half past six. We must be there
before the curtain rises. You must see her in the first act,
where she meets Romeo.'
  'Half past six! [says Lord Henry.] What an hour! It will
be like having a meat-tea, or reading an English novel.'

Not every echo is as clear as that, of course. But one might
wearily instance any number of other Wildeanisms in Amis's
prose. Plainly, Amis read Wilde with attention, and at a forma-
tive age. His response to Wilde's work goes far beyond the occasional borrowed witticism; his most basic aesthetic assumptions
are Wildean in timbre – and frequently, his prose is, too. Even at
its loosest, Amis's prose aspires to the condition of epigram. He
is forever looking to fix a perception in its final form – to trap
the truth in a sparkling phrase. This is what makes him so quotable. It is also what gives him away as a close student of Wilde
– as a nineteenth-century Aesthete in modern dress.

  The nineteenth-century Aesthetic Movement, beginning
with its Oxonian progenitor, Walter Pater, was in love with the
epigram. There were sound aesthetic reasons for this: Pater,
and Wilde after him, believed that one of the purposes of art
was to capture the essence of a fleeting perception, and for this,
the epigram was the perfect literary form. (Pater's most well-
known line is, of course, an epigram: 'To burn always with this
hard, gem-like flame, to maintain this ecstasy, is success in
life.') As Cyril Connolly put it in *Enemies of Promise* (1938), the
Aesthetes were 'obsessed with the beauty of the moment, and
not the beauty only, but the problem of recording that beauty'.

Pater and his lesser epigones are more or less unreadable today, largely because their aphoristic sallies exude the stale perfume of an affected 'decadence'. But in Wilde's work – particularly in *Dorian Gray* and *The Importance of Being Ernest* – the epigrammatic style achieves its purest consummation. This is because Wilde's Aestheticism was never 'mere' aestheticism – in other words, it was devoted to rather more than the capturing of a transient ecstasy. In fact, Wilde's Aestheticism was essentially political. His paradoxes subvert conventional morality by disclosing that conventional morality was paradoxical to begin with. (And even his lightest confections contain a secret poisoned centre: take Miss Prism's famous description of her three-volume novel, in which 'the good ended happily, and the bad unhappily. That is what Fiction means'. This is not just a joke about clichéd novels – it is a sly reminder that we are wrong to expect justice in the real, non-fictional world.) One definition of Wilde's mature style might, indeed, be 'politics by aphorism'. Wilde's oeuvre mounts a sustained assault on Victorian pieties in the name of a sophisticated radicalism. His *meilleurs mots* are quoted out of context so frequently that it is a shock to discover, on returning to the lengthy essays collected in *Intentions* (1891), that his work is in fact carefully argued, and crammed with interesting – and highly subversive – ideas.

Wilde's *mots*, in other words, were the slogans of a coherent political philosophy. 'Really,' says Algernon, in *The Importance of Being Earnest*, 'if the lower orders don't set us a good example, what on earth is the use of them? They seem, as a class, to have absolutely no sense of moral responsibility.' It is, of course, Algernon and his ilk who have no sense of moral responsibility: only the empty forms of a bankrupt propriety. Wilde's epigrams are glittering hand grenades lobbed in a kind of class war: each one points discreetly towards the possibility of a better world.

What, then, are Amis's epigrams? Here is a more or less random sampling of Amis in epigrammatical mode:

> Experimental novels may have a habit of looking very easy (certainly easier to write than to read), but their failure-rate is alarmingly high – approaching, I sometimes fear, 100 per cent. (*The War Against Cliché*)

> Reading is a skill: you have to be taught how to do it. (*The War Against Cliché*)

> In the rest of the developed world, the contest between brain and bowel was long ago revolved in favour of brain. In America the dispute still splits the nation. (*The Rub of Time*)

> In fact, every life is a tragedy, too. Every life cleaves to the tragic curve. (*Koba the Dread*)

> Writers' lives are all anxiety and ambition. No one begrudges them the anxiety, but the ambition is something they are supposed to shut up about. (*Visiting Mrs. Nabokov*)

> I satisfied myself that porno, naturally male-chauvinist in origin and essence, is now so baldly misogynistic that the only desire it arouses is a desire to be elsewhere. (*The Rub of Time*)

> Fictional divination will always be haphazard. The unfolding of world-historical events is itself haphazard (and therefore unaesthetic), and 'the future' is in a sense defined by its messy inscrutability. (*The Rub of Time*)

One of the key things about the epigrammatic style, of course, is that it is self-consciously superb: it brooks no argument; the appropriate readerly response is not critical engagement but simple admiration. Reading Amis is very much like reading Wilde, in the sense that one encounters dazzling formulation after dazzling formulation – a tapestry of finished thoughts, each expressed in a phrase of perfect rhythmic balance and deep linguistic richness.

Amis's prose is also marked by its regular deployment of the epigram-as-aside (that 'naturally male-chauvinist in origin and essence' dropped into the sentence about porn, for instance), which conveys, impressively, the sense of a great deal of casually mastered subsidiary thought ('naturally' Amis has already thought deeply about pornography's inherent male chauvinism, and now, of course, his meditations have been proved correct). And this leads us to the other key thing about the epigrammatic style, which is its regal assumption of authority. For both Wilde and Amis, the epigram is a means of exerting a stylish form of control over the material of an unruly world. As a rhetorical trope, the epigram appeals to writers who understand their work in terms of (in Matthew Arnold's resonant phrase) 'a criticism of life'. But it also appeals to writers – often the same writers – who understand their work as a project of self-fashioning: as an effort to elevate a personal style to the position of ultimate authority, and thereby to remake themselves into arbiters of the style of the world.

This is the essence of the Wildean project; a project from which Amis has learned almost everything he knows as a critic. Amis is never more Wildean than when he summarizes an aesthetic crux in a single virtuoso phrase: 'The apocalyptic-epiphanic mode in fiction is not for minor talents,' he writes, in his review of *Crash*, and who are we to disagree? The point is not the statement's (debatable) truth-value; the point is to win assent for an arguable proposition through sheer linguistic prestidigitation: to master the world through style.

When Amis writes about public affairs, he essays his own version of politics by aphorism. He doesn't do polemic – his political essays are not intended to change anyone's mind. Rather, Amis is superbly good at summarizing, as if for all time, a particular brand of received liberal wisdom. 'It has to be admitted,' he writes, in his piece on the 2012 GOP convention, 'that Uncle Sam is highly distinctive, even exotic, in his superstitious reverence for money.' And in a review of Donald Trump's two 'bestsellers', written for *Harper's Magazine* in 2016, he notes that 'every now and again Americans feel the need to exalt and heroize an ignoramus'. Fancy phrasing aside, these are unexceptionable observations; they lack entirely the paradoxical sting of Wilde's finest political squibs – as when Vivian, in 'The Decay of Lying', complains of politicians that they 'never rise beyond the level of misrepresentation, and actually condescend to prove, to discuss, to argue'. Amis doesn't bother to explain *why* Americans feel the need to heroize ignoramuses – analysis, after all, being of no concern of the epigrammatist, who, like Wilde's Vivian, would find the necessity of proving one's argument unspeakably vulgar, and whose true interest is in the perfect phrase.

More to the point, Amis's criticisms of Trump and the GOP might have been thought up (though ne'er so well expressed) by just about any liberal Western intellectual you could name – Americans love money! Sometimes they elect idiots! That Amis is a good old-fashioned mainstream liberal is hardly in doubt: in a 'You Ask the Questions' feature for the *Guardian* (included in *The Rub of Time*), he remarks that he has 'always been pallidly left-of-centre', and in *Koba the Dread* he describes his younger self as 'quietist and unaligned' (in contrast to the 'proselytizing Trotskyists' James Fenton and Christopher Hitchens, his colleagues at the *New Statesman*). Although some journalists have detected in recent years a rightward drift to Amis's politics, in fact he has remained more or less where he always was; it is the world that has changed around him, perhaps to the world's loss. Amis's essays on Trump and the GOP complacently adumbrate mainstream liberal viewpoints: Trump, he felt in 2016, would be defeated by Hillary 'and her innumerable sisters at the ballot box', and the GOP, he felt in 2011, would trouble us only with the 'rattle of its chains'. Amis's stance, as a political analyst, is *de haut en bas* – but the heights from which he condescends are not those of a gentleman radical, sworn to overturn the established order, but those of his version of aestheticism, from which all traces of radicalism have been drained. In other words, Amis approaches political analysis just as he approaches literary criticism: as an opportunity to coin more epigrams, to master the world through style. Amis's critiques therefore tend to reinforce the political assumptions of his liberal readers, who pause to savour his powers of expression and then pretty much carry on as before.

It should by now be clear that Amis's epigrammatic style differs from Wilde's in that it works not to demolish a bourgeois consensus but to uphold one. Where Wilde's epigrams sought to provoke and disturb, Amis's solicit a cosy agreement. His work therefore embodies a peculiar paradox: it represents an aestheticism of the liberal mainstream. If Wilde's Aestheticism was animated by a radical critique of culture and society, Amis's update jettisons the radicalism and keeps what is left over: a belief that the world, including the world of politics, can be mastered by style. The result is writing of a peculiarly limited brilliance, in which the fireworks of Amis's phrasemaking obscure significant areas of darkness.

There remains the mysterious question of why Amis has written no essays in praise of Oscar Wilde; why he has refused to acknowledge his debt to such an obvious, and obviously important, precursor. I think I can make a guess. Amis's brief list of literary-critical heroes – such a list might be distilled from the Foreword to *The War Against Cliché*, in which Amis mentions people like Edmund Wilson, William Empson and Northrop Frye – includes one especially significant figure:

F.R. Leavis, the Cambridge don and founder of *Scrutiny* (1932–
53). Amis's relationship with Leavis has always been uneasy
– he has mocked his 'impregnable humourlessness', as well as
'provincial, lofty, and fierce', and he has scoffed at the 'pitifully
denuded bookcase' 'okayed by Dr. L' (who basically approved
of George Eliot, Joseph Conrad, D.H. Lawrence, Henry James,
and no one else). And yet, there are nine entries for 'Leavis, F.R.'
in the index to *The War Against Cliché*, and two in the index to
The Rub of Time. And in *Experience*, Amis tells the following
anecdote about a literary lunch:

> I put to the table the following question: Who would you
> side with, if the choice were limited to Leavis or Bloomsbury?
> Everyone else said Bloomsbury. I said Leavis […] I had never
> been a Leavisite and I had written several attacks on his doc-
> trines and his followers. But I think I would cast the same vote,
> even today. What could be more antipathetic than Woolf's
> dismissal of *Ulysses* on the grounds of Joyce's *class*? No, give
> me F.R. and Q.D., give me Frank and Queenie, despite all the
> humourlessness, the hysteria, and the Soviet gloom.

'I had never been a Leavisite': no, but Leavis's work has left a
deep impression on Amis's criticism nonetheless. Leavis's
small handful of keywords – 'tradition', 'life', 'maturity' – crop
up again and again in Amis's essays and reviews. Of John
Updike's fiction: 'What we like is life.' The sentences of Thomas
Harris (author of *The Silence of the Lambs* and *Hannibal*) do
not contain 'the throb of life'; Bellow's *Augie March* is 'all about
life; it brings you up against the dead-end of life'; literature is
'among other things, a talent contest, and every reader must
find his personal great tradition'.

This is the other pronounced strain in Amis's critical
work: a Leavisite austerity that consorts surprisingly well, in
Amis's hands, with his Wildean hedonism. If Wilde is Amis's

literary father (setting aside, of course, his *actual* literary father), Leavis is a kind of stern uncle, offering a bracing moral corrective to the pleasure-seeking fripperies of the Aesthete. As he himself confesses, Amis has never been able entirely to shake off Leavis's reproving ghost (with its 'grimly secular creed', whatever that means). There is a highly Amisian moment in *The Great Tradition* (1948), when Leavis observes that 'major' novelists are major 'in the sense that they not only change the possibilities of the art for practitioners and readers, but that they are significant in terms of the human awareness they promote; awareness of the possibilities of life'. Doesn't this remind us of Amis's praise of Saul Bellow – his advocacy of 'a dynamic responsiveness to character, place and time'? It is, as they say, no accident that Leavis was one of twentieth-century liberal humanism's most important thinkers: his influence was as much political as it was literary, and Amis is hardly the only writer who imbibed his 'pallidly left-of-centre' politics through the medium of Leavisite literary criticism. I think we can say with confidence that Amis's own politics are essentially literary in character – that he learned his liberalism not from John Stuart Mill, but from F.R. Leavis – and that this partly explains his failure to replicate Wilde's radicalism, along with his emphasis on style.

Especially significant is the fact that Leavis disapproved of the Aesthetic Movement. He does not mention Wilde by name in *The Great Tradition*; instead he nominates Flaubert as the *fons et origo* of the Aesthetic approach. 'For the later Aesthetic writers,' Leavis wrote, 'represent in a weak kind of way the attitude that Flaubert maintained with a perverse heroism, "form" and "style" are ends to be sought for themselves, and the chief preoccupation is with elaborating a beautiful style to apply to the chosen subject.' For Leavis, the Flaubertian tradition was marred by 'disgust or disdain or boredom'. What was needed instead was 'a kind of reverent openness before life, and a marked moral intensity'. For Leavis, the Aesthetes simply weren't *serious* enough – and perhaps, for Martin Amis, the work of Oscar Wilde isn't *serious* enough, either. It is, after all, hard to defend a superficially trifling romantic comedy like *The Importance of Being Earnest* in the same lofty terms that you might use to defend *Herzog*.

In suppressing his debt to Wilde, Amis takes his cue from Leavis: he professes, at least overtly, to prefer a 'marked moral intensity' to the Aestheticism of Bloomsbury (and the Bloomsbury writers were themselves, of course, heavily in Wilde's debt). With Leavisite rigour, Amis denudes his bookcase: no Walter Pater, no Flaubert, no Oscar Wilde, no Virginia Woolf. Just Bellow and Nabokov and Updike, with their marvellous sentences – and their reverent openness before life. Thus Amis manages the trick that Gore Vidal once described as 'the simultaneous possession and ingestion of confectionery': on the one hand, Amis devotes himself exclusively to literary pleasure; on the other, he stakes a vague claim to moral seriousness (and makes a good deal of noise about it, too).

Amis's work has, he tells us, 'no purpose at all – except, I suppose, to give pleasure, various kinds of complicated pleasure'. *Pleasure* is Wilde; *complicated* is Leavis. Amis remains more or less loyal to Leavis; Wilde is visible, in Amis's work, almost entirely by his absence. Meanwhile, *The Rub of Time* (rich, funny, dense with lapidary *mots*) gives enormous pleasure – even if it is of an interestingly complicated kind.

The Dublin Review of Books, November 2017

HATING JONATHAN FRANZEN

It's okay to hate Jonathan Franzen. Exhibit A: In November 2018, to mark the publication of *The End of the End of the Earth*, Franzen's new collection of non-fiction pieces, the bookchat website Lithub republished '10 Rules for Novelists', a list that Franzen originally composed for a 2010 *Guardian* feature. Franzen's rules are as useful as these things generally are – that is to say, they are as useful as you find them to be. 'The reader is a friend, not an adversary, not a spectator.' 'When information becomes free and universally accessible, voluminous research for a novel is devalued along with it.' 'Interesting verbs are seldom very interesting.'

Unexceptionable stuff, you might think. But the online response was virulently hostile. According to the Lithub commenting fraternity, Franzen was 'an unbearably arrogant, pretentious twat' and 'a massive, self-important douche'. His rules were 'pretentious drivel'; 'pretentious, privileged nonsense'; 'self-indulgent, elitist nonsense with no basis in fact'; 'completely tangential to good writing'.

Meanwhile, over on Twitter, users ginned up parody lists: 'Jonathan Franzen's 10 Rules for Being an Absolutely Mediocre White Guy Who Writes Forgettable Books About Mediocre White Guys Who Are Depressed About Modern Existence and Also Birdwatching'. Or, if they weren't in the mood for gags, they denounced 'jonathan's franzen's latest piece of arrogant bullshit'. Jeff Pearlman, a novelist, opined: 'God, Jonathan Franzen is one arrogant fuck.'

The writer Chuck Wendig – author of the 2015 *New York Times* bestseller *Star Wars: Aftermath* – accumulated many thousands of likes for a point-by-point refutation of Franzen's precepts. Wendig was particularly exercised by Rule 7 ('You see more sitting still than chasing after'): 'what the crap does that even mean,' he tweeted. 'how does it relate to writing a story/ are the characters sitting/is the author sitting, I mean, I'm usually sitting/should I be chasing something/should something be chasing me/what the fuck, franzen'. Non-standard formatting [*sic*].

So: Jonathan Franzen is arrogant. He is privileged. He is mediocre. He is also – to step backwards in time and quote the author of a lengthy Medium essay ('Jonathan Franzen: The Great American Misogynist', 2015) – a misogynist: 'For years,' this author writes, Franzen has 'slathered his white maleness across the pages of such venerable publications as *Harper's* and *The New Yorker*,' and his books – the products of a 'rich male life' (perhaps not quite *les mots justes*, but never mind) – deserve only to be caricatured:

> His works are so varied and intense, in fact, that it's unreasonable for me to expect you to read through them all, so let me sum them up for you: A man runs into trouble with some woman (or women) in his life, thinks back to his college days in an attempt at self-reflection, fails miserably but misremembers a lot of nondescript sex to make it tantalizing,

gets upset about technology for no discernible reason, then comes to the conclusion that being an upper middle-class white man really is the truest tragedy of all.

I could, if I were feeling sadistic, catalogue numerous further examples of anti-Franzen sentiment – not all of them, by any means, culled from the trashier precincts of social media or from the comments sections of literary websites. But I think my point is made. It's okay to hate Jonathan Franzen. Everybody else is doing it. There is, in fact, a list of prefabricated terms that you can borrow in order to bolster your animus: elitism, arrogance, white male privilege, misogyny. It's the full charge sheet of contemporary crimes. On the evidence of the Medium essayist's *précis* of Franzen's fiction, it isn't even necessary to read his books. You can hate him without putting in the work.

Whence this hostility? It may, in part, be Franzen's own fault. His response to Oprah Winfrey's choice of *The Corrections* for her Book Club in 2001 (he said that appearing on Oprah's show might consort oddly with his status as a representative of 'the high-art literary tradition') did him no favours. 'Instead of rallying to Mr. Franzen, *The New York Times* remarked at the time, 'most of the literary world took [Oprah's] side, deriding him as arrogant and ungrateful.'

In Martin Amis's *The Information*, the literary agent Gal Aplanalp advises the failed writer Richard Tull that 'the public can only keep in mind one thing per writer. Like a signature. Drunk, young, mad, fat, sick: you know.' In the aftermath of the Oprah kerfuffle, Franzen's signature was established. He was arrogant. Almost two decades later, the familiar neurons still fire whenever Franzen's name is mentioned. He serves as a convenient shorthand for a certain kind of popular bogeyman: the smug elitist who disparages mass culture in the name of a snootily exclusive 'tradition'.

There is, as it happens, a certain amount of textual evidence to support this view – for instance, his remark in a 1995 essay ('The Reader in Exile', collected in *How to Be Alone* [2002]), that 'I understand my life in the context of Raskolnikov and Quentin Compson, not David Letterman or Jerry Seinfeld,' or his suggestion, in 'Pain Won't Kill You' (collected in *Farther Away* [2012]), that 'consumer-technology products' are 'great allies and enablers of narcissism'. It is certainly possible to construe these remarks as 'arrogant', especially if you take the precautionary step of divorcing them from their original contexts (respectively, an essay about how reading assuages loneliness and a commencement address about how difficult, and how essential, it is to truly love another human being).

But in fact, what's remarkable about the opprobrium heaped on Franzen by the online literati is that it seems to have very little to do with Franzen's actual work. The author of the Medium essay I quoted earlier clearly has not read Franzen's fiction (or if she has read it, she has failed to understand it). But she knows how she feels about the man. And this is typical. Successive waves of online Franzen-hatred have generally taken the form of *ad hominem* responses to essays, or to remarks made in interviews, or to his occasional appearances on television. That Franzen's opinions – expressed in forms, very much including the essay, that he has not mastered and that tend to serve him poorly – so often go against the contemporary grain (for instance, his distrust of social media) or situate him squarely in a trainspotterish cul de sac of hobbyism (all that birdwatching) mean that he is, from the point of view of the virtue-signalling culture warriors of Twitter, a soft target. Here, once again, Franzen may have to take some of the blame. It's difficult to think of another contemporary novelist who is served so poorly by out-of-context quotation, or by his own inability to craft acceptable soundbites.

There is also Franzen's whiteness. Here, perhaps, his critics (those of them, at any rate, who have actually read his work) are on firmer ground. His novels rarely feature non-white characters, and in a literary climate that has elevated 'representation' to the status of an aesthetic principle, this makes him look either obsolete or purblind, if not actively (the literary thoughtcrime of the moment) 'exclusionary'. But there is no point in defending Franzen's work on the grounds that writers are allowed to write about whomever and whatever they choose, in whatever fashion they prefer. Large swathes of the literary community no longer believe in this elementary principle of intellectual liberty, and saying that it doesn't matter that Franzen only writes about middle-class white people – that it only matters *how well* he writes about them – will only get me in trouble with the commissars of literary Twitter.

And then there is Franzen's maleness, which may get us closer to the heart of the matter. Franzen is a man – oh dear me, yes, he is a man – and he is also a novelist. For many of Franzen's enemies, this appears to be enough to damn him irretrievably on both moral and aesthetic grounds, as if Franzen were the sort of male novelist who went around shooting African megafauna (like Ernest Hemingway) or stabbing his wife (like Norman Mailer) or stalking his ex-girlfriends (like David Foster Wallace); or as if he were the sort of male novelist who wrote about tortured love affairs in such a way as conclusively to demonstrate his own sexual potency (like James Frey). But Franzen isn't like that. In actuality, Franzen (who has repeatedly called himself a feminist in essays and interviews) is at least as conflicted about maleness and male sexuality as the fieriest social justice warrior, and the fact that he finds unfettered male sexuality both funny and creepy is attested to in all three of his major novels (look at Chip Lambert in *The Corrections* [2001], humping his chaise longue in search of an olfactory memory of Melissa Paquette, or at Andreas Wolf in *Purity* [2015], telling himself that having sex with troubled teenage girls counts as an act of political subversion).

The problem, of course, is that all the male novelists who actually did terrible things, and then wrote about them, are now dead (or, as with James Frey, have subsided into irrelevance). You can't be angry at these guys on Twitter – what would be the point? Jonathan Franzen, on the other hand, is neither dead nor irrelevant – his books are bestsellers, his essays are widely disseminated. That he doesn't happen to fit the mould of 'toxic male writer' is, for many of his critics, beside the point. Certain intellectuals and other literati (and we might remember, at this point, that the original *literati*, in Ancient Rome, were slaves who copied out official documents, often without understanding what they wrote) are conducting a campaign against an extinct generation of white male novelists, with Jonathan Franzen as their proxy target. The sense of cognitive dissonance produced when a reader familiar with Franzen's work encounters the online commentary about him derives, in large part, from the gap between what Franzen actually is and what people want (or need) him to be. If Franzen were, in fact, a Norman Mailerish self-promoter, he might very well make some interesting art out of this crux. But Franzen is Franzen: an altogether more inward, and inwardly riven, figure.

In the literary sense, of course, the nature of the online discourse about Franzen means very little. As an interesting example of how corporate-owned social media outlets have mired our culture in a bitter and irresolvable Gramscian war of position over who gets to say what and how, it is certainly worth examining. But really, it falls under the heading of *local phenomena*, and will almost certainly have very little impact on what posterity makes of Franzen's work. There are more interesting questions, to wit: How good is Franzen, as a novelist? And, more to the immediate point, how good is he as an essayist?

Here's a summary (and very provisional) judgement: The first two novels, *The Twenty-Seventh City* (1988) and *Strong Motion* (1992), are no good: ponderously intricate and drab, they feel, on rereading, like nothing more than very strong apprentice work. *The Corrections* remains one of the best novels ever written about the ways in which the nuclear family shapes the individual self, even as the overlapping superstorms of hypercapitalist modernity threaten to tear the very idea of the nuclear family apart. *Freedom* (2010) and *Purity* are gripping, flawed, rich, memorable, occasionally great, and probably not destined to endure. [Hindsight note: *Crossroads* (2021) strips the Franzen Recipe back to its basic elements, and is, I think, his best novel since *The Corrections*.] Their best moments, which tend to occur when Franzen, after much delay, abruptly yokes his divergent plotlines together, evoke a distinctively contemporary dread. In other words, Franzen's fiction is at its best when its pages are animated by a sense that the ground-note of our times is an unappeasable anxiety. (From the opening paragraph of *The Corrections*: 'You could feel it. Something terrible was going to happen.') The omnipresence of this anxiety in *The Corrections* explains, I think, why the book still feels contemporary, two decades after publication.

Franzen's essays – collected in *How to Be Alone* (2002), *The Discomfort Zone: A Personal History* (2006), *Farther Away* (2012) and now *The End of the End of the Earth* – are, by turns, cogent, cranky, shapeless, brilliant, bewilderingly slight, sharply observed, fascinatingly confessional, beset by scruples, oddly informal and weirdly weightless. For a writer who has published four volumes of essays – five if you count *The Kraus Project* (2013), in which he swamped two slender pieces by the Viennese satirist Karl Kraus in 300 pages of anecdotal footnotes – Franzen has, rather surprisingly, not developed either a consistent essayistic style nor a particularly distinctive set of preoccupations (unless you count birdwatching, which, alas, you must).

This isn't necessarily a fault – a novelist is not, if the novel happens to be his or her thing, obliged to master other literary forms – but it does mean that Franzen's non-fiction volumes make for unsatisfactory reading experiences. Like the curate's egg, they are good in parts. Even individual essays ricochet disconcertingly between the sharply pertinent and the flatly circumstantial. Take 'Why Birds Matter', from *The End of the End of the Earth*. Half of it sounds like an ornithology textbook: 'To survive in so many different habitats, the world's ten thousand or so bird species have evolved into a spectacular diversity of forms.' There is, for the merely-averagely-interested-in-birds reader, only so much of this stuff you can take. The essay is almost over before does Franzen does any actual *writing* – which is to say, any actual thinking:

> The radical otherness of birds is integral to their beauty and their value. They are always among us but never of us. They're the other world-dominating animals that evolution has produced, and their indifference to us ought to serve as a chastening reminder that we're not the measure of all things.

In *The End of the End of the Earth*'s opening piece – a reflection on essays called 'The Essay in Dark Times' – Franzen makes some large claims for (explicitly) the essay as a literary form and (implicitly) the essays of his own that follow. Essays, Franzen says, 'force me to take my measure'. 'For the writer, an essay is a mirror.' 'I'd come to think of the essayist as a firefighter, whose job, while everyone else is fleeing the flames of shame, is to run straight into them.' These are admirable sentiments, and they prepare us for a volume of pieces that will expose Franzen in the act of self-scrutiny – that will allow us to watch the essayist watching himself in the mirror, and behold the intricacies of his shame as he rushes towards it like (in that rather self-flattering image) a heroic emergency responder.

But this isn't the book we get. Instead, we get a sequence of essays that aren't quite in the polemical mode and that aren't quite in the confessional mode but are more often something uneasily in between. There is, in *The End of the End of the Earth*, no extended treatment of shame as such (and we can infer, from the frequency with which he uses the word, that shame is one of the key elements in Franzen's writerly self-conception), though there are repeated avowals that shame has been felt (whenever he visits a bar, for instance, Franzen tells us, 'I become miserable with self-consciousness and thrift and shame and shyness and etiquette anxiety'). But to say that one has felt ashamed is not the same as to write about shame. If the essayist must, as Franzen avers, set a collision course with his own shame, then Franzen has largely shirked that duty, in favour of a general and rather *pro forma* invocation of shame as the emotion that *accompanied* the writing of certain essays. In other words, despite his assertions, shame isn't really Franzen's subject in *The End of the End of the Earth*.

So what is his subject? Well, in one sense, it's birds. Of the sixteen essays collected here, eight of them are largely or exclusively about birds and birdwatching. Of those eight, six follow a recurring template, *vide.* Jonathan Franzen travels to a place and looks at birds. In 'Postcards from East Africa', he goes to Ghana and looks at birds. In 'May Your Life Be Ruined', he goes to Egypt and Albania and looks at birds. In 'Missing', he goes to Jamaica and looks at birds. In the title essay, 'The End of the End of the Earth', he goes to Antarctica and looks at birds. (This template was first set in 'The Ugly Mediterranean', collected in *Farther Away*, in which Franzen goes to Italy and Greece and looks at birds.)

We know – because Franzen has told us repeatedly, for instance in 'Pain Won't Kill You' (*Farther Away*), where he says, 'it's very uncool to be a birdwatcher', that being a bird-watcher (or, if you must, a 'twitcher') causes Franzen to experience a certain amount of shame. Whether or not Franzen is right to feel ashamed of his passion for birds – and really, who cares if he's a birdwatcher? – we might legitimately expect him to realize that birds are what he's writing about, and that the shame he experiences in doing so is either an interesting subject in itself (in which case, he should write about it properly), or is entirely irrelevant, and should not be mentioned. This might seem like a small point, but in fact it brings up a larger issue with Franzen-as-essayist: he often doesn't seem absolutely clear about what his subject is.

This has always been a problem with Franzen's non-fiction. His most famous essay, 'Perchance to Dream' (revised for publication in *How to Be Alone* and retitled 'Why Bother?'), is a never-entirely-coherent discussion of several different, and not necessarily, related things: the fate of literature in a consumer-capitalist world; Jonathan Franzen's depression; the value of the 'social novel'; and so on. But this endemic lack of focus – this tendency to yoke together disparate topics and call the result an essay – is especially evident in *The End of the End of the Earth*. The pieces collected here tend to be about several things at once, and finally about no one thing in particular. There is a notional unifying theme: several essays feint in the direction of ecological polemic, most notably, and most successfully, 'Save What You Love', a lengthy critique of the Audubon Society's focus on climate change as 'the number one threat to the birds of North America', perhaps the collection's most focused and coherent piece.

Here, Franzen makes the entirely reasonable point that regional conservation projects are both more manageable and more effective ways of delaying climate change than doomed efforts to reduce world carbon emissions (the essay was, when it first appeared in *The New Yorker*, greeted with near-unanimous scorn from environmental activists and from the usual mob of Franzen-haters). In its clarity of argument and its idiosyncratic passion, 'Save What You Love' hints at the sort of book *The End of the End of the Earth* might have been: a book about climate change, seen through the lens of a single species (birds) and through the eyes of a single, largely depressive sensibility (Franzen's). Franzen's thinking about climate change is interestingly lateral. It is also deeply pessimistic – a short squib appended to the book notes that 'our reigning political and economic systems reward short-sightedness'. But at no point does he put together a Unified Field Theory of Climate Change According to Jonathan Franzen. Like other subjects raised but not really discussed in *The End of the End of the Earth*, climate change appears as simply one more item in Franzen's writerly rucksack – taken out when occasion demands, and otherwise ignored.

But here, perhaps, I'm guilty of the same error that Franzen's detractors make when they call him out as a toxic patriarch – that of mistaking his nature as a writer. Climate change per se isn't Franzen's subject – he isn't George Monbiot or Bill McKibben. He's under no obligation, in his non-fiction, to write about climate change coherently or at length. He is, in fact, obliged only to tell stories (if we grant him, as I think we should, the status not of essayist but of novelist-on-holiday: telling stories is what novelists, as opposed to essayists, traditionally do). And the best essays in the book are the ones that make use of Franzen's remarkable narrative gift. The title essay, in which he recounts both an Antarctic cruise and the life and death of the uncle who bequeathed him the money to pay for it, is an exemplary bit of storytelling. Here Franzen's true preoccupations (that is, the preoccupations that animate his fiction) work superbly in concert: the essay deals with nature, social and financial anxiety, and, most centrally, the meaning of family. In linking a memoir of his uncle Walt – who was, like Franzen's mother, 'an optimistic lover of life, long married to a rigid and depressive Franzen' – to a tragicomic history of his efforts to see an emperor penguin from the deck of a luxury liner, Franzen does what he does best: he situates a family history in the context of a guiltily superabundant, apocalypse-haunted, nature-defined modernity.

It is, I would argue, Franzen's extraordinary powers of narrative organization that make him an excellent novelist and a so-so essayist. The most remarkable thing about *The Corrections*, *Freedom* and *Purity* is how beautifully they choreograph their multistrand plots; the most notable thing about his essays is how often they default to a narrative mode, forgetting, in the process, their ostensible focus on argument or idea. Writing about his ideal novel in 'Perchance to Dream', back in 1996, Franzen said: 'I like maximum diversity and contrast packed into a single exciting experience […] I still like a novel that's alive and multivalent like a city.' As a form, the novel is well served by maximum diversity and contrast. But the same isn't necessarily true of the essay – or, at least, it isn't true of the not-quite-narrative essays that Franzen tends to write.

What holds maximum diversity and contrast together is, of course, story. Franzen-as-essayist appears to realize this only intermittently. It isn't a coincidence that 'The End of the End of the Earth' is the longest essay in the book. Franzen needs space in which to organize his grab bag of materials. He is a marathon runner, never at his best in the hundred-yard dash. If it's never entirely clear what he's writing about, that may be because, in a ten-page essay, he has barely had time to begin figuring out what his subject is. If his essays rarely assemble a coherent argument, that may be because he thinks through and with story – unlike the more traditional essayist, who thinks through and with ideas.

All of which is to say that Franzen's essays are epiphenomenal to his work as a novelist – occasionally interesting, sometimes spikily individual, but more often unsatisfactorily haphazard or dutifully fact-bound. The real Franzen is to be found elsewhere: in the pages of his fiction, with its omnivorous sympathies, its richly satisfying plots, and its profound comic vision of the contemporary world. There, his divergent interests cohere into meaning. In his essay collections, we must make do with mere assemblages of interesting fragments: sometimes illuminating, sometimes lively, but never, in the end, quite enough.

The Dublin Review of Books, February 2019

SUSAN SONTAG'S WILL

Was she a terrible person? Consider: to her partner of fifteen years, the photographer Annie Leibovitz, she was like 'an abusive mother' (this is according to Joan Acocella, who profiled her for *The New Yorker* in 2000). 'People couldn't bear to be at dinner when she was with Annie because she was so sadistic, so insulting, so cruel.' She explained to friends that Leibovitz 'would be the stupidest person' they had ever met. When Leibovitz served her son David shrimp at a Christmas party, she began to shout. 'David is allergic to shellfish! How could you be so stupid?' Leibovitz rushed out to buy a replacement appetizer. During these years, according to her accountant, Leibovitz gave her cash gifts totalling somewhere in the region of eight million dollars – to help support her writing.

To her son, she could be shockingly indifferent. 'I must think about David,' she admonished herself in a journal entry in 1971, when David was nineteen years old. A decade later, when David was undergoing dual traumas (the break-up of his relationship with the writer Sigrid Nunez and the surgical removal of a precancerous growth from his spine), she flew to Italy with her partner, the dancer Lucinda Childs. David recuperated in the house of the writer Jamaica Kincaid and her husband. 'It was just unbelievable that she went,' Kincaid said. 'We couldn't believe she was really getting on that plane.' Later, Kincaid would remark of her that she 'wanted to be a good mother, but it was sort of like wanting to be a great actress'. When David developed a cocaine addiction, his mother told friends that she found it 'unforgivable' (although she herself regularly took amphetamines to help with her long stints at the typewriter).

When she wasn't being indifferent, she could be stiflingly attentive. When David was a child, she groomed him to become her intellectual equal, leading him through 'a University of Chicago-like great books curriculum'. At four, David was reading Homer. A friend once asked the young David what he was up to. 'I'm writing a novel about the Spanish Civil War,' he replied. The friend asked if David had read Hugh Thomas's thousand-page book about the subject. 'Of course,' David said. He was eleven years old. Later, she got David a job at her publisher, Farrar, Straus & Giroux, and insisted that he be her editor. When he made an incorrect change to the proofs of her 1980 essay collection, *Under the Sign of Saturn*, 'she got him on the phone immediately, and started screaming'.

Friends were not spared. When the novelist Larry McMurtry was late for dinner (his flight was delayed), she ate a fortune's worth of caviar and went home, leaving McMurtry, when he finally arrived at the restaurant, to pay the bill. Klaus Biesenbach, a young German curator whom she befriended late in life, 'remembered Susan's screaming at him at four in the morning while they were buying French fries in Berlin: he had misused a word'. Alfred Chester, a writer who knew her in the 1960s, called her 'extraordinarily tactless'. Martie Edelheit, a friend from college, insisted that she didn't intend to hurt people – 'she simply was oblivious'. In her emeritus years, 'she constantly shed friends'. But she had been shedding them all along. She promised a short-term girlfriend, Eva Kollisch, that she would secure financial support for the PhD Kollisch needed to help support her family. 'I'm going to get you a scholarship from the American Association of University Women,' she said. 'All I have to do is write them.' But she never did. Kollisch was devastated: 'There was something very wrong with Susan.'

If there was indeed 'something very wrong' with Susan Sontag – and Benjamin Moser's authorized biography is not so much a dispassionate chronicle of Sontag's life and times as it is an eight-hundred-page bill of indictment against her – there was, equally, much that was right. Consider also the following. She had no patience with the milquetoast evasions (or the outright cowardice) of those who blamed Salman Rushdie for inciting the Ayatollah Khomeini to put him under sentence of death. At the time of the fatwa, Sontag was president of American PEN. She organized a reading of *The Satanic Verses* by famous writers, including Joan Didion, Norman Mailer and Edward Said. This was enough to persuade prevaricating US book chains like Barnes & Noble to sell the novel. It also reassured Rushdie that he was not alone: 'To have allies is very strengthening.'

In 1993 she followed her son, David, to Sarajevo, the Bosnian city then besieged by Serb military forces. (David had by this point become a war correspondent, perhaps as a relaxing alternative to life with his mother.) According to the theatre director Haris Pašović, '[Sontag] was the first international person who said publicly that what is happening in Bosnia in 1993 was a genocide.' She made many trips to Sarajevo during the siege (which lasted until 1996), risking death by sniper fire or shelling each time. She distributed money and food. She worked with primary-school children. She staged a production of *Waiting for Godot*, lighting local actors using a portable generator and, when that failed, candlelight. On return journeys to America she used her prominence to argue in favour of military intervention by NATO. (It is important to say that Sontag was right about this. US military estimates at the time projected that armed intervention would end the siege of Sarajevo in forty-eight hours. And when NATO forces did conduct a bombing campaign in 1999 to prevent the 'ethnic cleansing' of Kosovar Albanians by Serb coalition forces, it worked.)

It is strange, perhaps, to find Sontag, supposedly the arch-critic of the liberal consensus, arguing for a policy – liberal interventionism – that is now, in the world created by the Iraq War (2003–present), frequently reviled as the acme of liberal hubris. It is almost certainly the only thing that Sontag has in common with Tony Blair – except for one other strange coincidence. There are children in Kosovo named Tonibler. And there is a square in Sarajevo – in front of the National Theatre – named Pozorišni trg – Susan Sontag: Theatre Square Susan Sontag. Many citizens of Sarajevo remember her as a hero. Admir Glamočak, a prominent Bosnian actor who played Lucky in Sontag's *Godot*, said, 'I don't have my own square in front of the theatre [...] But I always think: if it's Susan Sontag, she deserves that damn square.'

So: on the one hand, we have Sontag's decades of disappointing behaviour – her condescension and misanthropy (she wrote in her journal that she found 'almost everyone with whom I have contact ugly and shallow'), her insecurity, her insanely high standards (congratulated on *On Photography* [1977], she sighed, 'But it's not as good as Walter Benjamin, is it?'), her poor personal hygiene (she had to remind herself to bathe), her habitual lying (she pretended to her oncologist that she hardly ever smoked), her unpredictable moods, her ingratitude, her vaunted humourlessness, and her inability to be alone ('Rather than live alone,' she told a friend in a Chinese restaurant, 'I could live – and would live – with any person in this room chosen at random'). On the other hand, we have the kind of moral passion that takes risks and, in doing so, effects real and beneficial change in the world. Do the scales balance?

What's missing from this particular bit of double-entry bookkeeping is, of course, Sontag's work. There were four novels, a collection of short stories, and a play. The novels appeared in pairs, one pair each at the beginning and the end of her career: *The Benefactor* (1963) and *Death Kit* (1967) open the parentheses closed by *The Volcano Lover* (1992) and *In America* (1999). In between was the collection, *I, etcetera* (1977). The play, *Alice in Bed*, premiered in 1993. There were four collections of essays: *Against Interpretation* (1966), *Styles of Radical Will* (1969), *Under the Sign of Saturn* (1980), and *Where the Stress Falls* (2001). And there were four monographs: *On Photography* (1977), *Illness as Metaphor* (1978), *AIDS and Its Metaphors* (1989) and *Regarding the Pain of Others* (2003). This was what she was doing, in the midst of all the erratic behaviour, all the campaigning for liberal causes: she was writing.

At first, she wrote in favour of 'the New Sensibility': a seductive aestheticism given a radical sixties burnish. The title essay of *Against Interpretation* argued for a sensuous criticism, in place of the 'reactionary, stifling' project that reduces us to merely 'interpreting' works of art. (Was the tank in Bergman's *The Silence* a phallic symbol? No: it was 'an immediate sensory equivalent for the mysterious abrupt armoured happenings going on inside the hotel'.) It was a renewed formalism, owing much to Oscar Wilde ('Notes on Camp' is dedicated to Wilde). Nobody listened, of course – least of all the academics who were her targets. And as Sontag's career progressed, she moved away from aestheticism and became something like a conservator of the lives and works of great writers: her essay-portraits of E.M. Cioran, Walter Benjamin, Roland Barthes, W.G. Sebald and others repay endless rereading. On the other hand, she never stopped being a formidable polemicist: her 1975 attack on Leni Riefenstahl, in the form of a vitiating critique of the fascist aesthetic ('Fascinating Fascism', collected in *Under the Sign of Saturn*), remains the final word on the subject. The closing lines are superb: 'The colour is black, the material is leather, the seduction is beauty, the justification is honesty, the aim is ecstasy, the fantasy is death.'

Although almost all of Sontag's work remains in print, fifteen years after her death, the current value of its stock is difficult to assess. Her showing on university reading lists is poor, especially in English departments. She is not really a hero of contemporary feminists, or of contemporary literary hipsters (they chose Joan Didion instead). It is rare, nowadays, to come across a reference to Sontag's ideas *qua* ideas. Much more common to find her invoked as an icon of something or other: sixties radicalism, perhaps, or modernist rigour, or the role of the public intellectual. More common still to find her cited as a locus of faded gossip (Moser adds his own titbit to the anthology of juicy Sontag stories: in the mid-1960s she had a brief affair with Robert Kennedy). But to some of us, the work, and the ideas, still matter very much. Almost all of Sontag's non-fiction is first-rate: each essay or monograph an exemplum of lucid, densely epigrammatic prose and elegantly marshalled argument. But more than this: Sontag was, and remains, an inspirer.

A personal interest is now declared: Sontag's work has been important to me for most of my adult life. In the summer of 2005 I sat down with my freshly bought copies of *Against Interpretation* and *Styles of Radical Will* and *Under the Sign of*

Saturn and made a list of the films and books that Sontag recommended. Following her syllabus, I worked my way through most of early Godard. I also watched *Rashomon*, *Throne of Blood*, *The Lady from Shanghai*, Bresson's *Les Dames du bois de Boulogne*, much of early Truffaut, Bergman's *The Silence*, *Through a Glass Darkly*, *Winter Light* and *Persona*, Renoir's *La Règle du jeu* and *La Grande Illusion*, Resnais's *Hiroshima mon amour*, *Night and Fog* and *Last Year in Marienbad*, Buñuel's *Un Chien Andalou* and *L'Âge d'or*. I was supposed to be working on my doctorate, but because I had just that year encountered Sontag's essays for the first time, and found myself utterly seduced by the authority of her style (itself an example of the 'erotics of art' that she called for in *Against Interpretation*), it suddenly seemed much more urgent that I shore up these embarrassing gaps in my cultural knowledge. Before me was the example of Sontag's avidity: her lifelong conviction that a writer is 'someone who is interested in "everything"'.

It is because of Sontag that I have seen Leni Riefenstahl's *Triumph of the Will* (looking carefully, as I watched, for the beauty that the earlier, more radical Sontag claimed to find there alongside the Nazi propaganda, and seeing, perhaps because I had also read 'Fascinating Fascism', only Nazi propaganda). It is because of Sontag that I have read Brecht's unreadable early play *Baal*, and because of her that I regard Ionesco as fundamentally second-rate. A list of writers whom I have read solely because Sontag wrote about them would include Paul Goodman, Glenway Wescott, Pauline Réage, Georges Bataille, Joseph Brodsky, Ortega y Gasset and (God help us) Georg Lukács, whom even Sontag cannot persuade me is worth the effort. And it is because of Sontag that I first began to think, in my amateurish way, about some of the classic questions: style versus content; tradition versus experiment; art versus life. In watching those films, and in reading those books, I hoped, I suppose, to learn to write with Sontagian authority. A man can dream.

This personal excursus is a roundabout way of suggesting that if Sontag's work can matter in this way to one reader, whom she never met and who had no personal stake in her life or career, then it matters *tout court*. To state the obvious: a writer is 'important' not because of who she is, but because of what she writes.

Sontag was (is) the kind of writer who inspires not public hosannas but passionate private emulation. To read her is to hunger for a wider, deeper knowledge of art, history, philosophy, literature, film – to seek to nourish one's mind in the way that Sontag nourished hers ('Art', she once wrote, 'is the intelligent gratification of consciousness'). In other words, Sontag was (is) the kind of writer fated to inspire individuals, rather than groups – the kind of writer whom, in our feverishly communitarian times, we least esteem. (In the late 2010s, if a writer isn't striding towards the culture-war barricades, we scarcely know what to do with her.) The significance of Sontag's work is therefore harder to quantify than her significance as a cultural phenomenon – her role, as Moser puts it, as 'America's last great literary star.'

Which doesn't excuse us from making the effort. Surely part of the interest in any biography of Sontag is the question of how she became what she was – not just an icon, but that much rarer thing, a writer with a genuinely distinctive style of being and thinking. Sontag understood herself to be engaged in a lifelong project of self-fashioning: becoming not just 'Susan Sontag' but learning always, as she put it in *Against Interpretation*, 'to *see* more, to *hear* more, to *feel* more'. Moser is good on Sontag's childhood; he is ready with his laundry list of anecdotes about her various inadequacies; but he gives us no real insight into how the work, and therefore the self, was made – the kind of insight which is, in the last analysis, the only real justification for any biography of a writer.

Moser's own style is prosecutorial. He comes armed with the morality of his time, and, judging Sontag by its standards, finds her severely wanting. He devotes many pages to Sontag's failure to out herself as bisexual during the early years of the AIDS crisis – although, by this stage, he has already given us irrefutable evidence that this was a gesture of which Sontag was simply not capable. (Surprised in the middle of a nap, she would aggressively insist that she had been not sleeping, but working; confronted with a subject of which she was ignorant, she would dismiss it and talk about something she had mastered. To fashion a self is also to become a slave to the self so fashioned. 'Susan Sontag' – all appetite and will – could not be permitted to look vulnerable.) But Moser is unforgiving. Sontag's monograph on the crisis, *AIDS and Its Metaphors*, reveals, he says, 'how quickly metaphor can slide into obfuscation, abstraction, lying'; her other responses are 'thin, dainty, detached'. But Sontag's own journals, which Moser quotes extensively throughout, reveal someone perennially at war with sex and sexuality – forever 'detached' from experiences that were simply not amenable to the forces of the radical will. 'What would it have meant,' Moser asks, 'for one of the most famous writers in the country, a writer whose cultural authority was unparalleled, to say that she was in a relationship with another famous woman?' For Sontag, it would have meant the collapse of a self built and rebuilt in a continuous attempt to escape from the neediness and unpredictability of an alcoholic mother (more on whom anon). But Moser does not allow the point.

This is literary biography as an act of generational (can we say Oedipal?) revenge. In making his case against Sontag so thoroughly, Moser inflicts upon his readers the sort of fruitless moral calculations with which I began this review: was Sontag a good person? Was she a bad mother? A faithless friend? Was she sufficiently committed to the right causes? Does she meet the stringent standards for private behaviour that we now impose on dead writers? Et cetera, et cetera. But if a biography defaults too readily to the business of moral judgement, then it has failed in its ideally appointed task: to recreate the inner life of its subject. It is despite Moser, rather than because of him, that we intuit the reasons for Sontag's refusal to come out during the AIDS crisis. 'The very nature of thinking is "but",' Moser quotes Sontag as saying. By this, she meant that the beginning of thought is to step, as Nietzsche insisted that we must, 'beyond good and evil'. Instead, Moser brings his 21st-century moralizing consciousness to bear, and gives us a portrait of the artist as a compromised diva.

People who remake themselves are perennially fascinating, especially to those of us who seem to grow less by conscious fiat than by chaotic improvisation. (How did I end up *here*?) Sontag's remaking of herself is the story of her life, and it is this story that makes *Sontag: Her Life and Work* (2019) worth reading, even if it isn't quite the story that Moser actually tells. She was born Susan Rosenblatt in 1933, descended, on her mother's side, from Polish immigrants (*In America*, her final novel, tells the story of a group of well-to-do Poles who travel to California and found a commune). Her father, Jack, died of tuberculosis in China when Sontag was five (*Illness as Metaphor* superbly anatomizes the artistic uses to which TB was put in the nineteenth century). Her mother, Mildred, drank. 'Don't leave me,' Mildred would beg her daughter. 'I'm afraid of the dark. I need you here.' Sontag developed childhood asthma – a disease that is frequently, as Moser notes, 'triggered by emotional turmoil'. As Susan 'stretched toward the ceiling in an effort to find breath', Mildred would leave the room, unable to cope. 'I had no mother,' Sontag would tell people, as an adult.

Sontag later wrote that she had experienced her childhood as a 'long prison sentence'. Her project of self-fashioning – or self-rescue – began, as such projects generally do, early. When Mildred married an ex-soldier named Nat Sontag, Susan happily changed her name. When the family moved to Tucson, Arizona, and Susan, aged eleven, entered a new high school, she made a 'conscious decision': 'I will be popular.' In becoming Susan Sontag, Moser writes, she 'did not want to feel like asthmatic, helpless, unpopular Sue Rosenblatt'. Many people make such promises to themselves. But not everyone is Susan Sontag. What made her different was the quality of her mind (or perhaps I should say the quality of her will: in Sontag's essays, 'mind' and 'will' are often more or less synonymous). Aged three, she had already learned to read. In school, she was, as a friend put it, not just a good student but 'a champion student'. Books did for her what books do for bright children: simultaneously offered her the promise of a glittering future and sealed her more thoroughly in her loneliness.

In 'Pilgrimage' (1987), a memoir, not entirely truthful, of her teenage years, she wrote: 'What other people thought of me remained a dim consideration, since other people seemed to me astonishingly unseeing and uncurious, while I longed to learn everything.' Compare Ryszard, the writer from *In America*, 'doomed to find no one clever enough'. High intelligence is itself deracinating. The extremely bright are more or less condemned to reject their beginnings and seek out a world in which people have read the same books, listened to the same music, seen through the same cant. Or, as Hannibal Lecter remarks to Clarice Starling in *The Silence of the Lambs*, 'Being smart spoils a lot of things, doesn't it?' An early encounter with a copy of *Partisan Review* – she was fifteen; the key essay was 'Art and Fortune' by Lionel Trilling – made her 'tremble with excitement'. Within a year, she had 'read all the New Critics and become a great fan of Kenneth Burke'. When she got to the University of Chicago she approached a lecturer, who had introduced himself as 'Mr Burke', and asked if his first name was Kenneth. Why did she want to know? 'Well, I've read *The Philosophy of Literary Form* and *A Grammar of Motives ...*' She was sixteen.

I don't mean to be patronizing when I say that, for all her ardent self-invention, Sontag never really stopped being the brightest kid in the class. Good writers usually do start out as the brightest kid in the class, and there is a sense in which literature is what happens when all the bright kids grow up and compare notes. But being the brightest kid in the class is a psychologically precarious business. Hypertrophy of intellect – necessary to keep you in the top spot – can cause starvation of the heart. Errors of judgement often follow. In Sontag's case, it happened when she was seventeen. At Chicago, she sat in on a sociology lecture taught by a young instructor, Philip Rieff. The next day, she had become his research assistant. A week later, they were married. The marriage lasted eight years. Towards the end of her life, Sontag wrote about reading *Middlemarch* at eighteen: 'a third of the way through the book I burst into tears because I realized not only that *I* was Dorothea but that, a few months earlier, I had married Mr. Causaubon.'

It was the marriage to Philip Rieff that produced her son, David. It also, according to Moser, produced her first book. *Freud: The Mind of the Moralist* (1959) is credited to Rieff, but Moser advances the theory that it is actually Sontag's work, and suggests that keeping shtum about its true authorship was part of the price Sontag paid for escaping the marriage in the early 1960s. In any event, once she had left Rieff and gone to Oxford, and thence to Paris, her self-fashioning could begin in earnest: she began to absorb the radical art of the 1960s (Happenings, the Cinémathèque Française, Willem de

Kooning, Jasper Johns, Andy Warhol), and to publish the essays that would make up *Against Interpretation*. In 1963 a novel, *The Benefactor*, appeared. (It was about a man, Hippolyte, who decides to live entirely in and for his dreams. Hannah Arendt liked it. No one else ever has.) She left academe as soon as she could, and never returned. 'Susan Sontag' was not an academic. She was a writer – 'someone who pays attention to the world'. She would spend the rest of her life as a star; the most glamourous public intellectual of them all. She did what she was best at: she transmuted her obsessions and experiences (photography, cancer, film) into those unglamorous things: works of criticism. There were also the novels – she won the National Book Award for *In America*, and *The Volcano Lover* was, improbably, a bestseller. It is impossible to imagine anyone else sustaining such a career – then or now. She has had, as Moser notes, no successors.

(A side note on Sontag's fiction: Moser convincingly argues that *The Volcano Lover*, a sumptuous retelling of the love triangle between Emma Hamilton, Lord Nelson and Sir William Hamilton, is her best novel. The others, especially the first two, are, to put it politely, heavy going. She was too wedded to the glamour of the avant garde – to the 'boring' art she extolled in 'The Aesthetics of Silence' (1967). When it came to fiction, Sontag thought that modernism was the point of art, when really, if this isn't too facile a reversal, art was the point of modernism – aesthetic experience being the destination, with the choice of conveyance (traditionalism, experimentation) up to you. It occurred to her only belatedly that the novel is not a plastic art – that it could not be revolutionized as easily or as completely as sculpture, painting, dance, or even film; that a novel is narrative or it is nothing. The last two novels do their best to escape the gravitational pull of the modern masters. Behind the metafictional prologues and the stream-of-consciousness divagations and the interpolated letters and diaries, old-fashioned stories are signalling wildly to be let out.)

How many lives could successfully withstand eight hundred pages of prosecutorial scrutiny? Perhaps the *sine qua non* of successful biography is the empathetic leap. What was it like to be my subject? How did it feel, to be Susan Sontag? *Sontag: Her Life and Work* tells us vividly what it was like to *know* Susan Sontag (it was a tough gig). But it doesn't tell us what it was like to *be* Susan Sontag (perhaps an even tougher gig, especially if her published journals are to be believed). As with all writers, the work is the best clue we have to the nature of the inner life: notes and drafts, materials published and unpublished. But *Sontag: Her Life and Work* tells us little about how the essays and books were made. Moser does discuss an unpublished essay, 'Sartre's Abdication', composed in the early 1980s, in which Sontag accuses Sartre of scrambling his mind with amphetamines: *Saint Genet* (1952), his elephantine biography of Genet, has, according to Sontag, 'the characteristic overexplicitness of writing done on speed'. Sontag knew whereof she spoke: she, too, was writing on speed (and in fact composed many of her most famous essays in this way). Robert Silvers at *The New York Review of Books* rejected the piece, pointing out, more or less tactfully, its incoherence. Moser cites the episode less for the insight it offers into Sontag's creative processes and more for the proof it seems to give of her lack of self-awareness (and of her need to create self-portraits in the guise of character studies of other writers).

Moser quotes Gary Indiana to the effect that 'Susan wrote in a way that no one I've ever known wrote or writes' – but leaves this tantalizing observation unelaborated. If Sontag's writing processes were distinctive, doesn't that tell us something important about the way she thought and felt about her work

– and about what that work might mean? (Incredibly, once, she invited her friend Michael Silverblatt to sit in her room as she wrote. 'I'm going to be writing. We can babble.' What was *that* like?) Compare Richard Ellmann's biography of Joyce, or Leon Edel's of Henry James: in each of these books, the story of how the work gets written *is* the story of the writer's life, with almost everything else relegated to ancillary status. In Moser's telling, the story of Susan Sontag's life is largely the story of how she failed to empathize with the people closest to her – how she disappointed and mistreated them. No responsible biographer would ignore such a rich vein of anecdotal evidence. But as the Age of Susan Sontag recedes in time (and what an age it was! What writers it produced!), the moral question (was she good or bad?) becomes less urgent. It is the work that lasts, if it lasts.

In 'Against Interpretation', Sontag wrote: '*Transparence* is the highest, most liberating value in art – and in criticism – today. Transparence means experiencing the luminousness of the thing in itself, of things being what they are.' In other words: experience first; morality later. Or, as Nietzsche put it: 'That which is done out of love always takes place beyond good and evil.' In his final sentences, Moser suggests that Sontag herself would warn us 'against the mystifications of photographs and portraits: including those of biographers'. That is well and decently said. Was she a terrible person? Moser seems to think so. But even if this judgement stands, it still feels necessary to argue that being terrible was the least interesting thing about her. Susan, *sui generis*. More's the pity.

The Dublin Review of Books, October 2019

ON JOHN GRAY

Why can't a person be more like a cat? More specifically: why can't *philosophers* be more like cats? John Gray is a philosopher, sort of. But in some ways he would rather be a cat. 'Seldom doing anything unless it serves a definite purpose or produces immediate enjoyment, cats are arch-realists,' he says. 'Faced with human folly, they simply walk away.'

John Gray is not a cat. ('Humans,' alas, 'cannot become cats.') Faced with human folly – by which he often means the ideas of philosophers – he does not walk away. Instead, he takes folly apart to see how it works. He is an anatomist of error, an encyclopaedist of asininity. Whatever it is, we've got it wrong: this is Gray's burden, his preachment. He does not philosophize, in the academic sense or in any other. He is an anti-philosopher, an enemy of philosophy as such.

Hired to restore the church's treasured stained-glass windows, Gray scrapes off the ancient smoke and dust, particle by particle. The glass is now clean, but – he finds – intolerably tinted by human artifice. Such a window, he says, can show us nothing. He takes the window out of its frame and smashes the coloured glass.

But no: there is still something in the way. Swinging his hammer, he demolishes the church and sweeps away the rubble. Now what remains is merely what was there in the first place: the world, seen clear. We may have nowhere in which to worship and no protection from the elements, Gray tells the outraged sacristan. But at least we have dispensed with our illusions.

For 'church', read any given system of faith or metaphysics; for 'sacristan', read human beings (or, as Gray insists on calling them, 'humans'). Gray would have us unsheltered and unfooled: unsheltered by systems, unfooled by our need for meaning. To read his books is to find oneself led by a calm, remorseless guide across a landscape of toppled ruins. Behind you lie the crushed temples of Judaism, Christianity, Islam, humanism, Marxism, Enlightenment rationalism. Up ahead, looming blackly, is the wrecked Death Star of Transhumanism. The guide seems affable enough: a bit humourless, perhaps, but excellent company nonetheless. On the other hand, he is the man who has caused all these ruins to fall. Can we trust him?

I see that I have twice now figured Gray as a wrecker, a demolition man. Is that fair? He's certainly not a builder, or even a repairer of damaged buildings. But there is more to his work than the smashing of icons. Let me shift the analogy. In Douglas Adams's *The Hitchhiker's Guide to the Galaxy*, there is an alien torture device called the Total Perspective Vortex that works by showing you precisely where you stand in relation to the cosmic totality. Most victims, perceiving their utter insignificance in the scheme of things, go mad. This is what Gray's work reminds me of. The ten books he has published since the beginning of the twenty-first century constitute a Total Perspective Vortex intended methodically to disabuse us of the more tenacious of our consoling fictions. *Straw Dogs* (2002) takes out humanism and secular progressivism. *Black Mass* (2007) rubbishes Christianity, Marxism and fascism. *The Silence of Animals* (2013) dismantles human exceptionalism. *The Soul of the Marionette* (2015) puts paid to free will and the self. *Seven Types of Atheism* (2018) points out that even getting rid of God represents a kind of faith. And now *Feline Philosophy* dismisses the enterprise of philosophy *in toto*.

The crucial difference between Adams's Total Perspective Vortex and Gray's is that to enter Gray's Vortex feels salutary, rather than deranging. Or salutary to some of us, at least. Plenty of people have, in fact, been deranged by Gray's work (though they do, now that I mention it, tend to be people who were pretty deranged to begin with). The libertarian columnist Tim Black, reviewing Gray's essay collection *Gray's Anatomy* (2009) for the formerly Marxist, now merely anti-woke website Spiked, found 'all the classic Gray components':

> the contrived aphoristic wisdom; the tedious, derivative anti-Enlightenment riffs; and, knitting it all together, the pompous insistence that humans, forever deluded by a mistaken, Christian-inspired sense of their uniqueness, will, in striving to shape the world in their image, only bring misery upon not just themselves but every living thing on Earth.

Critics who find their beliefs threatened by the book under review often adopt the classic pose of world-weary sophistication ('tedious', 'derivative'): much easier than refuting powerful arguments. And if Gray sounds pompous to the philistine ear, this is perhaps because he knows who he is and what he thinks – qualities that have always been caviar to the general. But this is by the by. Black's account of Gray is colourful (sorry) but misses the point superbly. As does the account offered by Ian Thomson in the *Catholic Herald*, which sums Gray up as a 'career misanthrope'. As, indeed, does the account offered by the left-wing website Open Democracy, in which Gray appears as a reactionary and 'one of the intellectual leaders of the nationalist Right'.

These accounts are representative of the elite response to Gray's work. For leftists, he's a rightist; for rightists, a leftist. He has, for instance, been accused of dragging the *New Statesman* to the right. But he could just as plausibly be accused of dragging the *Daily Mail*, for which he also writes, slightly to the left. The whole point of Gray is that he doesn't think in terms of right or left. He thinks in Gray-scale, perceiving colours beyond the visible political spectrum.

But let's say it again: to call Gray a misanthrope or a reactionary or a nationalist (or to apply to him any other term from the vocabulary of contemporary political morality) is to miss the point. His books are not attacks on humanity as such. Nor is he tub-thumping for a particular politics or even for a particular morality (I'll come in a moment to the question of whether or not a specific politics can or should be extracted from Gray's work). Instead, his books are in the first instance the record of an honourable attempt to discover what can be said about human beings if we dispense, as thoroughly as we can, with the things that human beings have said about themselves. To step out of Gray's Total Perspective Vortex and ask, 'But what's left?' is to misunderstand the purpose of the Vortex. What's left, when Gray is finished, is everything: life, death, nature, the universe. All there is, in other words. The point is the seeing. In the final sentence of *Straw Dogs*, he asks, 'Can we not think of the aim of life as being simply to see?'

Gray knows that for most human beings, the answer to this question is no. 'Human kind,' says T.S. Eliot's overquoted bird in 'Burnt Norton', 'cannot bear very much reality.' Gray, you feel, would get on famously with that bird ('Human beings,' he writes in *Straw Dogs*, 'cannot live without illusion'). What might it look like, a world without illusion? What might it mean to see clearly, or as clearly as we can, the reality that we cannot bear? Only secondarily does Gray propose a *modus vivendi* in response to unillusioned reality. And he isn't proposing it for the masses, either.

Feline Philosophy, a short book ostensibly about cats (Gray is a lifelong ailurophile, or, if you're feeling less pretentious, a lover of cats), in fact serves as a handy primer on Gray's thought – it is the Total Perspective Vortex in miniature. Hardened Gray-watchers will not be surprised to learn that, in his book about cats and philosophy, Gray turns out to be pro-cat and anti-philosopher. If this is so, it is because cats, according to Gray, do not philosophize. 'The source of philosophy,' he writes, 'is anxiety, and cats do not suffer from anxiety unless they are threatened or find themselves in a strange place. For humans, the world is a threatening and strange place. Religions are an attempt to make an inhuman universe humanly habitable.' By *religions* he means any human system that imposes meaning on the world, thereby endeavouring to annul 'the abiding disquiet that goes with being human'.

Cats, who 'thrive without anxiously inquiring how to live', are better off without philosophy. 'Philosophy testifies to the frailty of the human mind. Humans philosophize for the same reason they pray. They know the meaning they have fashioned in their lives is fragile and live in dread of its breaking down.' In *Straw Dogs*, Gray suggests that 'the examined life may not be worth living'. In *Feline Philosophy* (from dogs to cats) an echo appears: 'Cats do not need to examine their lives, because they do not doubt that life is worth living.'

Having seen off religion, Gray takes a quick tour of the history of philosophy, brandishing his hammer. Plato's 'doctrine of forms' is a 'mystical vision', a 'figment'. The Epicureans 'cannot secure their tranquil garden against the turmoil of history'. The Stoics advocated 'a pose of indifference to life'. Descartes, with his monstrous 'experiments' on animals, thought he had proved that only humans had souls; 'what [he] actually showed is that humans can be more unthinking than any other animal'. August Comte (an old enemy of Gray's), advocated with his Religion of Humanity 'a watery version of Christianity'. *Und so weiter.* For Gray, all philosophers commit the same error: 'they imagine life can be ordered by human reason'. In fact, 'Our lives are shaped by chance and our emotions by the body'. There are only biology and hazard: the twin sources of our 'abiding disquiet'.

All of this is more or less familiar from Gray's previous books. What's new in *Feline Philosophy* is precisely the feline element. Cats, Gray notes, 'do not exert themselves to improve the world, or agonise over what is the right thing to do'. (As the owner, or perhaps I should say the housemate, of two cats, I can confirm that this observation is correct.) Cats are therefore superior to Marxists, Christians, liberal meliorists and the other improvers of the human lot. Living without the fear of death, and without a distorting 'image of themselves', cats are free to realize their nature – to become, as Nietzsche might put it, what they are. They are therefore, for Gray, potentially the source of a superior approach to questions of morality and love.

Morality and love are, besides philosophy, Gray's chief targets in *Feline Philosophy*. Morality first. 'Morality has many charms,' Gray notes. 'What could be more captivating than a vision of everlasting justice?' But there is no such thing. What is construed as moral changes from one age to the next. Once people saw the building of empires as moral. Now imperialism is seen as a high-water-mark of human rapacity. Once homosexuality was immoral. Now it is normal, and good.

'What morality demands shifts across the generations and may change more than once within a single human lifetime.'

This seems like an unexceptionable truth – though it is, of course, perennially intolerable to the bridegrooms of meaning who constitute the majority of the human race. 'Relativism!' they cry, and demand to know how one is to live without morality. (As if relativism itself were morally 'bad', instead of simply the way things are.) We might begin, Gray suggests, by acknowledging that 'there is no such thing as a universal human agent. All that exists is the multitudinous human animal, with its many different moralities.' Instead of living for morality, or for any other idea, we might consider living in accordance with our natures, accepting a universe that is 'a purposeless process of endless change'.

Is this what cats do? Hmm. Gray's argument in favour of a 'feline ethics' hinges on what is essentially a thought experiment, and one that does not entirely refute charges of anthropomorphism (even the Total Perspective Vortex suffers the occasional breakdown). 'Simple-minded folk,' Gray writes, 'will say the reason cats do not practise philosophy is that they lack the capacity for abstract thought. But one can imagine a feline species that had this ability while still retaining the ease with which they inhabit the world.'

Can one? By 'abstract thought', Gray means, basically, language: 'Relying on what they can touch, smell, and see, cats are not ruled by words.' Wordless cats cannot live or die for ideas: fair enough. But it is not easy to imagine a species, or even an individual animal, which successfully combines the capacity to dream up ideas with the capacity to resist their allure. Of course, Gray doesn't mean it to be easy. He approves of Wittgenstein, who

> recognised that ordinary language is littered with residues of past metaphysical systems. By uncovering these traces

and recognising that the realities they describe are actually fictions, we could think more flexibly. Small doses of such a homeopathic remedy against philosophy – an anti-philosophy, one might say – might bring us closer to other animals.

In the contemplation of an imaginary race of conscious cats, we might find traces of a vaccine against the virus of thought. Here Gray, the aspirant cat, approaches something like a statement of first principles. Scrape the dirt from the stained-glass window of language; demolish the church of ideas; permit us to see ourselves as we are: animals, unbound by the strictures of a transcendent morality, tasked only with seeing what is there.

So far, so Gray. But *Feline Philosophy* does strike an interesting new note. Hitherto Gray, busy euthanizing religions and other illusory systems, has had scant time for the ultra-mundane – for, that is, the two things that in an everyday sense do the most to give human life meaning. I mean social life and love. Gray is not really interested in 'society' (not for nothing was he an early fan of Margaret Thatcher). When he occasionally turns literary critic, he scorns those writers who chronicle the social world of births, marriages and deaths, and praises instead novelists who work by parable, or by highly compressed imagery, or by both: Joseph Conrad, William Golding, J.G. Ballard, Philip K. Dick, M. John Harrison. But in *Feline Philosophy* he writes about love for, as far as I am aware, the first time. What happens when you put love in the Total Perspective Vortex?

Well. In the Vortex, of course, love stands revealed as yet another illusion. Summarizing Proust, Gray writes: 'Love erects a barrier against knowledge, against understanding – whether of others or oneself – that allows human beings relief from being themselves.' Speaking *in propria persona*, Gray is harsher still: 'In love, more than anywhere else, human beings are ruled by self-deception.' Reading this, I do wonder about those of us who have come to know parts of ourselves through love – who have learned, through loving another person deeply and being loved in return, to understand more about ourselves: where we are strong, where we are weak. Most married people would probably agree that it is, in certain crucial respects, much harder to fool yourself when someone knows you profoundly. Love may be a cultural response to biological necessity (we are gregarious animals; human children develop very slowly, and require, to say the least, a lot of tending, so it's a real plus if the parents stick together). But love does more than disguise an emptiness. At its best, love allows and encourages us to do precisely what Gray says we should: live in accordance with our nature.

For Gray, however, it might be wiser to eschew human love and reserve your deepest affections for your cat. When you love a cat, 'the intertwined emotions of vanity and cruelty, remorse and regret that are at work in love between humans [are] absent'. Is this wisdom? Human love may be, from the coign of cosmic vantage, an illusion. But it feels necessary to point out that not all love between human beings is a poisonous brew of vanity, cruelty, remorse and regret. Reading these pages, you reach for the charge, not of misanthropy, but of pusillanimity – for a writer and thinker, a far graver crime.

So. You reel out of the Total Perspective Vortex, having rid yourself of faith, the dream of utopia, morality, love, the hope of progress … 'But what do we *do*?' you ask. 'How shall we live?' Not by politics, Gray says – unless, of course, you choose to embrace such folly as a form of distraction from the void. (And if you do so choose, Gray will not judge you – at least, not to your face.) How, then?

The commentariat persists in reading Gray as if his books resembled other books about the state of the world and the human predicament. In the common run of such books, our condition is deplored, and a solution is advanced (empower workers; disempower workers; destroy privilege; create more privilege). But Gray's books are not polemics. They do not tell you how to vote, or whether you should delete your social media accounts, or whether you should organize a grass-roots campaign for social justice.

If we look to Gray's method, we can, I think, come closer to ascertaining his exact nature. The books are tricked out with all the usual scholarly apparatuses: quotations, endnotes. But they are not really works of scholarship. The prose is clear – hypnotic, in fact, in its clarity. The tone is one of numinous certainty. But Gray doesn't do *belles-lettres* or *bon mots*. Nor does he invite argument or rebuttal. He is not making a case or erecting an aesthetic monument – his values are not the values of the artist. His books proceed, rather, by parable and flat statement: now an aphorism, now a story that encodes his meaning. What else works this way?

Parable and flat statement. Isn't this how holy books work? The Bible. The *Analects* of Confucius. The *Tao Te Ching* of Lao Tzu (Gray's favourite, and the source of the phrase 'straw dogs'). Take your pick. 'To subdue one's self and return to propriety is perfect virtue.' In tone, if not in content, that sounds like Gray – but it's Confucius.

'How shall we live?' Gray is here to tell us. His books are not interventions in an ongoing political debate but handbooks for a style of life – call it the life of unillusioned contemplation. Gray's books are really meant for the few, not the many. They are aimed not at the millions who seek clarity about contemporary world events, but at the handful of individuals who might be capable of living such a rigorously denuded interior life. Gray's sense of mission, and his certainty that his mission is foredoomed, explains both the flatness and the numinosity of his prose; it also explains the weary-but-undaunted tone, misread by the unwary as misanthropy, that characterizes all of his books.

At the end of *Feline Philosophy* Gray comes out, as it were, of the closet: he offers, as an epilogue, a brief series of ana-lects, ostensibly the lessons that cats might teach us. 'If you are unhappy, you may seek comfort in your misery, but you risk making it the meaning of your life. Do not become attached to your suffering and avoid those who do.' (Incidentally, as I think most of us would agree, avoiding people who have become attached to their suffering is more or less a full-time job.) 'It is better to be indifferent to others than to feel you have to love them.' Gray has rarely been so openly instructive.

Feline Philosophy permits us to see more clearly than any of Gray's previous books his true nature. He is not really the enemy of the prophets but their competitor. Where they seek to seduce the multitude, Gray seeks to console the few. His books are designed to strengthen you against the slings and arrows; to teach you to live, insofar as it's possible, without the need for meaning.

What about the cats? *Feline Philosophy* collects many moving and provoking anecdotes about cats, real and imaginary: Mary Gaitskill's Gattino, who appears in her memoir *Lost Cat* (2020); the kitten that the war reporter Jack Laurence rescued from the battlefield in Hue during the Vietnam War; Saha, the feline protagonist of Colette's novella *La Chatte* (1933). But it behoves me to say that nothing here measures up to one throwaway line in Saul Bellow's *Humboldt's Gift* (1975): 'The cats came and glared through the window, humourless.'

In one word – *humourless* – Bellow makes what is, for me, an irrefutable argument for the human over the feline. Cats may not suffer from illusion or from the fear of death. But they are incapable of finding anything funny, or beautiful. (I find I can't resist quoting another Bellow phrase, a few lines later, in which the cats enter the kitchen 'bristling with night static'.) An aspiring cat himself, and a prophet for the contemplative few, John Gray does not do humour. He would probably suggest that jokes are merely another form of displacement activity – merely another illusion. And of course reality, seen from inside the Total Perspective Vortex, may not, in fact, be a particularly amusing thing to contemplate. But I can't help suggesting, in valediction, that some illusions may be worth hanging on to, after all.

The Dublin Review of Books, January 2021

ZADIE SMITH'S UNCERTAINTY

How has your pandemic been, so far? Have you been writing about it? If so, has it helped? 'Writing is control,' Zadie Smith observes in the first piece in *Intimations*, her slender collection of lockdown essays. 'The part of the university in which I teach should properly be called the Controlling Experience Department.'

Out there, in 'the field', there is 'Experience': a 'largely shapeless bewilderment', with 'no chapter headings or paragraph breaks or ellipses in which to catch your breath'. Experience 'just keeps coming at you', perhaps especially in 'this strange and overwhelming season of death'. But at the desk, on the page, 'space and time itself [*sic*] bend to my will'. Writers, therefore, are in the business of exerting control over experiential flux – over the blooming, buzzing confusion of the real. In a time of crisis, writing helps. Or so the theory goes.

And yet, and yet. Isn't the shapeliness and order offered by literary prose a kind of cheat? 'To write,' Smith observes, 'is to swim in an ocean of hypocrisies, moment by moment' – to offer attitudes and insights as if they were final, or true, and then to discover, 'out in the field', that they 'cannot be relied upon.' That everything we encounter is in fact more complex, offers more subtle valences to the interpretative mind, than even the most capaciously well-intentioned prose can encompass. 'Is it possible to be as flexible on the page – as shamelessly self-forgiving and ever-changing – as we are in life?'

Who better to write about lockdown than Zadie Smith? Which living essayist is less likely to bombard us with the heavy ordnance of epigram, or to enlist us peremptorily in a political argument, for or against? Smith's great achievement as a writer of non-fiction prose is to have made a virtue of uncertainty. Which is not to say that she lacks ideas, or to suggest that she arrives at no firm conclusions. Rather, it is to say that she distrusts the traditional essayist's will to mastery. For Smith, mastery of this sort – in which each essay, and perhaps even each sentence, offers implicitly the essayist's final word on her subject – is a shirking of ethical responsibility, even a kind of lie. Hence *Intimations*, and not *Assertions* or *Persuasions*. From her brief Foreword:

> There will be many books written about the year 2020: historical, analytical, political as well as comprehensive accounts. This is not any of those – the year isn't half-way done. What I've tried to do is organize some of the feelings and thoughts that events, so far, have provoked in me, in those scraps of time the year itself has allowed. These are above all personal essays: small by definition, short by necessity.

Notice is served: we are entering the country of the provisional, the personal, the pointedly unassuming. It is typical of Smith that she follows this statement of studiously modest aims – a promise 'to organize some of the feelings and thoughts that events, so far, have provoked in me' – with an essay devoted to the proposition that writing cannot really organize anything; that the essayist is necessarily a hypocrite, someone who builds a house in which they do not intend to live.

To acknowledge one's own hypocrisy, of course, is to attempt to outwit it. This is Smith's signature move, as an essayist. She repudiates herself. Later essays repudiate earlier ones. Individual essays, especially the more recent pieces, tend to become self-repudiating. Did I once think that? Now I think this; and I may yet think something else, if you catch me in another essay, written on another day. (Her novels, too, have tended to repudiate their predecessors. *NW* [2012] rejects the cartoonish realism of the first three novels; *Swing Time* [2016] cancels the modernist experimentation of *NW*.)

Smith's first collection of essays was called *Changing My Mind* (2009); her second, *Feel Free* (2018). The titles are cannily chosen. She is large; she contains multitudes. She is neither a polemicist nor a Theorist. She has no vested interests, no axes to grind. She almost never speaks or writes *ex cathedra* – and if she does, it is usually for reasons of expedience. In the Foreword to *Feel Free*, she writes:

> Writing exists (for me) at the intersection of three precarious, uncertain elements: language, the world, the self. The first is never wholly mine; the second I can only ever know in a partial sense; the third is a malleable and improvised response to the previous two.

Precarity. Uncertainty. Improvisation. This is the essay as humanist inheritance, the tradition of Montaigne: *Que sais-je?* What do I really know? Note that careful parenthesis: 'Writing exists (for me) ...' Always, Smith resists the lure of epigram. Some essayists are great foreclosers (Emerson, Sontag, Didion). Smith is a great opener-out, a refuser of final thoughts. This is what I think. Feel free to argue.

Smith herself has suggested that this emphasis on the provisional has to some degree been forced upon her by success. But it is a mark of her intellectual integrity that this is the path she has chosen. In the Foreword to *Feel Free*, she records a quip made by an old friend: 'But of course your writing so far has been a fifteen-year psychodrama.' The obtuseness of this (rather cruel) remark lies partly in its failure to acknowledge that every literary career, and indeed every life, is a 'psychodrama' (how could it be otherwise?), and partly in its blindness to the honesty that animates Smith's work. In the Foreword to *Changing My Mind: Occasional Essays*, Smith writes: 'When you are first published at a young age, your writing grows with you – and in public.' She was not obliged to own up to this aspect of her fate; and she was certainly not obliged to derive an ethic from its lessons. That she has done both of these things is proof of the quality of her mind.

It is a mind superlatively well suited to our present moment, precisely because it eschews settled positions and embraces flux. If you could generalize successfully about the Age of Covid (and Smith would probably say that you couldn't, or shouldn't), you might say something like this: the advent of the disease has been a lesson in contingency, and our collective response to it has been a lesson in the fear of contingency. Not for us Keats's negative capability, 'when man is capable of being in uncertainties, Mysteries, doubts, without any irritable reaching after fact and reason'. Give us facts. And if you can't give us facts, give us polemic: opinion stated as fact. Confronted by a future filled with radical doubt (how long will it take to find a vaccine? Is a vaccine even possible?), we have been navigating by the fixed stars of ideology, *faute de mieux*.

The effect has been to harden discourse, to purge it of nuance. Online culture wars have turned internecine. Electoral politics in the West has become a pageant of scandals. High moral dudgeon is the preferred rhetorical mode. In flight from uncertainty, we have abjured the ethical obligation to be uncertain – to pause and say maybe, rather than simply to scream yes or no.

Enter Zadie Smith, the essayist of maybe – the essayist, that is, of contingency. The third of *Intimations'* six short essays is called 'Something to Do', and it is about contingency. More precisely, it is about the ways in which Covid-19 has disclosed to us all the essential emptiness of pretty much everything we do. 'Why did you bake that banana bread? It was something to do. Why did you make a fort in your living room? Well, it's something to do. Why dress the dog as a cat? It's something to do, isn't it? Fills the time.'

You might, perhaps, have expected writers, those professional solitaries, to turn their lockdown sentences to account – to find meaning in the newly empty hours. 'Instead, in the first week I found out how much of my old life was about hiding from life. Confronted with the problem of life served neat, without distraction or adornment or superstructure, I had almost no idea of what to do with it.' Under lockdown, not simply trivial activity (baking, building a fort) but activity as such stands revealed as contingent. From this perspective, 'There is no great difference between novels and banana bread. They are both just something to do.'

Smith is less interested in redeeming this perception of futility – in torqueing it, as another writer might, until it gives up some specious meaning ('How Writing My Novel Got Me Through Lockdown') – than she is in simply formulating it, or inhabiting it – living with it, in order to see how it feels. She permits herself, and her readers, to dwell in shared doubt. 'I do feel comforted,' she writes, 'to discover I'm not the only person on this earth who has no idea what life is for, nor what is to be done with all this time aside from filling it.'

And that's it – that's the closing line of the essay. If the doubt is shared, the comfort is, too (and reading Smith is often a comforting experience, even when she is at her most pessimistic). Not just doubt, and not just comfort, but both at once, and each arrived at honestly. This is Smith's basic affect, as an essayist. Entertaining extreme views, she is the opposite of an intellectual extremist.

In fact she occupies the space once described by the contrarian novelist and critic Renata Adler as 'the radical middle'. This is where humanism lives, of course, if it lives at all; and in calling Smith an heir to the humanist tradition, I certainly don't mean to dismiss her as either a fusty traditionalist or a wishful liberal. Genuine humanist thought is radical almost by definition (*nihil humanum mihi alienum* remains a highly subversive notion, after all), and in an age of proliferating anti-humanist radicalisms, Smith's work is salutary.

Like all humanists (and, I'm tempted to say, like almost all good novelists), Smith writes as if the individual were the basic unit of meaning. The fifth piece in *Intimations* consists of pen-portraits of strangers (or near-strangers); people Smith encountered in the weeks and days before the lockdown. A local bum, wheelchair-bound, shouting into his cell phone about Covid: 'I ain't running from no cold. I survived worse. I survived WAY worse shit than this.' An apparently hard-edged New York matron, who tells Smith, as the lockdown begins, 'Thing is, we're a community, and we've got each other's back.'

Smith evokes each individual in a few superb paragraphs, and moves seamlessly from these evocations to larger questions about inequality, community, style, family, violence, madness, history. A sketch of Ben, the masseur at her local nail parlour, prompts a brief rumination on economic injustice. At their weekly sessions, they talk about school closures, snow days – each a financial disaster for Ben, who will lose work in order to take care of his son, but each merely a minor inconvenience for Smith. The closing lines of this sketch are worth quoting at length, because they show us Smith's method in action: begin and end with the individual, because it is the individual who will tell us what all the socioeconomic structures and strictures really mean:

> How high are the rents on 6th Avenue below 14th Street? High enough that the closed Barnes & Noble has stayed shuttered now for a decade, for as long as I've lived here. High enough that it's difficult to imagine how such an operation as this nail place could survive for even a week without the daily turnover. High enough that even when the nail place was two thirds full sometimes I would walk past (always being careful to cross the road to the opposite side beforehand) and see Ben standing anxiously by a hand-dryer, looking out on the street, his optimistic face transformed from the cartoon I thought I knew into a stern portrait of calculation and concern, at once mercantile and intensely humane, backlit like a del Piombo, and evidently weighed down by far more than, solely, his boy. Responsible, rather, for the fifteen white-trousered livelihoods behind him – and God knows how many more. There he stood, scanning for customers, hoping for walk-ins – or wondering where I was, maybe.

We are already, as Smith says, deluged with sociopolitical analyses of the consequences of Covid – the unemployment statistics, the lists of small businesses going under, the editorials on economic policy. But Smith's humane eye, deployed here in a few hundred words about a particular individual, reveals more about our historical moment than all of them put together. She does not begin with policies or structures. She defaults to the individual – which is another way of saying that she defaults to empathy.

The most overtly sociopolitical piece in *Intimations* is a short postscript to her pen-portraits called 'Contempt as a Virus'. Here Smith responds to the death of George Floyd and the subsequent protests. Her central conceit is characteristic. What others call racism, Smith calls contempt – a quietly brilliant move. 'Racism', as we have come to use the word, is abstract; it is, as we so often hear, 'structural'. But 'contempt' is personal. 'Contempt' particularizes.

In the piece's first sentences, Smith condenses the logic of her pen-portraits: 'You start to think of contempt as a virus. Infecting individuals first, but spreading rapidly through families, communities, peoples, power structures, nations.' Individuals first; structures later. This is not to deny the importance of structural thinking – and Smith's précis of what it means to be Black in America is both percipient and morally unerring. But Smith wants us to understand that there are no structures without individuals, and that to start our analysis with structures is to get everything backwards – to miss the particular in the flood of the general.

To understand the individual as the basic unit of meaning, as Smith does, is to understand even racism as originating in a single heart, at a given moment. Again, she is worth quoting at length:

> Patient zero of this particular virus stood on a slave-ship four hundred years ago, looked down at the sweating, bleeding, moaning mass below deck, and reverse- engineered an emotion – contempt – from a situation, he, the patient himself, had created. He looked at the human beings he had chained up and noted that they seemed to be the type of people who wore chains. So unlike other people. Frighteningly unlike! Later, in his cotton fields, he had them whipped and then made them go back to work, and thought: They can't possibly feel as we do. You can whip them and

they go back to work. And having thus placed them in a category similar to the one in which we place animals, he experienced the same fear and contempt we have for animals.

We might note, here, the use of novelistic techniques – the free indirect style ('So unlike other people'), the clinching details ('the sweating, bleeding, moaning mass') – that is intrinsic to Smith's particularizing method as an essayist. And we might also note the quiet radicalism of this passage, in which Smith, the child of a Jamaican mother and an English father, imagines herself into the mind of a slaver in order to articulate a fresh vision of what racism is: not a structural abstraction but a human choice, and hence evil in a way that no merely Theoretical analysis can ever grasp. This is an enormously powerful piece of writing. The pessimism of the essay's conclusion ('I used to think that there would one day be a vaccine [...] I don't think that any more') feels earned, even if Smith herself, the exemplary mind-changer of contemporary letters, has taught us to view all such conclusions as provisional, temporary, open to debate.

'Early on in the crisis,' Smith writes in her Foreword, 'I picked up Marcus Aurelius and for the first time in my life read his *Meditations* not as an academic exercise, nor in pursuit of pleasure, but with the same attitude I bring to the instructions for a flat-pack table – I was in need of practical assistance.' The final essay in *Intimations* homages the opening sections of Marcus Aurelius, in which the emperor lists the significant people in his life and speculates about what he has learned from each ('Of my grandfather Verus I have learned to be gentle and meek,' and so on). Smith's significant people include her parents; Zora Neale Hurston; Mohammed Ali ('"No Vietcong ever called me nigger." Therefore: solidarity'); Virginia Woolf ('To replace that missing layer of skin with language. For as long as that works'); and many others. The final entry in this list is headed 'CONTINGENCY'. From which, Smith says, she learned that she is 'a case of relative historical luck' – meaning that she 'grew up in a moment of social, religious and national transition', and that 'my physical and moral cowardice have never really been tested, until now'.

If it is our bad luck to find ourselves living in the Age of Covid-19 (and we are still half-crazed with mourning, are we not, for the world that we've lost?), it is unquestionably our good luck to find ourselves alive at the same time as Zadie Smith, and able to console ourselves with these essays – the work of a writer whose bravery, on the page at least, is beyond question.

The Dublin Review of Books, September 2020

NORMAN MAILER
The Almighty

In 1954, on holiday in Mexico, Norman Mailer discovered weed. He had smoked it before, but this time was different. He experienced 'some of the most incredible vomiting I ever had [...] like an apocalyptic purge'. But soon, 'I was on pot for the first time in my life, really on.' In fact, he felt a bit like God. His second wife, the painter Adele Morales, was sleeping on a couch nearby. 'I could seem to make her face whoever I wanted [it] to be,' Mailer wrote later, in the journal he kept during his marijuana years. 'Probably could change her into an animal if I wished.'

After that, Mailer got high on a regular basis. On 'tea' (Mailer called his weed diary 'Lipton's Journal'), he felt that 'For the first time in my life, I could really understand jazz.' He also got to know the mind of the Almighty, which bore, he discovered, a marked resemblance to his own. Hotboxing his car every night for a week, Mailer groped his way to the ideas that would shape his work during the 1960s and beyond. They were not, on the whole, very good ideas. But by 1954, Mailer was a desperate man. He was thirty-one and had published two novels. *The Naked and the Dead* (1948), which had been a smash, and *Barbary Shore* (1952), which had tanked. He felt like a failure. He needed 'the energy of new success'. Eventually, of course, new success would come. But things had to get a lot worse before they could get better.

As the 1950s turned into the 1960s, an increasingly stoned and drunk Mailer cooked up a feverish vision of a world in which Western Man was challenged by the 'Faustian' forces of technology and capitalism to remake himself at every moment of existence into either a devil or a saint. It was, he wrote in an essay called 'The White Negro' (1957), a vision of

> the inner life and the violent life, the orgy and the dream of love, the desire to murder and the desire to create, a dialectical conception of existence with a lust for power, a dark, romantic, and yet undeniably dynamic view of existence for it sees every man and woman as moving individually through each moment of life forward into growth or backward into death.

It was, in plainer terms, a farrago of Marx, Freud, and the easier bits of Heidegger and Sartre, with some Old Testament monotheism thrown in here and there to shore things up. This vision, as it grew, led the Mailer of the late 1950s and early 1960s to make a number of large and confusing statements about capitalized abstract nouns: Sex, Time, God, Cancer, the Mass Media, Psychopaths, the Hip and the Square, and so on. The final paragraphs of his third novel, *The Deer Park* (1955), offer a fair example of Mailer in Gnomic Existential Visionary mode. These lines, Mailer later confessed, were written 'at the end of a long and private trip' on mescaline:

There are hours when I would have the arrogance to reply to the Lord Himself, and so I ask, 'Would You agree that sex is where philosophy begins?'

But God, who is the oldest of the philosophers, answers in His weary cryptic way, 'Rather think of Sex as Time, and Time as the connection of new circuits.'

Then for a moment in that cold Irish soul of mine, a glimmer of the joy of the flesh came toward me, rare as the eye of the rarest tear of compassion, and we laughed together after all, because to have heard that sex was time and time the connection of new circuits was a part of the poor odd dialogues which give hope to us noble humans for more than one night.

Poor odd dialogues, indeed. When *The Deer Park* mysteriously failed to revolutionize the popular consciousness, Mailer sank even further into addiction and despair. By the autumn of 1960 he was, according to his sister Barbara, 'surly and difficult' (these details are taken from J. Michael Lennon's gripping and exhaustive 2013 biography, *Norman Mailer: A Double Life*). It was around this time that an increasingly deranged Mailer looked into running for mayor of New York. 'I thought I was unique,' he said, a decade later. 'I had something to do in the world.' Scraping together support for his mayoral bid, writing little, 'bombed and sagged' on pot, booze, Miltown and Benzedrine, and burdened with the task of bearing 'God's message', Mailer went looking for trouble. He got into scraps in bars and spent a few nights in jail.

On 19 November 1960, Mailer and Adele threw a birthday party for a friend in their Greenwich Village loft. Mailer was drunk and stoned from early on that day. At one point, he went out onto the street and invited the bums he met there to crash the party. The evening descended into a free-for-all. At around 3 am Mailer ordered his remaining guests to divide themselves into two groups: supporters and enemies. An hour later, Mailer's shirt was bloody and he had a black eye. Adele began to taunt him: 'Come on you little faggot, where's your *cojones*?' Mailer produced a two-and-a-half-inch penknife and stabbed Adele twice. 'By great luck,' J. Michael Lennon writes, 'he missed his wife's heart by a fraction of an inch.' Adele was hospitalized. When she awoke from life-saving surgery, Mailer was standing by her bed. 'Do you understand why I did it?' he said. 'I love you and I had to save you from cancer.'

Adele concluded that Mailer was 'hopelessly crazy'. But when Mailer was arrested, she declined to press charges. Mailer spent three weeks in Bellevue, under observation. In the opinion of the assistant district attorney, Mailer was in the middle of 'an acute paranoid breakdown with delusional thinking'. After spending time in Bellevue – where he played pinochle and extracted the life stories of his fellow inmates for later use in his fiction – Mailer was declared 'not psychotic' and released on parole. A few months later, Mailer wrote a short poem: 'So long as you use a knife,' it said, 'there's some love left.' It is entirely characteristic of Mailer that he went on to include this poem in a 1962 book called *Deaths for the Ladies (and Other Disasters)*. By then, Mailer and Adele's marriage had ended. In 1997 Adele published an angry memoir, *The Last Party*, in which she blamed Mailer for ruining her life. Susan, Mailer's daughter by his first wife Beatrice Silverman, would describe the stabbing as 'the single most painful thing in my childhood'. Mailer himself occasionally commented on the assault. 'It was madness,' he once wrote of the stabbing itself, which he claimed not to remember in detail. 'I was pretty drunk at the time and probably on pot.'

This story is the one thing that everybody knows about Norman Mailer: he stabbed his wife at a party in 1960. In 2018 this may in fact be the *only* thing that many people know about a writer who was once regarded as a totemic presence in American literature. In the current intellectual climate, wife-stabbing is not likely to be looked upon with indulgence; it seems fair to say that many 21st-century readers are content to dismiss Mailer as a violent misogynist and to leave his work unread.

Certainly, since his death in 2007, the value of Mailer's stock has collapsed. The literary Mount Rushmore on which his face was engraved, alongside those of John Updike, Saul Bellow and Philip Roth, has succumbed to the forces of ideo-logical erosion; round the decay of that colossal wreck, bound-less and bare, the lone and level sands stretch far away. Writing in 2011 Jonathan Lethem, a former fan, ruefully admitted that Mailer was now 'fatally out of fashion [...] Mailer is as much on the skids as the world of referents in his work is evaporat-ing.' The appearance of *A Double Life* sparked a brief revival of interest in Mailer's work. Graydon Carter, writing in *The New York Times*, praised Mailer's 'thrusting, lapidary prose', but concluded that Mailer had written 'no single volume that captured and continues to capture the hearts and minds of successive generations'. This is true: for Mailer, there was no *Herzog*, no *Slaughterhouse-Five*, no *Catch-22*. Between 1948 and 2007 Mailer produced over forty books, some of them enormously long; but if his name still rings a bell, it is largely for extra-literary reasons (he stabbed his wife; he punched a lot of people).

This was not the sort of immortality that Mailer craved. In what is almost certainly his best book, *Advertisements for Myself* (1960), he confessed that

> I am imprisoned with a perception that will settle for nothing less than making a revolution in the consciousness of our time [...] I would go so far as to think it is my present

and future work which will have the deepest influence of any
work being done by an American novelist in these years.

During the years he spent popping pills and smoking pot,
Mailer had made contact with the mind of God; he had also
discovered that it was his destiny 'to write a novel which
Dostoyevsky and Marx; Joyce and Freud; Stendhal, Tolstoy,
Proust and Spengler; Faulkner, and even moldering old
Hemingway might come to read, for it would carry what they
had to tell another part of the way'.

Mailer's error, during these years, was this: he decided that
he could only be a great and original novelist if he could invent
some great and original ideas. He expended vast energies
trying to gin up a metaphysics, drawing on his reading and his
stoned perceptions about an existential deity. He then spent ten
years wondering why his great novel was proving so difficult
to write. But this isn't really how literature operates. Writers
can get along just fine without a Theory of Everything. And
contra Sartre, we don't need to grapple with a writer's metaphysics before we can embrace his or her work. (You don't, for
example, need to be persuaded by the tenets of High Church
Anglicanism to be moved by *Four Quartets*.) Literature is about
responding to the given world.

But by 1960, this was no longer enough for Mailer. He
doubled down on his mistake, and made his stoned visions the
centre of his work. When a male novelist starts talking about
Time with a capital T (or Sex with a capital S), you know that
he has forsaken literature as such for the grander shores of
unmoored metaphysical speculation – and that the quality of
his work will now sharply decline. The good bits in Mailer –
and there are many, many good bits – are never the pages in
which he expounds his ideas. The good bits are the moments in
which he forgets about Sex and Time and the Existential Hero

and applies his senses to the world around him. Responding to the world, Mailer was a kind of genius; when he was busy being a genius, he was all but unreadable.

It seems safe to say that Mailer's ideas – both the ones that he professed to hold and the ones that he held unknowingly – were at the root of the psychotic episode that sent Adele to the hospital and led Mailer himself to Bellevue, and public disgrace. His ideas also explain why Mailer is little read today. Novels of ideas tend to suffer from built-in obsolescence, after all; and many of the ideas that Mailer expressed – particularly those about men and women, homosexuality, religious belief, and contraception – make him seem, in 2018, Palaeolithically out of touch.

It is therefore an interesting moment to find Mailer enshrined in the official US literary canon by the Library of America. *Four Books of the 1960s* has been edited by J. Michael Lennon, Mailer's stalwart biographer; Mailer's presence on the LoA list is presumably the result of some dedicated campaigning by Lennon and others, and may come as a surprise to those who had written Mailer off as a relic of the bad old days. The Library of America was originally an idea of Edmund Wilson's – he envisioned an American equivalent of the French *Bibliothèque de la Pléiade*, which keeps the canon of French literature in print in sturdy, attractive volumes. Saul Bellow and Philip Roth have already been included in the LoA; it was by no means inevitable that Mailer would join them – but here he is, with four of his 1960s hits printed on onionskin paper and given a light sprinkling of editorial fairy dust. Omitted is the seminal *Advertisements for Myself*; instead, Lennon has chosen two novels (*An American Dream* and *Why Are We in Vietnam?*) and two works of reportage (*The Armies of the Night* and *Miami and the Siege of Chicago*). The resulting volume is, as the French might say, *une salade mixte*.

An American Dream was Mailer's fourth novel, and a best-seller at the time. He wrote it as a stunt: *Esquire* serialized it in eight instalments between January and August 1964, and Mailer revised it for hardcover publication in 1965. Writing for serial publication, Mailer said, was 'like playing ten-second chess. You have to take the bold choice each time.' He churned out ten thousand words a month; the final instalment clocked in at 22,000 words, and delayed the presses until the last possible minute.

Alas, the circumstances of its composition are probably the most interesting thing about *An American Dream*. A lurid mishmash of pulp diabolism and bargain-basement Kierkegaard, the book will find, I suspect, few champions among 21st-century readers and critics. To read *An American Dream* now is to wonder at the distance we have travelled since 1964: Mailer's primitivist fantasy of male empowerment feels as out of date, in 2018, as the thrillers of Mickey Spillane. Plenty of second- and third-rate books have, of course, been immortalized by the Library of America; but none, I think, has been as grossly prurient or as philosophically unsound as *An American Dream*.

The book borrows its structure from *Crime and Punishment*. Former congressman Stephen Richards Rojack is now 'a professor of existential psychology with the not inconsiderable thesis that magic, dread, and the perception of death were the roots of motivation'. Not inconsiderable, perhaps; but not very original, either. Rojack is married to, but separated from, an heiress named Deborah Caughlin Mangaravidi Kelly, whose spirit animal, we're told, is 'a violent, brutish beast'. As the novel begins, Rojack is suicidal. His career has stalled. Deborah is stiffing him for alimony: 'I was something like $16,000 in the hole already and probably worse.' More outrageous still, Rojack has taught Deborah an unnamed sexual technique – 'something she had done with me and never with anyone else' – that she is now performing with her 'new beau'. (In one of the more entertaining conjectures in *A Double Life*, J. Michael Lennon suggests that what Rojack and Deborah are discussing here is female-to-male analingus, a pastime that makes an encore appearance in the equally murderous *Tough Guys Don't Dance* [1984].) This clinches it ('Shut your fucking mouth'): Rojack strangles Deborah to death. 'I was trying to stop, but pulse packed behind pulse in a pressure up to thunderhead; some black-biled lust, some desire to go ahead not unlike the instant one comes in a woman against her cry that she is without protection came bursting with rage out of me.' Soon, 'She was dead. Indeed she was dead.' But Deborah's death has – wouldn't you know it? – given Rojack supernatural powers. Freshly virile, he pauses to sodomize Deborah's German maid, Ruta, before throwing the cops off the scent and embarking on a two-day bender, encountering along the way a nightclub singer named Cherry, a pimp named Shago Martin, and Deborah's father, Barney Oswald Kelly, with whom, it is strongly hinted, Deborah was having an incestuous affair. (Oh, and Ruta the maid turns out to be working for the CIA – bet you didn't see that coming.)

An American Dream contains more outright nonsense than anything else Mailer ever published. 'Murder offers the promise of a vast relief,' Rojack reflects. 'It is never unsexual.' Sure. Or how about this? 'Murder sounds like a symphony in your head, and suicide is a pure quartet.' Okay then. 'Ideally a Great Bitch delivers extermination to any bucko brave enough to take carnal knowledge of her.' I needn't go on. *An American Dream* also contains some of the very worst prose that Mailer ever wrote. From the murder scene: 'She gave one malevolent look which said: "There are dimensions to evil which reach beyond the light," and then she smiled like a milkmaid and floated away and was gone.' As Rojack copulates with Ruta, the German maid: 'I felt for the first time in my life like a healthy alley cat, and I stroked at her with a delicate hatred lacquered clean up to a small flame by the anticipation of my body.' Switching between Ruta's vagina and her anus: 'Like a thief I was out of church again and dropping down for more of that pirate's gold.'

The dialogue is frequently risible. Here's a sample of Deborah's verbal style: 'I mean, *figure-toi*, pet, I had to keep up a conversation with the detective, a *horrible* man, and he was laughing at me.' Here's Cherry: 'Chookey-bah lamb. Gigot!' And here's a specimen of the excruciating repartee that Mailer gives to Shago Martin, the Black pimp whom Rojack bests in a bout of highly suspect wish-fulfilment fisticuffs: 'What about you, uncle, going to give a kid with a white ass, with a white diarrhetic old ass? Kiss my you-know-what.'

Elizabeth Hardwick, reviewing *An American Dream* for *Partisan Review* in 1965, called it 'an assortment of dull cruelties and callous copulations'. Reassessing the book in 1981, Martin Amis wrote that it was the work of 'a man in a transport, not of sexual excitement so much as the tizzy of false artistry'. These judgements stand. But we must add two further charges to the indictment: as well as being cruel and badly written, *An American Dream* is flatly racist and misogynist. It evokes a humid, cloistral world of wounded narcissism, sexual violence and fear of the other. Nowhere in its pages does Mailer put to use his extraordinary gift for writing about real people and real places; the America of *An American Dream* – with its incestuous tycoons, Bitch-Goddess heiresses and cannibalistic Knights of Faith – never existed outside of a pulp magazine. It is somehow fitting that the 1966 Warner Bros film of the book was called *See You in Hell, Darling* – the sort of title the book should have been given in the first place.

Why Are We in Vietnam? (1967) is a better book than *An American Dream*, though not by much. It recounts the story of Ranald 'D.J.' Jethroe and his friend Tex Hyde, scions of wealthy Texas families, as they hunt bears in Alaska before shipping out to fight in Vietnam. The style of the book was inspired by *Naked Lunch* (which Mailer believed entitled William S. Burroughs to 'a purchase on genius') and by the routines of Lenny Bruce; it takes the form of a scatological hepcat monologue that has dated exceptionally badly. Here's the opening paragraph:

> Hip hole and hupmobile, Braunschweiger, you didn't invite Geiger and his counter for nothing, here is D.J. the friendLee voice at your service – hold tight young America – introductions come. Let go of my dong, Shakespeare, I have gone too long, it is too late to tell my tale, may Batman tell it, let him declare there's blood on my dick and D.J. Dicktor Doc Dick and Jek has got the bloods, and has done animal murder, out out damn fart, and murder of the soldierest sort, cold was my hand and hot.

Later, Mailer would suggest that *Why Are We in Vietnam?* was, of his novels, 'the least alienated from genius'. He also thought: 'I had never written a funnier book' (or so he told J. Michael Lennon). He was wrong on both counts. *Why Are We in Vietnam?* is not a work of genius; and it is not funny. Its many 'experimental' riffs on flatulence, faecal matter, masturbation, blood, gore and phallic insecurities scarcely repay the effort they require to construe. And yet, despite its fossilized pop-cultural references and its achingly sixties bebop daddy-O affectations, *Why Are We in Vietnam?* does gather an eerie emotional power as it nears its climax. Even at the peak of his culture-prophet narcissism, Mailer never lost his gift for describing American landscapes, and his paragraphs about the final bear hunt are potently evocative:

And the ridgelines, the ridgelines now beginning to dance
in the late afternoon with transparencies behind turns of
transparency and sunlight rising up straight from the snow
in lines of razzle reflection, their eyes gritted, and afternoon
chill was still good on them yes, and yes, for the colors began
to go from snow gold and yellow to rose and blue, coral in
the folds of the ridges where the sun still hit.

If *Why Are We in Vietnam?* is a more affecting book that *An
American Dream*, it may be because it takes cognizance of
an America that actually existed. Hovering over the whole
book is Mailer's tragic sense of what the war in Vietnam was
doing every day to kids like D.J. and Tex. The book's last line
is 'Vietnam, hot damn'; in context, it is savagely ironic, and
awakens us to a painful truth. This is the sort of stuff that Great
American Novels are made of. But in 1967, Mailer had long
since been derailed by his quest to clobber America over the
head with his ideas. He didn't publish another novel for thirteen years; when he returned to fiction, it was with *Of Women
and Their Elegance* (1980), an imaginary memoir supposedly
written by Marilyn Monroe (it is as bad as it sounds).

In the meantime, he did what he should probably have
been doing all along: he looked out at the world around
him and wrote a series of unique, supercharged books about
American politics and culture. Two of the best of these appear
in *Four Books of the 1960s*. In *The Armies of the Night* (1968),
Mailer delivers his report on the March on the Pentagon, organized in October 1967 by an ecumenical assortment of anti-
war groups. In *Miami and the Siege of Chicago* (1968), he writes
about the 1968 Republican and Democratic conventions; the
latter, of course, descended into chaos when Chicago's union-
boss Mayor Richard Daley ordered his cops to round up anti-
Vietnam protesters by any means necessary.

Both of these books are written in an ironized third person (the technical term is 'illeism'; Mailer said he got the idea from *The Education of Henry Adams*). In *Armies*, Mailer refers to himself as 'Mailer', and in *Miami*, he goes by 'the reporter'. It was a simple idea. But it released Mailer's energies in an unprecedented way. He wrote the first part of *The Armies of the Night* in six weeks; the Chicago section of *Miami and the Siege of Chicago* was composed in eighteen days – and Mailer performed both of these feats in the same nine-month period. That these books contain some of the best writing Mailer did in the 1960s is not a coincidence: it was already clear from *The Naked and the Dead* that Mailer's true gifts were as a stenographer of the real. He had an uncanny ability to capture in prose the sensory affect of being in an American city – the true essence of what it felt like on the ground. This is his description of Chicago, from *Miami and the Siege of Chicago*:

> The reporter was sentimental about the town. Since he had grown up in Brooklyn, it took him no time to recognize, whenever he was in Chicago again, that the urbanites here were like the good people of Brooklyn – they were simple, strong, warm-spirited, sly, rough, compassionate, jostling, tricky and extraordinarily good-natured because they had sex in their pockets, muscles on their back, hot eats around the corner, neighbourhoods which dripped with the sauce of local legend, and real city architecture, brownstones with different windows on every floor, vistas for miles of red-brick and two-family wood-frame houses with balconies and porches, runty stunted trees rich as farmland in their promise of tenderness the first city evenings of spring, streets where kids played stickball and roller-hockey, lots of smoke and iron twilight. The clangor of the late nineteenth century, the very hope of greed, was in these streets. London one hundred years ago could not have looked much better.

Mailer's visit to Miami is equally prodigal of memorable *aperçus*:

> The vegetal memories of that excised jungle haunted Miami
> Beach in a steam-pot of miasmas. Ghosts of expunged flora,
> the never-born groaning in vegetative chancery beneath the
> asphalt came up with a tropical curse, an equatorial leaden
> wet sweat of air which rose from the earth itself, rose right
> up through the baked asphalt and into the heated air which
> entered the lungs like a hand slipping into a rubber glove.

The political analyses Mailer propounds in *Armies* and *Miami*
are now chiefly of historical, as opposed to literary, interest.
But he was a shrewd observer of American politicians – Nixon
was 'like an actor with good voice and hoards of potential, but
the despair of his dramatic coach' – and a reliable witness to
scenes of conflict. Here he is, watching the Chicago protesters
clash with police:

> The action went on for ten minutes, fifteen minutes, with the
> absolute ferocity of a tropical storm, and watching it from a
> window in the nineteenth floor, there was something of the
> detachment of studying a storm at evening through a glass,
> the light was a lovely gray-blue, the police had uniforms of
> sky-blue, even the ferocity had an abstract elemental play
> of forces of nature at battle with other forces, as if sheets of
> tropical rain were driving across the street in patterns, in
> curving patterns which curved upon each other again.

Mailer went on to write several more books in his by now pat-
ented third-person style: *Of a Fire on the Moon* (1970) was com-
missioned by *Life* magazine and ruminates upon the Apollo 11
moon shot; *St. George and the Godfather* (1972) visits the party
conventions of 1972. There are marvellous things in both books
(Mailer's account of the Apollo 11 launch at Kennedy Space
Center is Melvillean in its grandeur and eloquence); but soon
Mailer was humping his way back to the idea-mines, in search

of more grand notions with which to alter the consciousness of his age.

Styles, of course, are born in human postures, of which there are only a limited number. Mailer's posture was essentially Romantic. He had a Romantic's proneness to solipsism and histrionics. He needed to step outside of himself before he could produce work that spoke urgently to the world he lived in. In other words, he was not a natural novelist. (His novels, Clive James once wrote, 'stretch out in a line that only a tenured academic could love'.) After *Advertisements for Myself*, Mailer's best book is probably *The Executioner's Song* (1979), a monumental account of the life and death of Gary Gilmore. In the austerity of its prose, and in the plangent power of its empathy for the suffering of ordinary Americans, it bears little resemblance to Mailer's other work – which should have told him something, but didn't. His later career included the unreadable *Ancient Evenings* (1983), the cheesy *Tough Guys Don't Dance* (1984) and the embarrassing *The Gospel According to the Son* (1997). His last novel, *The Castle in the Forest* (2007), was narrated by an existentialist devil tasked with influencing a young Adolf Hitler. To the end, Mailer remained faithful to his ideas, even as they prevented him from understanding the true nature of his talent.

I met him once, at a party in his house in Provincetown, MA, in 2006. His eyes were a very pale blue and he gave the impression of being vastly more intelligent than anyone I had ever met. He was kind to me – I asked him for writing advice, and he gave it. Over the last fifteen years, I have read everything Mailer published, and I don't regret the effort. Every age assumes that its judgements are final – otherwise, why get out of bed in the morning? Mailer's untimely meditations are not what we want to hear right now. But fashions change, and writers can wait decades before finding a secure nook in the canon. For now, we must perforce think of Mailer's career much as the Victorians thought of the dinosaurs: as an alluring and terrible story that just might tell us the truth about where we've been – and where, in this minatory new age, we think we're going.

The Dublin Review of Books, May 2018

Crisis Chatter

APOCALYPSE NO

A few aphorisms, to start with: There is no such thing as the apocalypse. It is always the age of the apocalypse. If the apocalypse didn't exist, we'd have to invent it.

Of course, the apocalypse doesn't exist, so we *do* have to invent it. We're forever inventing the apocalypse. Some people deplore this, on grounds of political pragmatism. A catchphrase of the contemporary left, adapted from Fredric Jameson by way of Mark Fisher, holds that 'it is easier for us to imagine the end of the world than it is for us to imagine the end of capitalism'. But since it is, in fact, very easy for us to imagine the end of the world, I wonder how much this *aperçu* really tells us about capitalism's obduracy. Doesn't it tell us more about the pleasure we take in imagining the end of the world?

Especially the end of the American world. As the New Zealander, in Gustave Doré's 1872 illustration, is witnessing the ruins of British power, so we like to witness the ruins of American power. The apocalyptic *mise en scène*, American-style, tends towards the operatic, the globe-encompassing, and the Manichean. There are good historical reasons for this. Speaking to his Puritan flock aboard the *Arbella* in April 1630 as they sailed towards the New World, John Winthrop imagined America as the place where the City of God might at last be built. The American imagination thus grows out of teleological Christianity, with its promise of the Messiah's return (though, as one minor prophet reminds us, 'He may tarry'). The stakes for the American project are high, and getting higher all the time.

It remains a shaping paradox of the American experience that the New World should also think of itself as the country of Last Things. In America, the title bout between good and evil always looms. In 1949, for example, when Harry Truman revealed that the Soviets had just tested a nuclear weapon, a young Billy Graham told a revival meeting that this was a sure sign of the imminence of the end times: 'I am persuaded that time is desperately short!'

Time was short then. Time is short now. According to a YouGov poll conducted in March of this year, 17 per cent of Americans have an 'apocalypse survival plan' for their families. Twenty-nine per cent of Americans say they believe 'an apocalyptic disaster' will occur in their lifetimes. American politicians invoke the apocalypse routinely. 'Into the hands of America, God has placed the destiny of an afflicted mankind.' That's Ronald Reagan, in 1974. 'We stand at the birth of a new millennium, ready to unlock the mysteries of space, to free the Earth from the miseries of disease, and to harness the energies, industries and technologies of tomorrow.' That's Donald Trump, in 2017.

Destiny. Millennium. That's apocalypse talk. Both Reagan and Trump depended, for their electoral success, on white Christian evangelicals, who expect the politicians they vote for to address themselves to eschatological business as a matter of day-to-day policy. If America enjoys imagining the apocalypse, evangelical America is where the apocalypse gets real.

As of 2016, one in four American adults claimed membership of an evangelical church. Much of Trump's presidency has traded on symbolic messaging directed at this electorally potent minority. Mike Pence, twice-born since his college days, was carefully chosen to reassure evangelical voters made nervous by Trump's complete failure to act like even a once-born Christian. In May 2018, when Trump moved the US Embassy in Israel from Tel Aviv to Jerusalem, this was understood, by grateful evangelicals, as a fulfilment of end-times prophecy. One evangelical told the *Washington Post* (26 November 2019): 'Now, I don't know about you, but when I heard about Jerusalem – where the king of kings, where our soon coming king is coming back to Jerusalem – it is because President Trump declared Jerusalem to be [the] capital of Israel.' Thus Republican state Senator Doug Broxson of Florida, demonstrating that he thinks the US president has the power to confer capital-city status on what was already a capital city.

At moments of crisis Trump has tended desperately to signal evangelical voters. On 2 June this year [2020], when, in response to the Black Lives Matter protests, Trump had himself filmed walking from the White House across Lafayette Square to St John's Church – where he then posed holding a Bible upside down – many people were baffled by the apparent oddity of the gesture. But, as an article in the *Guardian* published two days later made clear, this was a message intended specifically for evangelicals. According to that article, Benjamin Horbowy, a 37-year-old evangelical from Tallahassee, Florida (what *is* it about Florida?), watched Trump's stroll to the church live on TV with his mother. 'My whole family was flabbergasted,' said Horbowy. 'My mother just shouted out, "God give him strength! He's doing a Jericho walk!"'

As the *Guardian* noted, 'A Jericho walk, in some evangelical circles, refers to the Biblical book of Joshua, where God commanded the Israelites to walk seven times around the opposing city of Jericho, whose walls then came crashing down.' Trump's Jericho walk was Ivanka's idea. Left to his own devices, the president might have replaced the Bible with a copy of his own (ghostwritten) *How to Get Rich*: something he used to do in the bedrooms of hotels he owned.

Benjamin Horbowy and his mother represent a large group of evangelical Christians who interpret not just Trump's presidency, but American history in general, in terms derived from dispensationalist theology. As Matthew Avery Sutton notes in his history of modern evangelicalism (*American Apocalypse*, 2014), evangelical audiences continue to 'devour the most daring and radical expressions of apocalypticism'.

The YouGov poll tells us that 13 per cent of Americans believe that the 'apocalyptic event' that will take place in their lifetime will be 'Judgement Day', or an aspect of Judgement Day known as 'the Rapture'. The Rapture is a concept from dispensationalist Christianity. To simplify, dispensationalism holds that God has divided history up into seven stages or dispensations. The last dispensation ends with a series of events that fulfil Biblical prophecy. Once these events have taken place, a climactic miracle called the Rapture will occur. This will be followed (or, according to some believers, perhaps preceded) by the Tribulation, a period of worldwide disaster, war, famine, suffering and general calamity, presided over by the Antichrist. After which interlude, God arrives to tidy everything up.

The words 'Rapture' and 'Tribulation', used thusly, appear nowhere in the Bible. Their popularity among American evangelical Christians derives from a Biblical commentary published in 1909 by a Christian minister named Cyrus Ingerson Scofield. Scofield, born in Michigan in 1843, was a former lawyer, ex-alcoholic and (once he had hit rock bottom and been born again) a general doer of good works. Scofield spent seven years annotating the Bible – drawing on extant Biblical scholarship and on the teachings of a peripatetic Anglo-Irish divine named John Nelson Darby – and published the results as *The Scofield Reference Bible* with Oxford University Press. Within twenty years of its first publication, the Scofield Bible had sold over a million copies. As Todd Mangum and Mark Sweetnam write in their history of the Scofield phenomenon, '*The Scofield Reference Bible* permeates evangelical culture and thought.' It is no exaggeration to say that when evangelicals refer to the Bible, they mean, more often than not, the Scofield Bible.

It was Scofield's dispensationalism that the evangelical writer Hal Lindsey popularized in his multimillion-copy bestseller *The Late Great Planet Earth* (1970). Lindsey mapped recent history onto certain prophecies from Ezekiel, Daniel and Revelation, and concluded that the Second Coming of Christ was due any day now. Here he is on the Rapture:

> It will happen! Some day, a day that only God knows, Jesus Christ is coming to take away all those who believe in Him. He is coming to meet true believers in the air. Without benefit of science, space suits, or interplanetary rockets, there will be those who will be transported into a glorious place more beautiful, more awesome, than we can possibly comprehend. Earth and all its thrills, excitement, and pleasures will be nothing in contrast to this great event. It will be the living end. The ultimate trip!

More recently, the extremely popular *Left Behind* novels (1995–2007), by Tim LaHaye and Jerry B. Jenkins, translated Scofield and Lindsey's apocalypticism into the idioms of the airport blockbuster. Prose-wise, the *Left Behind* books are remedial stuff. (Sample sentence: 'Irene was attractive and vivacious enough, even at forty.') Collectively, the series has so far sold 80 million copies. A 2014 film, starring Nicolas Cage, grossed €27 million worldwide. *Left Behind* follows various good-but-not-sufficiently-Christian Americans, like rugged airline pilot Rayford Steele, through the post-Rapture Tribulation period: war, famine, Antichrist, et cetera. The books are at once narratively compelling and morally purblind. At one point a baby is raptured from its mother's womb in the instant before birth. The mother's stomach becomes immediately 'flat', demonstrating, if nothing else, the authors' firm grasp of obstetrics. The message is clear: the unrighteous do not deserve to raise their own children. We are deep in the land of moral derangement here. For LaHaye and Jenkins, the Rapture is an authoritarian's ecstatic dream of the final ordering of the world.

It's difficult to exaggerate the power and appeal that this story possesses for American evangelical Christians. From a certain perspective, the Rapture is a promise that history *is* a story, and a story that will end happily, especially for evangelical Christians. (As Miss Prism notes in *The Importance of Being Earnest*, 'The good end happily, the bad unhappily. That is what fiction means.')

But from another perspective, the Rapture is also a secret dream of revenge – as all apocalyptic thinking is a secret dream of revenge. (The doomsday prepper, for instance, with his canned food and his semi-automatic rifle, is just waiting for the chance to avenge himself on a world that spotlights unbearably his emotional inadequacies. And Mark O'Connell, in *Notes from an Apocalypse* [2020], observes that if you're preparing for the end of civilization, you have already, in an important sense, given up on the idea of having a civilization at all.) When doomsday supervenes, good guys (evangelical Christians) are

Raptured heavenwards. Bad guys (everyone else, but especially Jews and atheists) will be tossed into the lake of fire.

There's more than a suggestion, here, I think, that the secret inner life of evangelical Christianity is to some degree built on fantasies of dominance and submission, of punishment and reward. A film like Mel Gibson's *The Passion of the Christ* (2004) shows us another facet of this retributive pathology. The film's prurient focus on the flensing, beating, whipping and crucifixion of Jesus – its relentless, obsessive interest in persecution, bodily damage and debasement – says less about Christianity's redemptive promise than it does about the evangelical interest in pain, in the ecstasy of submission, and in the intoxication of eventual dominance (when Trump told the state governors to 'dominate' the Black Lives Matter protesters, he was channelling the secret heart of white Christian America).

It's also worth noting that the suffering undergone by Christ in Mel Gibson's film doesn't come close to representing the white American experience, but it *does* precisely represent the Black American experience. White evangelicals have not, historically, suffered in this way. But Black Americans have. Looked at in a certain light, *The Passion of the Christ* is actually a recension of the historical experience of African-Americans, dehumanized by violence, reduced to tormented bodies. Thus white evangelicals co-opt actual suffering for their mythographical purposes, and the suffering of the Black body – the great repressed truth of white American history – is, as usual, visible mainly by its absence.

But American evangelical Christians are not the only people living in the end times. Nor are they the only people constructing apocalyptic narratives about Donald Trump. Secular liberals are living in the end times, too. And secular liberals have also tended to see Trump's presidency as an omen of doom. The narratives are isomorphic. The difference is one

of style. Not the Bible but Yeats's 'The Second Coming' provides the sacred text.

In the century since its first publication (in the American
magazine *The Dial*, in November 1920), 'The Second Coming'
has come to occupy the top textual spot in that strange zone
where the secular imagination overlaps with apocalyptic politics. The poem is always returning to public consciousness.
According to the *Wall Street Journal* (23 August 2016), analysis from the media database Factiva reveals that 'The Second
Coming' was 'more quoted [in American media] in the first
seven months of 2016 than in any other year of the past three
decades'. Fintan O'Toole, addressing the Yeats International
Summer School in 2018, formulated a law in response to this
statistic: 'The more quotable Yeats seems to commentators and
politicians, the worse things are.'

By this metric, America is currently in serious trouble.
Media references to 'The Second Coming' have spiked all
through Trump's presidency. Two recent instances. First, *The
Boston Globe* (30 March 2020): '"Things fall apart; the center
cannot hold," wrote W.B. Yeats in 1919. A century later, it's clear:
The epicenter cannot hold. Catastrophic decisions in the White
House have doomed the world's richest country to a season of
untold suffering.' And here's the foreign policy news website
Modern Diplomacy (14 April 2020), observing: 'The poet Yeats'
"rough beast" portends a monster, and monster is the only correct
term of judgement for an American president who encourages
manifold egregious crimes against the United States and other
nations.' Both of these articles were written before the filmed
death of George Floyd and the protests it ignited. It seems that
a certain end-times mood was already in the air.

But of course it was. It always is. And, like the apocalypse,
'The Second Coming' is always with us. Joan Didion's 1968 collection of reportage, *Slouching Towards Bethlehem*, prints the

poem in its entirety as an epigraph. In the introduction to that book, Didion writes:

> This book is called *Slouching Towards Bethlehem* because for several years now certain lines from the Yeats poem which appears two pages back have reverberated in my inner ear as if they were surgically implanted there. The widening gyre, the falcon which does not hear the falconer, the gaze blank and pitiless as the sun; those have been my points of reference, the only images against which much of what I was seeing and hearing and thinking seemed to make any pattern. 'Slouching Towards Bethlehem' is also the title of one piece in the book, and that piece [...] was the first time I had dealt directly and flatly with the evidence of atomization, the proof that things fall apart.

The piece Didion is describing here is her classic account of the hippies and dropouts of the Haight-Ashbury, a piece that ends, unforgettably, with a description of a five-year-old girl wearing white lipstick, reading a comic book, and tripping on LSD. This description climaxes a piece that begins 'The center was not holding' and that goes on to describe a country of 'commonplace reports of casual killings', 'misplaced children' and 'abandoned homes'. Apocalypse 1968?

Not everyone was persuaded. Taking Didion to task for the *London Review of Books* in 1980, Martin Amis wrote: 'Probably all writers are briefly under the impression that they are in the forefront of disintegration and chaos, that they are among the first to live and work after things fell apart.' His point isn't that the centre did, in fact, hold, in 1968. His point is that there *is* no centre. To Amis, Didion is succumbing to the lure of a distorting apocalypticism, and finding her objective correlative in 'The Second Coming'. The signs of the end are all around us: discord, alienation, acid in the kindergarten. Surely some revelation is at hand?

There is, of course, a big difference between how secular commentators use 'The Second Coming' and how evangelical Christians use the Bible. For one thing, Yeats's poem is generally not understood, by its readers, as a literal forecast of coming attractions. Yeats himself equivocated about how literally the poem was meant to be taken. 'They give me metaphors for poetry,' he said, of the intricate symbolic systems outlined in *A Vision* (1925). And if 'The Second Coming' is constantly being invoked as a powerful description of our present moment, this might tell us just as much about Yeats's genius for the lapidary phrase (and for the generally applicable metaphor) as it does about the state of our politics, or our culture.

The poem was composed in a moment of crisis. 1919: the Armistice was less than a year old. A global pandemic prospered. (In November 1918 Yeats's wife Georgie caught the Spanish Flu while pregnant with the couple's first child.) Yeats, as he wrote his great poem, might have approved of the sentiment expressed by the protagonist of Saul Bellow's *Mr. Sammler's Planet* (1970): 'Like many people who had seen the world collapse once, Mr. Sammler entertained the possibility it might collapse twice.'

In common with all apocalyptic works of art, 'The Second Coming' evokes a shiver of mingled foreboding and pleasure that we might call the chiliastic frisson. Experiencing the frisson is inarguably a rush. Not just American evangelicals, but our entire culture is addicted to the chiliastic frisson. 'Of course, we have it now, the sense of an ending,' Frank Kermode writes, in his 1967 book of that name. But: 'There is nothing at all distinguishing about eschatological anxiety.' It is common to almost every culture and to almost every historical epoch. As the year 1000 approached, people throughout Europe abandoned their homes to follow lunatics who declared themselves the Messiah, or the reincarnation of Frederick Barbarossa, or who interpreted current events as the fulfilment of sibylline prophecy. And that was just one calendrical crux, of many.

The star cliché of prose about the apocalypse is the observation that people have always believed that the end of the world was nigh. It's also then customary to note that, while every previous generation of human beings has obviously been wrong about this, *our* generation stands a much better chance of being right. For one thing, we're much further along in history now. And look at the gathering signs: fire, flood, earthquakes, plagues, rioting in the streets, monsters in power! A universal feeling of end-times dread! Surely *this*, our time now, at long, long last, is really it!

But this is the wrong inference to take from the fact that people have been expecting the end of the world to occur any day now for at least the last two thousand years. The correct inference is the statement I began with: There is no such thing as the apocalypse. It is easy for us to say that the evangelical Rapture will not take place. Less easy, perhaps, for us to say that climate change – scheduled to inflict lasting damage on the surface of the earth sometime in the next half-century – will not mean the end of the world either. (It will mean crisis, and change. But crisis and change are the rules of history, not the exceptions.) We would struggle, perhaps, to admit that the apocalypse is one of our hardiest fictions – one of the stories that we tell ourselves, as Joan Didion put it in *The White Album* (1979), in order to live – or, perhaps, in this case, in order to die.

Let's go back, one last time, to that YouGov poll. It tells us that 29 per cent of Americans say they believe 'an apocalyptic disaster' will occur in their lifetimes. And of course, the people who say this are correct: an apocalyptic disaster *will* occur in their lifetimes. They themselves will die. Things will fall apart. The centre will not hold. The world ends for each of us. Matthew 24:35–6: Heaven and earth will pass away, But of that day and hour no one knows.

The world ends for each of us. But not for all at once. In *The Sense of an Ending*, Frank Kermode (quoting Spenser) writes: 'Men, like poets, rush "into the middest", *in medias res*, when they are born; they also die *in mediis rebus*, and to make sense of their span they need fictive concords with origins and ends, such as give meaning to lives and to poems.' It is scarcely a coincidence that predictions of apocalypse tend to situate the ultimate hour within the lifetime of the person doing the predicting. The apocalypse is the individual death, rendered generally inclusive. Our lives have beginnings, middles and ends. But the flux of the world does not – or at least, none that we are privileged to witness. In the mirror of apocalypse, we see the image of our death. And since we always die, it is always the age of the apocalypse.

There are implications to this fact that go beyond aesthetics or philosophy. Narratives of apocalypse may give solace to individual lives. But they have powerful distorting effects on politics. The idea that we are close to the end is politically demoralizing. Why bother to change things, when the end of the world is near? A politics of last things is also a politics of discord and defeat. Politicians know this. They manipulate apocalyptic imagery to rouse the faithful, and to sow confusion among their enemies. Trump and Pence are masters of this game. But their opponents among the liberal commentariat have fallen for the romance of their own Rapture: Trump as the 'rough beast', the centre failing to hold, mere anarchy loosed upon the world. This vision, too, is disabling. A functioning politics begins by eschewing the chiliastic frisson. And knows that the world will keep on ending until we remind ourselves that the only real ending is ours, and ours alone.

The Dublin Review of Books, November 2020

THE MEANING OF GRETA THUNBERG

The coronavirus – but no. Let's not talk about the coronavirus. Let's talk about the other crisis instead: the supervening crisis, the crisis to which all the other crises are as mere *hors d'oeuvres*: 'the crisis that surrounds and affects us all. The one we humans have created through our way of life: beyond sustainability, divorced from nature, to which we all belong. Some call it over-consumption, others call it a climate crisis.' Thus Malena Ernman, who is the narrator, though not solely the author, of *Our House Is on Fire: Scenes of a Family and a Planet in Crisis* (2020).

This odd, disjointed book originally appeared in Sweden in 2018, a few days before, it is worth noting, Malena's daughter Greta Thunberg first took up her post outside the Swedish parliament buildings and inaugurated the 'school strike for climate' that is the basis of her global fame. The date of publication is worth noting because non-Swedish readers, who may have become aware of Greta only in December 2018, when she addressed the UN Climate Change COP24 Conference ('Our civilization is being sacrificed for the opportunity of a very small number of people to continue making enormous amounts of money'), might assume that *Our House Is on Fire*, appearing in English for the first time in 2020, was composed in the aftermath of Greta's rise to global prominence.

Not so. In its Swedish incarnation, *Our House Is on Fire* was published to capitalize not on Greta's celebrity but on her mother's. In Sweden, Malena Ernman is famous not just as a respected mezzo-soprano but as the performer chosen, via a televised contest, as the country's 2009 Eurovision entry. Malena has also worked as a newspaper columnist, stage actor and climate-change campaigner. Greta's father, Svante Thunberg, is an actor and producer. In fact it was Malena and Svante's popularity, coupled with their media connections, that guaranteed Greta a certain amount of attention when she first sat down outside the Riksdag in August 2018 accompanied by her handwritten sign. When Greta's strike began to trend on social media, and was picked up by newspapers and television, it was partly because Anders Hellberg, a family friend who happened also to be a professional photographer, shared for free his now-iconic shot of Greta hooded in her yellow rain slicker, staring, like the image of moral integrity itself, into the camera, with the strike sign just slightly out of focus in the background. And it was partly because the documentary film-maker Peter Modestij, another family acquaintance, brought a film crew along to record the strike's first days.

In other words, Greta Thunberg – with her famous and well-connected parents, and her growing prominence in the Swedish media (long before the school strike, Malena had placed stories by and about Greta in national newspapers) – was unusually well positioned to become the face of a new and powerful international movement. (It didn't hurt, of course, that Greta herself is almost hypnotically photogenic and articulate. But context counts, in every case.)

These facts run counter to the popular myth of Greta Thunberg, which tends to suggest that she sprang fully formed, like Athena from the head of Zeus, from the hearth of an ordinary Swedish family, impelled by nothing but her passion and her remarkable charisma, and borne aloft by a growing sense, among ordinary people, that their leaders were ignoring the most significant crisis in human history. This is an appealing story, of course. But its very appeal is what might lead us to examine it more closely, if we feel so inclined. Like all popular stories, it simplifies something that is actually extremely complicated, and like all popular stories, it answers a variety of compulsions and needs, often unconsciously held.

Even before Greta made her zero-emissions yacht trip across the Atlantic in August 2019 (now semi-officially memorialized on Wikipedia as 'The Voyage of Greta Thunberg' – and note the epic cadence of that phrase), it was becoming clear that the popular response to Greta's message of reason and togetherness ('Unite behind the science') may certainly have been about togetherness but was only ever fitfully about reason. Within a month of the school strike's inception, Greta's story had made the journey from the Stockholm dailies to *The New Yorker*; Masha Gessen, having interviewed Greta, remarked that 'Thunberg's is a voice of unaccommodating clarity that reminds me of Soviet-era dissidents.' The epic tone was set.

And once she disembarked in New York to address the UN Climate Action Summit, the fact that the popular response to Greta, her mission and her voyage was essentially cultic in nature became even clearer. Her arrival in New York harbour was live-streamed online and covered by major media outlets, who reproduced another iconic photo, this time of Greta smiling, with the Manhattan skyline behind her and a turbulent sky above. She was greeted by a 'welcome flotilla' and cheering crowds. Reporters sought the high style: 'Greta Thunberg arrived in New York on Wednesday, stepping on to dry land after crossing the Atlantic in a sailboat with a passionate message to tackle global heating' (*Guardian*).

Greta's braided hair had already led to comparisons with 'a straightforward, stubborn and deeply reflective Pippi Longstocking' (this was Abba's Björn Ulvaeus); now more overtly intellectual commentators (like David Wallace-Wells, author of *The Uninhabitable Earth* [2019]) began to compare her to Joan of Arc. Melana Ernman compares her daughter to the boy who points out that the emperor is naked. (From the start, Greta and her story have been understood in terms of a narrow range of fictional and historical analogues, almost always young women or children who are felt to exemplify either innocence or purity of purpose or both.)

Greta has been welcomed as a 'prophet'; as 'Earth's saviour'; as a 'true teen role model'; as a 'role model for kids on the autism spectrum'. Other teenage girls have published essays online explaining 'Why Greta Thunberg Is My Idol'. The hourly progress of her journey across the Atlantic was monitored on social media using the hashtag #Malizia (the name of the yacht on which she sailed). On International Women's Day this year, a sixty-metre portrait of Greta, properly visible only from above, was inscribed on the playing field of a school in Hebden Bridge in West Yorkshire. In the more left-leaning quadrants of non-social media, heart-warming stories about Greta's human side have been appearing regularly since 2018. Of Greta's visit to Capitol Hill, the *Guardian* wrote: 'Photographers hoping to get a shot of Swedish climate change activist Greta Thunberg had to contend with a young boy who attempted to shield the often shy teenager from the media. The spontaneous act elicited a smile from Thunberg.'

What does this remind you of? Well, in one sense, it reminds you of something like Beatlemania (the minute-by-minute tracking of an idol's progress, the grandiose gestures of homage, the insatiable appetite for humanizing detail). And in another sense, it reminds you of a phenomenon more obviously religious in nature: the recurrent elevation, throughout the history of Christianity, of children and other politically marginal individuals to the status of seer or saint. To say, with David Wallace-Wells (and with Margaret Atwood, and with op-ed writers for publications as geographically diverse as the *Daily Telegraph* and the Australian *Courier Mail*), that Greta is our Joan of Arc is to confess, willingly or not, that our response to her mission has less to do with science and reason than it has to do with superstition, hero-worship and hagiography.

Indeed, from the beginning, the popular response to Greta Thunberg has displayed some of the characteristics of a millenarian movement, as described by Norman Cohn in his classic study *The Pursuit of the Millennium* (1957). The millenarian movements of the Middle Ages, Cohn writes in that indispensable book, appealed to 'an unorganized, atomized population'; they tended to take place 'against a background of disaster' (plague, famine, economic crisis); they were 'salvationist' in tendency (imagining the redemption of the world through struggle); they convocated around 'intellectuals or half-intellectuals', figures of humble rank perceived by their followers as prophets or messiahs, leaders who possessed 'a personal magnetism which enabled [them] to claim, with some show of plausibility, a special role in bringing history to its appointed consummation'.

We live, of course, against a background of disaster. In fact, in the age of climate change, this background threatens increasingly to become the foreground. As we preside over the mass extinction of animal species, the infiltration by micro-plastics of our oceans, and the irrevocable heating of our planet's surface, surely some revelation is at hand? As the Irish essayist Mark O'Connell writes in his superb new book, *Notes from an Apocalypse*:

> It has always been the end of the world. Our entire civilisa-tion – from Ragnarok to *Revelation* to *The Road* – rests on a foundation of flood and fire. But what if now it's *especially* the end of the world, by which I mean *even more* the end of the world: really and truly at long last the end (or something like it)?

The message we've been hearing from climate scientists for half a century now tells us that there's no *what if?* about it: anthropogenic climate change really *does* portend, if not the end of the world as such, then certain radical and irremediable changes to all of human experience. (David Wallace-Wells: 'the world has, at most, about three decades to decarbonise before truly devastating climate horrors begin'.) Under the auspices of this message, Greta's elevation to the status of saviour or saint is completely intelligible. It's just one of myriad ways in which the religious imagination continues to shape the secular world, like a restless sleeper disturbing a thin blanket.

There is also Greta's immense symbolic usefulness to our contemporary demonologies of left and right. If Greta has con-jured up thoughts of salvation for the climate-conscious left, for the climate-ignoring right she has instead evoked a language of fear, manipulation and scorn. 'Fears Greta Thunberg is being manipulated on climate change by pushy parents,' wrote the *Sun* in August 2019. 'Greta the Teenage Climate Puppet' is the preferred epithet of one fringe right-wing website. In January of this year US Treasury Secretary Steven Mnuchin remarked, in response to Thunberg's call for governments to cut back on fossil fuel use: 'Is she the chief economist? Who is she? I'm confused [...] After she goes and studies economics in college, she can come back and explain that to us.' And these examples are relatively benign in comparison to the stickers circulated in February by Canadian oil concern X-Site Energy Services, which depicted a pigtailed woman with a *Greta* tattoo being sexually assaulted. Nor should it surprise us that the right has produced an 'anti-Greta' in the form of nineteen-year-old German think-tank employee Naomi Seibt, who suggested at CPAC this year that 'climate change alarmism at its very core is a despicably anti-human ideology'.

That the right's response to Greta is just as irrational as the left's is less significant, I think, than the widespread perception of Greta's viability as a totem in the culture wars (climate-change division). It's not really a coincidence that Greta achieved global fame in the aftermath of Trump's election, when 'carbon ideologies' (in William T. Vollmann's phrase) were everywhere ascendant, and a demoralized left was casting around for some equivalent of Masha Gessen's 'Soviet-era dissidents' to rally behind in dark times. Cue Greta: here was a neurodiverse teenage girl equipped with heroic resources of patience, concentration, moral integrity and intellectual clarity: in every way the human opposite of Donald Trump (with his incuriosity, his oil-man attorney general and his apparently non-functional moral compass).

All that was left was for these two opposites to meet, which they did, sort of, in September 2019, when a video, widely shared on social media, depicted Trump's arrival at the UN Climate Action Summit. As Trump enters the foyer – waddling along in his odd, penguin-like way – Greta can be glimpsed in the background, her face set in an expression of thunderous disapproval. Here it is: Greta versus the carbon ideologies, live from New York. It was widely felt, by people who shared the video, that Greta had scored a victory here; just as she was felt to have scored a victory when, in response to Trump's suggestion that she had an 'anger management problem' and should go to 'a good old-fashioned movie with a friend', she changed her Twitter biography to read, 'A teenager working on her anger management problem. Currently chilling and watching a good old-fashioned movie with a friend.' Boom!

That climate change – the issue, after all, on which Greta and Donald most forcibly differ, and the issue that they were both in New York to publicize – was scarcely mentioned at all in the online coverage that followed these smackdowns tells us a great deal about the roles played by Trump and Greta in our collective imagination. No victories had been won, in these online spats, for climate consciousness (or for climate ignorance). In fact what had happened was just another skirmish in the culture wars, in which two people, elevated (or reduced) to the status of symbols, were moved around like counters in a high-stakes board game. Or, more to the point, like two figures acting parts in a story – a classically Manichean drama of good versus evil, innocence versus complicity, integrity versus corruption, enacted on the world stage, with everyone on earth taking a side.

It shouldn't be surprising that this is the story we choose to tell, in the shadow of climate change. As an issue, climate change has proved fatally storyable – perhaps one of the reasons that we have been, and will continue to be, weirdly passive in the face of the dangers it represents. To hear that we have poisoned the world, and that the world will soon turn against us and all our works, is to hear an apparently simple message. It's a message that lends itself to fables of guilt and redemption ('We are all guilty, but if we act now, we might just save ourselves') just as readily as it spurs us to tell stories of good and evil ('The oil companies are the baddies and the environmental activists are the goodies'). Partly this urge to simplify arises because climate change, as a phenomenon, is so ungraspably huge and totalizing in its consequences that the mind quails before its ramifying complexities. There is a tremendous urge to reduce these complexities to easily understood demonological narratives, or to a blindingly obvious set of 'scientific facts' ('Listen to the science').

But nothing is simple. If stories are the tool we use to reduce the world's illimitable complexity to a graspable size, they are also, famously, the thing that prevents us from seeing how complex things really are. Ironically, it's Greta Thunberg herself – in her human particularity, rather than in her symbolic simplicity – who might be able to help us put aside the stories, or at least help us to replace the crude epics of public life with a perhaps more nuanced account of human frailty, blindness and love.

Which is to say that there are two stories about Greta Thunberg – the public and the private – and that, in muddling the two for the purposes of public symbology, we are doing ourselves a disfavour. On the other hand, in making this muddle, we are also following very much in the footsteps of Greta's parents, Malena and Svante, who have produced, in *Our House Is on Fire*, a book that attempts to connect the trauma experienced by a single Swedish family to the climate crisis, and in so doing, to find a universal and potent meaning in the family's pain.

'Scenes of a Family and a Planet in Crisis', says the subtitle, and by the end of this strange, haphazard memoir, we are left in no doubt that the Ernman-Thunberg family believes that both family and planet have been stricken by the same crisis ('Some call it over-consumption, others call it a climate crisis'). But the connection between the troubles undergone by Malena, Svante and their two daughters (Greta has a younger sister, Beata) and the dangers posed by anthropogenic climate change isn't so much proved, here, as it is forged by an act of will.

Famously, it was Greta's discovery of climate change – via a school video about the Pacific trash vortex – that offered her a means of engaging with a world that had once seemed to her incomprehensible and malign. Aged eleven, Greta had stopped eating; she experienced severe isolation at school; she had suicidal thoughts. It took Malena and Svante several years of meetings with various representatives of the Swedish medical establishment (harrowingly chronicled here) to procure for Greta a diagnosis of Asperger's Syndrome, obsessive-compulsive disorder and selective muteness. With a diagnosis at last in hand, it was possible to make various accommodations to Greta's needs, at school and elsewhere; but it was her interest in climate activism that empowered her, in Malena and Svante's telling, to begin meaningfully to grapple with the problems her disorders had created. 'Greta's energy has increased a little every day since last spring,' Malena writes, towards the end of *Our House Is on Fire*. 'Since [she won] the writing contest in the newspaper *Svenska Dagbladet*'(for an essay about climate change). 'Since she started planning her school strike.'

This, too, is an established part of the public myth of Greta Thunberg: that climate activism saved her life. It's a powerfully resonant idea, because it chimes with the general hope that climate activism will save all of our lives, if we pursue it diligently enough. The transformation dramatized in *Our House Is on Fire* – as Greta gradually evolves from a malnourished and inward child who dawdles for two hours and ten minutes over five individual gnocchi to a self-possessed young woman who eats Thai food and chats to strangers – is enormously moving, not just because of Greta's own bravery and passion but because of the heroic patience and fortitude demonstrated, along the way, by her parents. Observing Greta's awakened interest, and taking note of its salutary effects, Melana and Svante did what any loving mother and father would do: they joined in, reading books about the climate crisis, arranging for Greta to meet with climate scientists, and campaigning themselves for climate awareness. Soon Malena and Svante were abjuring plane travel (Svante, flying home with the troubled Beata after an abortive therapeutic holiday to Sardinia, is welcomed by Greta with the words, 'You just released 2.7 tonnes of CO_2 flying there and back'). Malena was chastised by her editor for writing too often about climate change.

But by this point in the book, we are completely on her side. After a hundred pages about the Ernman-Thunberg family's grinding struggles with 'meltdowns' and noise sensitivity (Beata), anorexia and depression (Greta), hyperactivity (Beata) and mutism (Greta), we are left in no doubt whatsoever that climate change has been the salvation of this family – that, in an irony unremarked upon by Malena, general catastrophe has rescued them from particular catastrophe.

In other words, the implicit story told by *Our House Is on Fire* is not global but local – indeed, familial. Roughly half of the book takes the form of a memoir about the pains and triumphs of raising children who suffer from a range of emotional and sensory disorders (this is the good half). The remainder of the text is about climate change, and the West's response to it (this is the bad half). The bad half – amid much staccato citing of scientific evidence and much humourless hectoring about governmental responsibility – advances an explicit story about the Ernman-Thunberg family's relationship to climate change in which the chronology of the implicit story is reversed. In these latter sections, it turns out that climate change was the family's problem all along.

'I should not have written a book about how I felt,' Melena reflects:

> I should not have written a book about how my family has
> felt for long periods during the past few years.
>   But I had to. We had to. Because we felt like shit. I felt
> like shit. Svante felt like shit. The children felt like shit. The
> planet felt like shit. Even the dog felt like shit.
>   And we had to write about it.

The vertiginous move, here, from the micro ('we felt like shit')
to the macro ('the planet felt like shit') is characteristic of the
arguments advanced by *Our House Is on Fire*. At various points,
the text suggests that the disorders suffered by the Ernman-
Thunberg children should be understood as local instances of a
general response to those aspects of our civilization (industrial
pollution, technological consumerism, the savage inequali-
ties promoted by unfettered capitalism) that have caused and
continue to exacerbate the climate crisis. In fact, the book
elides the climate crisis with another crisis (call it the crisis of
neo-liberalized humanity), and says it's more or less all the one
thing. Malena:

> If landslides in West Africa are one consequence of this
> crisis, drought in the Middle East another, and rising water
> levels for the island nations in the Pacific Ocean a third, then
> the crisis is expressing itself in our part of the world in the
> form of stress disorders, isolation and growing waiting lists
> within paediatric and adolescent psychiatry.

This is a rather jumbled remix of a familiar argument – perhaps
most eloquently advanced in recent years by Mark Fisher, who
in his short book *Capitalist Realism: Is There No Alternative?*
(2009) proposed that free market ideologies, having eroded
traditional community values and promoted the idea of the
solitary consumer, had caused a worldwide boom in mental
health disorders. Malena Ernman's contribution to this analysis
is to suggest that the climate crisis and the triumph of capitalist

realism are in fact the same thing, and that this thing, whatever you want to call it, is the root cause of the various troubles experienced by her family over the last few years.

We can disagree over the merits of this argument – though I would suggest that lumping climate change together with capitalist realism and suggesting that there is nothing to distinguish them is not a strategy calculated to improve our understanding of either. It's more to my immediate purpose tactfully to note that perhaps Malena and Svante's need to find an explanation for their trials has led them to engage in some high-level rhetorical fudging, and that what this means is that the explicit story told by *Our House Is on Fire* – a story about a family damaged by climate change who have set out to redress their grievances by battling climate change itself – is much less interesting, and much less true, than the implicit story it tells, which is a fragile, hopeful tale about a group of wounded people struggling to redeem their private suffering.

What is the meaning of Greta Thunberg? Despite her parents' best mythographical efforts, Greta emerges from the pages of this book not as an icon or as a symbol but rather as a human being as helplessly individualized and particular as the rest of us. She is, *in propria persona*, neither media-friendly nor divinely inspired. In fact, *Our House Is on Fire* frequently makes Greta sound like a total pain in the ass. She is, in other words, often just a completely normal teenager. This should serve to correct the public myth of Greta Thunberg. But it won't. We need the myth too badly, or so it seems.

So, what is the meaning of the myth? The critic and novelist Joan Smith, reviewing *Our House Is on Fire* for *Literary Review*, wrote:

> [Greta's] public persona is unusual and inspiring, and it offers an alternative to the pornified images of teenage girls that dominate popular culture. She also, I'm afraid, deserves

a better book than this messy melange of painful self-exposure and naive exhortation.

But the union of painful self-exposure and naive exhortation is the style of our times. Scroll through your social media newsfeed of choice. Attend a Trump rally or watch American cable news. Read a collection of personal essays. What do you see? Painful self-exposure and naive exhortation. The Greta Thunberg myth has been fashioned according to this style – a style that is also profoundly hospitable to older ideas about sainthood, the sanctity of confession, and the promise of salvation, and that permits us, whether we know it or not, to tell religious stories about the age of secular doom.

Greta the prophet appeared amongst us with a message: we must change our lives, or the climate emergency will change them for us. But the meaning of her myth is that the human response to climate change will be as irrational – will be as volatile and improvisatory – as the human response to everything else has been. Here we are. The clock is ticking. The falcon cannot hear – but you already know the rest.

The Dublin Review of Books, April 2020

JORDAN PETERSON'S 'JORDAN PETERSON'

The unreliable narrator, as a concept in fictional poetics, is frequently misunderstood. It refers not to a narrator who deliberately omits or distorts information (as, say, the narrator of Agatha Christie's *The Murder of Roger Ackroyd* pretends to us – spoiler! – that he is not the murderer of Roger Ackroyd). Rather, it describes a narrator who fails to make proper sense of the story he or she tells. The governess who narrates Henry James's *The Turn of the Screw* (1898) reveals to us, helplessly, that *she* is the evil haunting Bly; but it is up to us to draw this inference. Barbara, the prying teacher who narrates Zoë Heller's *Notes on a Scandal* (2003), is so lonely that she has been driven to cruelty and madness; but again, it's up to us to work this out.

A true unreliable narrator is one of the most difficult tricks to pull off, in fiction. To inhabit successfully a narrator who lacks self-knowledge requires achieved mastery – of character, tone, voice, structure. We should applaud, therefore, the

Canadian clinical psychologist Dr Jordan Peterson, who in two mainstream novels (and one obscurely published prequel) has presented a fictionalised alter ego, 'Jordan Peterson', in the mode of classic unreliable narration.

'Peterson' (we had better use inverted commas to keep author and character distinct) bears many similarities to his creator. They were both born and grew up in Alberta, Canada. They both studied at McGill and taught at Harvard. Peterson (the author) and 'Peterson' (the character) have family members with identical names. Both are professors of psychology at the University of Toronto. Both have enjoyed a successful clinical practice.

It is, however, 'Peterson' who interests us, as readers and critics. Brilliantly, and with painstaking care, Peterson has built up, across one fake academic text and two novels written in the mode of oracular self-help manuals, the portrait of an utterly un-self-knowing, pompously precise, bewildered, helplessly erroneous student of human nature: 'Jordan Peterson'. The portrait is both hilarious and heartbreaking – and all the more so because 'Jordan Peterson' never for one moment suspects that the joke is on him.

12 Rules for Life, the breakthrough novel in what we must think of as 'the Peterson Trilogy', riskily set forth Peterson's fictional strategies. Bravely eschewing traditional narrative for long stretches of the book, Peterson created, in *12 Rules*, a hybrid form: half deluded autobiography, half Jungian self-improvement guide. The joke, of course, was that 'Jordan Peterson', in explaining his theories of order and chaos, of hierarchical lobsters and postmodernist nihilism, in such a way as to spread his gospel of meaning, was speaking only to himself – for who could ever be taken in by such a hodgepodge of errors and unfounded assertions, such a desperate attempt to shore up the narrator's own confusion?

Of course, some reviewers *were* taken in – a testament, perhaps, to Peterson's genius. The normally perceptive Pankaj Mishra, in a significant misreading of *12 Rules* published in the *New York Review of Books*, seemed to take 'Peterson' seriously, and decried his 'fascist mysticism' (as if 'Peterson', that addled buffoon, could represent a serious political threat!). On the other hand, Hari Kunzru, reviewing the book for the *Guardian*, seemed in on the joke: 'He appears sincere,' Kunzru wrote, 'and in some ways admirable in his fierce desire for truth, but he is much less far along his journey than he thinks, and one ends his oppressive, hectoring book relieved to be free of him.' Confusingly, it isn't entirely clear whether Kunzru is referring here to 'Peterson' or Peterson; but he is right, of course, to call attention to the disjunct between what 'Peterson' says and the actual state of his knowledge of the world – the essence of the unreliable narrator trope.

Perhaps these critics weren't familiar with the first volume in the Peterson trilogy, a more daring and experimental work first published by Routledge in 1999, which went unreviewed in mainstream venues. *Maps of Meaning: The Architecture of Belief* (oh, the deliberately comic emptiness of that title!) is massively long, and eschews narrative altogether, in homage, one assumes, to the great modernist masterpieces in whose shadow it was undoubtedly composed. It replicates 'Peterson''s first ambitious attempt to create, Casaubon-like, a key to all mythologies.

The book's recreation of pretentiously unreadable academic prose is so uncannily accurate that it is perhaps not surprising that it did not meet with mainstream success. On the other hand, *Maps of Meaning* does include one passage that we must regard as central to Peterson's aesthetic project – a moment in which 'Peterson' inadvertently reveals himself as hilariously misguided in his megalomaniacal intellectual ambitions. This passage is called 'Letter to Dad' (but of course it is), and takes the form of a rambling, incoherent, but rather touching attempt by 'Peterson' to explain his great project to his father:

> I don't know, Dad, but I think I have discovered something that no one else has any idea about, and I'm not sure I can do it justice. Its scope is so broad that I can only see parts of it clearly at one time, and it is exceedingly difficult to set down comprehensibly in writing. You see, most of the kind of knowledge that I am trying to transmit verbally and logically has always been passed down from one person to another by means of art and music and religion and tradition, and not by rational explanation, and it is like translating from one language to another. It's not just a different language, though – it is an entirely different mode of experience.

The ventriloquism, here, of the voice of an alienated, insecure, but majestically ambitious idiot is Dostoevskian in its pathos: when 'Peterson' tells his father, 'it was sheer unconscious arrogance that made me posit to begin with that I had half a notion of who or what I was, or what the processes of history had created, and how I was affected by that creation', we hear the pure note of unreliable narration. 'Peterson' cannot help but write the words 'sheer unconscious arrogance', betraying himself and his whole specious project to the alert reader. This is high comedy; but, as few readers were willing to slog through five hundred pages of fake academic theorizing to get the joke, the book sank more or less without trace.

12 Rules for Life represented a softening of Peterson's aesthetic rigour. No more modernism. No more pseudo-academic anti-narrative. Suddenly 'Peterson' is telling autobiographical stories about growing up in Alberta; suddenly we're reading fake case studies in the Freudian manner, ostensibly drawn from 'Peterson''s clinical practice. Peterson is no longer parodying dry academic prose. Now his target is the self-help book trade, with its glib nostrums extracted from the works of complex thinkers, its pseudo-authoritarian lists of instructions, and its tendency towards messianic totalities.

In retrospect, the move makes sense. Of *course* 'Peterson' is now in the rules racket – how else could this hyperambitious, baffled weirdo get his 'message' across? Peterson's audience correspondingly expanded. There was, it appeared, a hunger out there for a self-help book that mocked the very idea of self-help books, and 12 *Rules*, with its obviously daft and maladroitly phrased guidelines ('Pet a cat when you encounter one on the street), fit the bill.

Audaciously, Jordan Peterson carried his aesthetic project one step further, and began publicly to appear in character as 'Jordan Peterson', at first making incoherent remarks to journalists about gendered pronouns (canny, this: of course 'Peterson' would have the answers to a complex subject like gender) and then going on rock-star-like tours, where, in virtuoso three-hour performances, he kept up the 'Peterson' facade, discoursing nonsensically on vast topics like myth, history and sexuality, knocking down straw men left and right, and never cracking a single knowing smile as he did it.

Perhaps the peak of 'Peterson''s performing career occurred when he shared a stage with 'Slavoj Žižek', another spoof academic character played by the Slovenian writer Slavoj Žižek; the resulting 'debate' read superbly as a parody of the shoddy condition of popular intellectual discourse.

On the other hand, it was 'Peterson''s very success that brought the character to the attention of large numbers of people who didn't quite get the joke. Serious articles began to appear, chastising 'Peterson' for the incoherence of his ideas, or for their underlying reactionary import – as if, for all the world, 'Peterson' wasn't undermining *himself* at every turn. Critics on the left, in particular, scolded 'Peterson' humourlessly, and wrote whole books to prove him wrong – as if there was anything in 'Peterson''s message to prove or disprove! Ben Burgis, for instance, one of the contributors to *Myth and Mayhem: A Leftist Critique of Jordan Peterson* (2020), fell wholesale for the gag when he observed that 'Peterson isn't just an unusually literate uncle saying some controversial things at Thanksgiving dinner. He has some serious intellectual chops. And therefore needs to be taken seriously.'

But of course to say this is to miss the point entirely. 'An unusually literate uncle saying some controversial things at Thanksgiving dinner' describes precisely the 'Jordan Peterson' character, as he has evolved across three books and a plethora of public performances. Like the boorish bloviator that Stephen Colbert used to play on *The Daily Show*, 'Peterson' has entered middle age as an inflexible blowhard, more divorced than ever from the reality he purports to explain.

This is where we find him in the new 'Peterson' novel, *Beyond Order* (subtitled, of course, *12 More Rules for Life*). In an ingenious twist on the 'Peterson' story, Peterson has put his self-duped narrator through hell: after the success of *12 Rules for Life*, 'Peterson' has succumbed to benzodiazepine addiction (the inspiration here is surely the case of Jason Russell, who, after the viral success of his *Kony 2012* video, suffered a breakdown that saw him ranting naked in the streets of San Diego). Increasingly depressed, suffering from 'hypersomnia', 'Peterson', the prologue to the new book reveals, was eventually brought by his family to a Moscow hospital and put in a medically induced coma to treat his withdrawal. Battling through a painful recovery, he managed to write *Beyond Order*, which explains at numbing length a new suite of supposedly helpful maxims ('Do not carelessly denigrate social institutions or creative achievement', 'Do not hide unwanted things in the fog').

Whereas *12 Rules for Life* was, 'Peterson' tells us, about 'how the consequences of too much chaos might be remediated'

(remediated!), *Beyond Order*, conversely, is about 'how the dangers of too much security and control might be profitably avoided'. 'Peterson' does not, of course, remark upon the irony that his life went catastrophically off the rails precisely because of a lack of security and control. He remains, in the new book, as he was in the previous two, hilariously insensitive to the ways in which his own behaviour and experience pointedly refute his grandiose theories.

The inconsistencies in 'Peterson''s responses are beautifully done. Peterson allows 'Peterson' to insist that his breakdown was the result of family trauma; only in a parenthetical aside does he permit his narrator to mention 'the period when my life changed from the quiet existence of a university professor and clinician to the tumultuous reality of a public figure'. It is, of course, a brilliant move: the author of a book about how to cope with chaos, unable himself to cope with chaos, and furthermore incapable of recognizing his own incapacity!

There is also 'Peterson''s voice – that inimitable self-betraying mishmash of cod-academic specificity and motivational business guff: 'I hope, in consequence, that I have managed to clarify some of the issues that were perhaps left less than optimally developed in my previous work, as well as presenting much that is original.' Our protagonist's unhappy way with the English language is in full flower in the pages of *Beyond Order*. 'Peterson' refers to his wife as 'someone whom I had befriended for fifty years and been married to for thirty'. His anti-talent for epigram – familiar to us, of course, from *12 Rules* – makes a welcome encore appearance: 'People exist among other people and not as purely individual minds.'

This last non-zinger is, typically, doing quite a lot of work. Because the joke, throughout *Beyond Order*, is that 'Peterson' himself only exists as an individual mind, and has zero sense of how to exist among other people. Time and again he grapples with ordinary human experience; time and again, it defeats his interpretative powers. Here's 'Peterson' observing his granddaughter:

> I have watched her carefully while she develops, trying to understand what she is up to and playing along with it. When she was about a year and a half old, she engaged in all manner of unbearably endearing behaviors – giggling and laughing when she was poked, high-fiving, bumping heads, and rubbing noses. However, in my opinion, the most noteworthy of all the actions she undertook at that age was her pointing.

However, in my opinion, the most noteworthy of all the actions she undertook at that age was her pointing. Set aside the spectacularly maladroit construction for a moment, and observe how precisely Peterson recreates the voice and mindset of someone who has *no grasp of human experience or behaviour whatsoever.* Through 'Peterson''s eyes, ordinary human activities come back to us as if seen through the eyes of an alien or an android. It is precisely the sort of effect praised by the Russian formalist critic Viktor Shklovsky as *defamiliarization*; precisely the effect evoked by Craig Raine and the 'Martian School' of poetry. Seen though 'Peterson''s eyes, the human world once again looks strange, even baffling. Who are these peculiar creatures? What are the hidden rules by which they live?

The 'Rules' themselves – 'Peterson''s desperate attempt to codify and control the incomprehensible behaviour of ordinary people – strike superbly the same defamiliarizing note. Rule X (ah, those Roman numerals!) 'notes the importance of explicit negotiation to maintenance of the good will, mutual regard, and heartfelt cooperation without which no true romance can be sustained'. This is 'Peterson''s recipe for a happy marriage. Pity poor Mrs 'Peterson' – and be glad she isn't real.

Contemplating Peterson's achievement in *Beyond Order*, we are moved to reflect on the wholeness of his conception

– on the depth of *his* grasp of human psychology. 'Peterson' is, of course, a successful clinical psychologist. He is therefore a credentialed expert on human behaviour. But *of course* he is! As we read *Beyond Order*, it dawns on us that 'Peterson' became a clinical psychologist because he doesn't understand the first thing about human behaviour. He has, in fact, spent his whole misbegotten career trying desperately to explain it to himself. Now, a hundred journal articles and three books later, he is no closer to succeeding.

Thus the scope of Peterson's vision becomes clear. 'Jordan Peterson', the narrator of *Maps of Meaning, 12 Rules for Life* and *Beyond Order*, is perhaps one of the most fully rounded, and most tragically conceived, literary characters ever created. We know this man. We know how he thinks (more precisely, we know how he doesn't think). He feels startlingly real. The sheer length and density of the 'Peterson' books contributes to this feeling, of course; it also contributes to a feeling, detectable as you turn the closing pages of *Beyond Order*, of slightly soiled weariness. 'Jordan Peterson': yes, a wonderful literary character. But you wouldn't necessarily want to be trapped in a lift with him. And you wouldn't necessarily want to spend yet another 400 pages in his company (let's hope for no more 'Peterson' books, after this one). 'Peterson' knows himself too poorly. Signalling to us wildly from between the lines of his ludicrous, grandiose texts, he asks plaintively for our help. However (as he might himself say), our sympathy for his plight must inevitably remain, after three exhausting books, less than optimally developed.

The Dublin Review of Books, June 2021

Short Takes

WILL SELF
Umbrella

Will Self's Booker-shortlisted new novel is unreadable in two senses: it is difficult to read, and it is almost unbelievably bad. The plot has been borrowed from *Awakenings* (1973) by Oliver Sacks. In 1922 a young woman named Audrey Death is admitted to Friern Barnet Mental Hospital with a diagnosis of 'Primary Dementia'. Audrey languishes on the wards until 1971, when Dr Zack Busner (a Self regular) theorizes that she may in fact be a victim of *encephalitis lethargica*, the 'sleeping sickness', which Sacks was then treating with the dopamine precursor L-Dopa. Busner administers the new medication and Audrey, briefly, awakes.

Umbrella thus sets out to embrace the passage of time, the history of psychiatry, the legacy of the First World War, the sedimentary accumulations of London culture and much more besides. Self's ambition, here, is not at fault. What is at fault – grievously, bafflingly – is his aesthetic technique. 'I don't write for readers,' Self told the *Observer* recently. He wasn't kidding.

For one thing, the whole book is done as a kind of down-market pastiche of James Joyce (the epigraph comes from *Ulysses*: 'A brother is as easily forgotten as an umbrella'). Every sentence is burdened with its own italicized scrap of interior monologue: '*a jolly arsehole, his long face a fraction: eyes divided by moustache into mouth*'. There are sub-Joycean compound words: 'claybrown', 'marblewhirl', 'earthsea', 'goldensmoky'. There are nouns used as verbs: 'his splayed shoes crêping along the floor', 'his pen *morsing* from box to box'. There are obscure words: 'hebephrenic', 'neoplasm', 'quoins', 'festination', 'kyphotic', 'kinetomic'. There is Joycean onomatopoeia: 'his fork negligently *sccccrrrraping* gravy shapes'. Self has hauled out every rusted old spanner and blunted chisel in the modernist toolbox and put them, wearily, to use. This stuff was brand new ninety years ago. By now, it has hardened into cliché.

None of this would matter if the verbal texture of Self's novel could be relied upon as a source of sentence-by-sentence pleasure. But the prose is often bad: 'Even so, Busner has noticed these others, caught sight of them with the eternal evanescence with which the eyes *capture a shape in water*.' Lengthy sections of phonetically rendered Cockney speech are particularly excruciating: 'There's summat wrong wiv you, carncher see yer father's wantin'izale?' And (alas): 'Ordree's mammy gorrersel knocked up by a navvy!' There are rhymes: 'its ticcing picking off the enemy', 'morphologies for new pathologies'. And finally there is the sheer unrelenting density of the thing, page after page of stuff like, '*Along comes Zachary, my tremolo arm vibrating as I sing to my own don't-step-on-the-cracks self …*' Worse: there are no chapter breaks. The book is, in effect, a single paragraph that goes on for 400 pages. That's 400 pages of lines in which the strain threatens to crack the spine of the book from within: 'He puffed small and aromatic clouds of *cosmic faux pas ...*' Whatever that's supposed to mean.

In Martin Amis's *The Information*, the failed writer Richard Tull produces a novel with 'an octuple time-scheme' and a 'rotating crew of sixteen unreliable narrators'. Richard's book is so bad that no one can read it without suffering some awful physical symptom – a nosebleed here, a brain tumour there. Will Self, we know, has read *The Information* – he interviewed Amis when it came out in '95. He must not have understood the gag.

The Sunday Business Post, 29 September 2012

HOWARD JACOBSON
Zoo Time

Howard Jacobson is not, at heart, a satirist. He is a comic tragedian, like Philip Roth (whom he so admires). He has written one masterpiece: the novel *Kalooki Nights* (2006). Set among Manchester's Jewish community, it is about the cartoonist Max Glickman's attempts to understand why his friend Manny murdered his parents by gassing them in their beds. It is a raging, torrential performance, powerfully moving, deeply felt. It is also – and this is not incidental – extremely funny. ('Gassed?' Max demands of his appalled mother, when she tells him about Manny's crime. 'You don't say "gassed" to a Jew if you can help it.') Jacobson's other novels tend towards the effortfully 'comic'. In much of his fiction – notably in the Booker-winning *The Finkler Question* (2010) – Jacobson has flouted, to his cost, one of literature's great paradoxical truisms, the one that goes: the funniest books are the ones that are saddest at heart.

Certainly *Zoo Time*, Jacobson's new one, is a pretty unfunny book. Heavily voice-driven, like all of Jacobson's work, it is narrated by Guy Ableman, a fortyish novelist who divides his hours between fretting over the state of publishing and lusting after his mother-in-law, Poppy. The thematic link between these two preoccupations is never clearly drawn, though we do learn that Guy plans to write a novel about a novelist who wants to sleep with his mother-in-law. In cod-meta style, Jacobson lets us know how thin the ice looks from where he's skating: 'This is when you know you're in deep shit as a writer – when the heroes of your novels are novelists worrying that the heroes of their novels are novelists who know they're in deep shit.' Quite.

Poppy is 'in her middle sixties', which is, Guy remarks, 'a wonderful age for a woman who has kept an eye on herself'. Poppy's daughter, Vanessa, is forever upbraiding Guy for his failings as a husband. She gets burdened with lines like, 'This isn't a green light for one of your literary flings.' On holiday in Australia, Guy and Poppy enjoy a brief erotic *frisson*. Guy resolves to elaborate upon this situation in his new book. Oddly, he believes that stand-up comedians have now replaced novelists as the guardians of the old *épater la bourgeoisie* aesthetic. So he makes the hero of his novel a stand-up comedian who sleeps with his mother-in-law. 'I had it in me to write the seamiest novel of an admittedly exceedingly tame century.' (A peculiar remark, this. You could call our young century many things, but 'exceedingly tame' probably shouldn't be one of them.) Guy believes that his book will install him finally and forever in the Canon (Male Sexuality Division), right up there with D.H. Lawrence and Henry Miller. 'She was sixty-six and out of bounds,' Guy declares. 'I'd show them fucking transgression!'

How funny you find all of this stuff is, I suppose, largely a matter of taste. More straightforwardly unamusing (and shrill) are Guy's many thoughts on the condition of the world of letters. Great tracts of *Zoo Time* are given over to an *ubi sunt* lament for the lost Golden Age of When Howard Jacobson Was Young and Publishing His Early Novels. 'Reading as a civilised activity was over,' Guy insists. The barbarians have gathered at the Gates of Literature, and Guy must resist such ignominious encroachments as 'library closures, Oxfam, Amazon, eBooks, iPads, Oprah, apps, Richard and Judy, Facebook, Formspring, Yelp, three-for-two, the graphic novel, Kindle, [and] vampirism'.

Yes, books are going down the tube, and Guy is here to preside at the wake. At a book club (where all the readers are women), he is asked: 'Why do you hate women so much?' His publisher, Merton Flak, has committed suicide. 'Even those publishers who still had writers, even those writers who still had readers, knew the game was up.' There is much exhilarating crankiness in these pages, much justified bewilderment at the lurid grotesqueries of contemporary life. But Jacobson's prose is not really up to the job of withstanding the tide of junk culture that threatens to sweep Guy Ableman away. When he attempts a satirical sally, we get stuff like this: 'Displayed face out on [the bookshop] shelves was a new TV tie-in cookery book by Dahlia Blade, a bulimic Kabbalist from an all-vegan girl band.' This is merely a catalogue of thin exaggerations: the language is not nearly sharp enough to draw blood.

Zoo Time is a pessimistic book. But this time out we are dealing with the shallow pessimism of the grouch, rather than the resonant fatalism of the tragedian. Jacobson's voice remains a marvellous instrument, but he has not, here, come close to replicating the dark laughter he attained to in the finest pages of *Kalooki Nights*.

The Sunday Business Post, 6 October 2012

ALAN SHATTER
Laura

There are, at present, two reasons why a publication may be outlawed in the Republic of Ireland. The first is if that publication is judged (by, presumably, a panel of highly qualified experts) to be obscene. The second is if it 'advocates the procurement of abortion or miscarriage' (meaning that a fun-sounding tome called *How to Drive Your Man Wild in Bed* remains inaccessible to Irish readers, doubtless to our considerable loss).

Recently, some wag noticed that the Justice Minister, Alan Shatter, had published a novel in 1989 that featured a randy TD impregnating his parliamentary secretary and suggesting she abort the child. A complaint about Shatter's novel, *Laura*, was submitted to the Censorship of Publications Board earlier this year – whether on the grounds of obscenity or the suspected advocacy of abortion, we don't know. But this particular bit of political mischief has, of course, backfired: here is *Laura*, billed (inaccurately) as 'A Novel You Will Never Forget', in a shiny new paperback edition, just in time for the summer holiday market.

The villain of the piece is fiercely pro-life TD Sean Brannigan: 'a handsome man whose athletic appearance was more like that of a footballer than a politician'. Sean's parliamentary secretary is 'a slight blonde girl' named Colette James. 'Colette found [Sean] to be a very conscientious deputy.' So conscientious, in fact, that you can hardly blame her for what happens next: 'Their relationship rapidly deepened [...] He told himself that it was not his fault that the young secretaries of Leinster House were attracted to him.' Indeed not. Two breathless and slightly squicky pages later ('When he entered her, he knew it was her first time'), the worst has happened: 'Brannigan had assured her that he always withdrew in time and that she was not at risk. She now knew this to be untrue. Colette James, convent educated, twenty years of age and unmarried, was going to be a mother.'

Potent stuff, back in 1989. The crux of the matter, as far as the Censorship Board may or may not be concerned, occurs when Colette tells Deputy Brannigan that she's pregnant and he ungallantly asks, 'Have you considered an abortion?' Given that Colette appears unable to tell if her pro-life lover has ejaculated inside her or not, it seems unlikely that she's gotten as far as considering an abortion, and so it proves: 'How could he of all people suggest an abortion? She would not have an abortion.'

Phew! But the question remains: what to do with the baby? Well, little Laura is adopted by a preternaturally bland middle-class couple named John and Jenny, who are so thrilled to hear that the agency has found them a child that 'their bodies joined together in a passionate celebration'. But then disaster strikes: Colette decides that she wants Laura back. Everyone ends up in court. The prose scales fresh heights of tedium: 'In Colette's presence a letter was dictated to the adoption society stating that if Laura was not returned to Colette within ten days, court proceedings would issue, seeking a court order granting custody of Laura to Colette.'

I don't mean it as a criticism, except in the literary sense, when I say that *Laura* is in every way a book written by a lawyer. Whether or not you support his politics, Alan Shatter is clearly a fine legislator with a distinguished career behind him. But his novel has all the zing and pep of a legal brief. It is hilariously literal-minded (there isn't a metaphor in sight). It is populated by triple-ply cardboard characters. It is drier than the Gobi Desert. But then, there are really only three questions worth asking about *Laura*. 1) Is it obscene? Absolutely not. 2) Does it advocate the procurement of abortion or miscarriage? Absolutely not. 3) Is it a good book? I think we already know the answer to that question, don't we?

The Sunday Business Post, 7 July 2013

DAVID MITCHELL
The Bone Clocks

There's a (possibly apocryphal) anecdote about Bertrand Russell that goes like this. After giving a public lecture, Russell was approached by a woman who said, 'Mr Russell, I'm afraid you're quite mistaken about the nature of reality. I have it on good authority that the world rests upon the back of an enormous turtle.' Russell, who almost certainly recognized this common aboriginal creation myth, had his counterargument at the ready. 'But madam,' he said, 'what does the turtle rest upon?' 'Oh,' said the woman airily, 'it's turtles all the way down.'

I thought of this when I read David Mitchell's million-selling epic *Cloud Atlas* (2004), which takes the form of six distinct but interlocking narratives and moves through time from the eighteenth century to an imagined post-literate future. The six strands of *Cloud Atlas* are nested inside one another in a feat of structural daring – and Mitchell's ability to summon a range of voices and styles is heavily impressive. But when you put all six strands of *Cloud Atlas* together, the point of the whole elaborate picture becomes rather difficult to see. More troublingly, there seems to be no clear ground upon which this marvellous tiered confection might stand: if the stories are all stories within other stories, then what, as Russell might have put it, do the turtles rest upon? Is Mitchell making some sort of grand point about the essentially recursive nature of late capitalism/postmodernity/The Way We Live Now? Scrutinized closely, *Cloud Atlas* seems, after all, to boil down to a vast self-referential toy, a game of stories with nothing too urgent at stake. So what is the ultimate import of Mitchell's undeniable storytelling gift? Is it just turtles all the way down?

In *The Bone Clocks* we arrive, as it were, at David Mitchell's final turtle. Here Mitchell's prodigious prose gifts are put at the service of a story about two groups of near-immortals, the evil Anchorites and the good Horologists, engaged in a centuries-long psychic war for the souls of ordinary, mortal human beings (i.e. us: the 'bone clocks' of the title). This, it turns out, is what has been giving a secret shape to Mitchell's novels all along.

The Bone Clocks is composed of six novella-length chapters. Almost every chapter is blindingly well-realized: furnished with convincing characters and scrupulously rendered settings. We begin in Gravesend in 1984 with Holly Sykes, who as a child, once upon a time, heard transmissions from mysterious voices whom she called the 'Radio People'. Now fifteen, Holly runs away from home, and encounters – almost fatally – the evil Anchorites. Skip forward – next novella – to 1991, and we're in the louche company of Cambridge rake Hugo Lamb, who finds himself – after a spree of nastiness reminiscent of the sort of shenanigans Patricia Highsmith's Tom Ripley used to get up to – willingly recruited to the Anchorite cause. Then – next! – it's 2004, and Holly's husband, war journalist Ed Brubeck, has his own mysterious run-in with the immortal predators. A pattern is forming.

The book's fourth (and best and longest) section follows English novelist Crispin Hershey, readily identifiable as a parody of Martin Amis (he wrote a novel called *Dessicated Embryos*, ho ho). Crispin – embittered, saddled with writer's block – befriends the now grown-up Holly at a series of literary festivals, as the Anchorites loom. The book's final two sections take us forward in time, to the final showdown between Horology and the Anchorites, and onward, to the 'Endarkenment' of the 2040s, when Holly, now an old woman, lives in an environmentally ravaged Ireland.

Endarkenment indeed. There is some superb writing in this book. Mitchell can apparently make English prose do anything he wants. He can tell you what it's like to snort cocaine: 'Tiny lights I can't quite see pinprick the hedges of my field of vision. I emerge from the cubicle like the Son of God rolling away the stone.' He can describe a post-industrial city at night: 'Shanghai by night is a mind of a million lights: of orange dot-to-dot along expressways [...] animated ad-screens for Omega, Burberry, *Iron Man 5*, gigawatt-bright, flyposted onto night's undarkness.'

But in the book's climactic pages, as the Horologists confront the Anchorites in a bullshit-storm of plot-coupons, Mitchell's style undergoes its own Endarkenment. 'He enters the female officer's chakra-eye and I now have access to her sensory input.' 'As a parting gift, Oshima redacts a broad swathe of Nancy's present perfect and induces unconsciousness before egressing her and ingressing the traumatized Holly.' 'Sadaquat flees for the exit but Pfenninger pscholassos him, reeling him in with mighty pulls, then kinetics him twenty feet high.' 'Incorporeally, I pour psychovoltage into a neurobolas and kinetic it at our assailants.'

The penultimate chapter, 'An Horologist's Labyrinth', is crammed full of this guff – and guff it is, since for most of the length of his book Mitchell has sensibly lavished his gifts on constructing realistic interior lives for his human characters, instead of using them to bolster his tortured and (let's be honest) horribly clichéd fantasy-novel superstructure. As a result, the book feels stupefyingly unbalanced: the realistic parts, nourished and fattened by Mitchell's flawless prose, gobble up the thinly realized fantasy elements, like an Anchorite gobbling up a bone clock (or should that be the other way round?). More seriously, it comes as a terrible disappointment to find that under all those turtles, holding up David Mitchell's entire fictional edifice, is a half-baked pulp story about 'apex predators' 'fuelling their atemporality by feeding on souls'.

Mitchell is – no denying it – one of the most talented novelists alive. Time spent reading his pages is never entirely wasted. But you can't show us the good stuff up front and then reward us with nothing but 'the psychodumdum semi-inverts my colleague's body', and all the other clangers that make up the climax of this glittering folly of a book.

The Sunday Business Post, 5 October 2014

MICHEL FABER
The Book of Strange New Things

The guardians of science fiction – critics, reviewers, fans – tend to get a bit tetchy when mainstream novelists make a move to colonize the genre. The SF community has never really forgiven Paul Theroux for his 1986 novel *O-Zone*, in which he wrote about rich people walling themselves off from a post-nuclear wasteland as if no one had ever written about such things before. SF critics like to point out that, unless writers are intimately familiar with the history of the genre – with its long-established codes and shorthand descriptors – they tend to find themselves reinventing the wheel, causing embarrassment all round.

Michel Faber is not, on the face of it, a typical mainstream interloper in the coded world of science fiction. His first novel, *Under the Skin* (2000), was straight-up SF: a quadrupedal alien, disguised as a beautiful human woman, prowls the dismal highways of Scotland, seducing men to be stored and eaten as food. Faber's 2002 magnum opus, *The Crimson Petal and the White*, relied on an essentially science-fictional conceit: explaining the Victorian period as though to a time traveller from the future. Faber, we could assume, knew his stuff. He was as *au fait* with the protocols of SF as he seemed to be with the protocols of every other genre he wrote in. (Like David Mitchell, whom he sometimes resembles, Faber is a kind of prodigy, a narrative wizard who can summon scenes and construct stories with an eerie fluency.)

Faber's new book – his first full-length novel since *The Crimson Petal* – is, we quickly realize, a work of pure science fiction. It opens with a couple, Peter and Bea, on their way to Heathrow in the dead of night. Peter, it transpires, is a Christian missionary. He has been hired by a powerful but rather mysterious corporation, USIC, to travel to a planet called Oasis, where human beings are constructing the rudiments of a colony. The Oasan natives – strange, genderless, softly spoken humanoids – have asked for a pastor to teach them about what they call 'The Book of Strange New Things' – the Bible. On Oasis – where the air is oppressively moist and the sun shines for seventy-two hours at a stretch – Peter (as in 'Thou art Peter and upon this rock I build my church') sets about teaching the Oasans about Christ.

But, of course, all is not as it seems. Why, precisely, is USIC building a colony on Oasis? Why are all the USIC employees so sinisterly bland? What happened to Peter's predecessor, the resonantly named Kurtzberg, who has disappeared without a trace? Why do USIC keep delivering antibiotics and analgesics to the Oasan village? Why are the Oasans so keen on Christianity that they rename themselves 'Jesus Lover One', 'Jesus Lover Two' and so on? Much of the novel consists of messages between Peter and his wife, Bea, who remains on Earth. As Bea's messages grow increasingly disturbing – as the situation on Earth turns genuinely apocalyptic – Peter sinks into a passive admiration of the Oasans. As he grows more and more obsessed with this strange, dull planet, he thinks: 'It was as benign as benign could be.' The sense of wrongness, subtly conveyed, is intense. Surely some revelation is at hand?

First, the good bits: the atmosphere of Oasis is conjured with real brio and skill. Faber's ability to summon imaginary landscapes recalls William Golding (Faber also calls to mind Golding's tendency to lapse into parable). The story is, for most of its 548 pages, profoundly gripping: Faber establishes his mysteries with such deftness and power that you're compelled to keep turning the pages.

But there are problems. For one thing, Faber is telling a story that feels like it's been told before. The basic situation is very similar to that of James Blish's 1958 novel, *A Case of Conscience*, in which a Jesuit missionary to the planet Lithia concludes that an alien race without any sense of Original Sin can only have been created by the devil. In its pulpy way, the Blish novel achieves a real sense of mythic power. But Faber's novel, as it goes about solving its various mysteries, simply fizzles out. The ending – which I won't spoil but which is seriously anticlimactic – leaves you with the feeling that you've read the first half of a good science fiction novel, and that the second half, in which the moral, theological and scientific implications of Peter's discoveries will be properly explored, has been inexplicably removed.

Faber is a novelist of immense, even freakish, skill. He can create a world on the page with vigour and force. His imagination is fabulous. But in *The Book of Strange New Things*, he has failed to provide a revelation equal to the extraordinary world he summons, and what might have been a great SF novel ends up as a sputtering firework.

The Sunday Business Post, 11 October 2014

MARILYNNE ROBINSON
Lila

Vladimir Nabokov once wrote an essay about the tribulations involved in finding a publisher for *Lolita*. One particular editor, Nabokov recalled,

> suggested that his firm might consider publication if I turned my Lolita into a twelve-year-old lad and had him seduced by Humbert, a farmer, in a barn, amidst gaunt and arid surroundings, all this set forth in short, strong, 'realistic' sentences ('He acts crazy. We all act crazy, I guess. I guess God acts crazy.' Etc.).

Remove the theme of pederasty from this grim conjuration and you will end up with something closely resembling Marilynne Robinson's new novel. 'The preacher said things that bothered her, she couldn't make sense of them. Resurrection. But she guessed she liked the candles and the singing. She guessed she didn't have a better place to be.'

Or a better novel to be in, I guess. *Lila* is a companion piece to Robinson's two previous novels of religion and guessing in rural Kansas, *Gilead* (2004) and *Home* (2008). Our eponymous heroine, Lila, is a waif, neglected by her family of origin and rescued by a kindly migrant worker named Doll. After many years of wandering, Lila ends up in Gilead, where she marries the Reverend John Ames (who narrated the first novel in the trilogy). The structure is elliptical, refractory. Narrative development is slow. Lila reflects on her past; worries, in *faux naif* fashion, about historical events ('Lila heard about the Crash years after it happened, and she had no idea what it was even after she knew what to call it. But it did seem like they gave it the right name'); muses on her husband's poignant past ('He looked as if he'd had his share of loneliness, and that was all right'); and frames glib little not-quite-*aperçus* about the way of the world ('For a woman being old just means not being young, and all the youth had been worked out of her before it had really even set in').

Marilynne Robinson is, of course, basically a religious writer. Her subject is the way in which the divine manifests itself in the habitual, the banal. In the earlier novels – particularly in *Gilead* – there are moments when Robinson's prose reveals these manifestations with such beauty and force that they can be felt even by the secular reader: 'Light is constant, we just turn over in it. So every day is in fact the selfsame evening and morning. My grandfather's grave turned into the light, and the dew on his weedy little mortality patch was glorious.'

That is wonderful writing. Regrettably, *Lila* is starved of comparable ascensions. Robinson's prose, here, has a fatal sameness throughout. There are too many middle-length sentences full of short, similar words – there is nothing for the eye to snag on. 'The next day was a Sunday, and she had waked up early and slipped out of the house and walked away past the edge of town and followed the river to a place where the water ran over rocks and dropped down to a pool with a sandy bottom. She could watch the shadows of catfish there once the sun had come up.'

There is also a deadening lack of irony – the inescapable flaw of devotional prose. Literary irony has come in for a hard time of it lately – the late David Foster Wallace spent his last years calling for a return to 'single-entendre' fiction, and academic critics are busily heralding the arrival of a 'New Sincerity' – but literary irony (i.e. the ability to mean two things at once and to take pleasure in the tonal contradiction) is one of the novel's most profound resources. Single-entendre novels are novels that can hear only one meaning at a time – and no novelist should willingly invite such a deprivation.

Amidst the gaunt and arid surroundings of Gilead, Lila learns about Christianity. 'She thought, What would I pray for, if I thought there was any point in it? Well, I guess the first thing would have to be that there was some kind of point in it.' *Lila* sure does contain an awful lot of guessing and an awful lot of God. It might have been a better book if it had a little bit less of both.

The Sunday Business Post, 9 January 2015

WILLIAM GIBSON
The Peripheral

Critics who don't read much science fiction tend to call successful science fiction writers 'prophets' – as if science fiction
were a set of Tarot cards, or as if J.G. Ballard (say) were seriously warning us that the planet might one day turn into a
giant maze of crystals. But SF has never been about prediction.
Kingsley Amis came closest to articulating SF's true purpose
when he called his 1961 study of the genre *New Maps of Hell*. SF,
at its best, is the visionary literature of our time, charting the
infernos that we have already made. Set alongside the retro-
grade medievalism of contemporary fantasy, SF starts to look
like the most grown-up of popular genres.

If this is so, it's largely thanks to William Gibson. Gibson,
of course, began as a science fiction writer – maybe the most
important science fiction writer of the 1980s. He minted new
words ('cyberspace', 'microsoft') that sounded like they'd been
around forever. More vitally, with his first novel, *Neuromancer*

(1984), he minted – or consolidated – a brand-new style: a noir-ish high-tech vision of the very near future. Critics at the time called it cyberpunk, a word that now comes wrapped in its own nimbus of fuzzy nostalgia. Cyberpunk mapped a very 1980s hell, all matte-black hardware and corporate malfeasance. It didn't seem like where we were going; it seemed like where we already were.

It was a high point. For much of the 1990s, Gibson seemed to be marking time. But with the advent of the new century his focus shifted: the SF hell he was interested in charting now looked almost exactly like the contemporary world. The Blue Ant Trilogy – *Pattern Recognition* (2003), *Spook Country* (2007) and *Zero History* (2010) – gave us a new Gibson: main-stream heir to Pynchon and DeLillo, tech-savvy tracer of the shimmering horizons of our mediated globe.

Fredric Jameson has pointed out that in a postmodern age (evacuated of meaning, lacking in affect, deprived of motive), we can experience the world only as a series of self-conscious postures or styles. The Blue Ant Trilogy embodies this *aperçu* with eerie grace: in these novels everything – character, setting, plot, theme, imagery – boils down to an encounter with style. Gibson's protagonists are hyperalert to the material circum-stances of their alienated worlds: they clock the shiny limou-sines, the microfibre jackets, the bleeding-edge computer tech. They observe things like polymers (in *Pattern Recognition*, Cayce Pollard notices that an empty refrigerator smells of 'long-chain monomers'). They drift through Gibson's weirdly suspenseless narratives like freelance style journalists (Hollis Henry, in *Spook Country*, is literally a freelance style journal-ist), taking the temperature of the contemporary, never seri-ously threatened by the buoyantly Pynchonian conspiracies in which they find themselves enmeshed.

Now, with *The Peripheral*, Gibson has returned to full-fledged science fiction. The new novel is set unequivocally in the future – in two futures, to be precise. For hardcore Gibson fans, this will be an exciting prospect. For the general reader, however, it will probably feel like a large step backwards.

The plot of *The Peripheral* is complicated without being particularly involving. There are two time zones: Near Future and Slightly Farther Future. In the Near Future, dropout Flynne Fisher's army vet brother, Burton, beta-tests virtual reality games for shady operators. As the novel begins, Flynne finds herself covering for Burton. Piloting a drone in what she takes to be a boringly realistic game, she is drawn into an assassination. Meanwhile, in the Slightly Farther Future, international spook Wilf Netherton finds himself investigating, via an internet connection to the past, the assassination Flynne committed in what was (of course) not a virtual reality game. Got that? Me neither; and after 496 pages, I was scarcely the wiser.

At his best (as in the Blue Ant novels), Gibson's pages audition image after fugitive image of our money-glazed, post-everything century. At his worst – as in *The Peripheral* – his sentences stumble over their own too-cool-for-school feet. 'They didn't think Flynne's brother had PTSD, but that sometimes the haptics glitched him.' 'Netherton was fully as annoyed with the bohemian nonsense of Ash's workspace as he would have expected to be.'

Gibson's vaunted stylishness has always been a matter of carefully managed ellipsis: the know-it-all asides, the tough-guy imagist poetry. In the early novels this could engender moments of epigrammatic richness (*Neuromancer:* 'In an age of affordable beauty, there was something heraldic about his lack of it'). But in *The Peripheral,* Gibson's obliquity has become a hindrance to readerly pleasure. The prose is chequered with neologisms ('klept', 'polt', 'moby', 'patchers') and opacities ('haptics', 'thylacine'), and the syntax is riddled with needless conditionals. Simply put, it's often hard to tell what's going on. Worse, it's even harder to care. The vision that gave rise to Gibson's style has gone AWOL, leaving only the style behind – a very Gibsonian predicament.

The Sunday Business Post, 22 February 2015

DOUGLAS CORLEONE
Robert Ludlum's The Janson Equation

Daydream fiction has, or should have, an honourable place in the culture. To complain that popular fiction is escapist is to seriously undervalue the pleasures of escaping reality. Reality is tax returns and who cooks dinner – two things that neither James Bond nor his identically initialled descendant Jason Bourne ever have to worry about, as they cut their stylish swathes of destruction across an array of exotic locales. There's nothing wrong with fiction that feeds the dream life – thrillers, for instance, that allow us to imagine ourselves spies, or international assassins, or what have you. Much more fun than feeding the cat.

Until his death in 2001, Robert Ludlum was one of the great purveyors of this sort of escapist fiction. During his heyday in the 1980s and 1990s, Ludlum wrote dozens of deforestation-sustaining thrillers with three-word titles like *The Parsifal Mosaic* and *The Aquitaine Progression* (Salman Rushdie once quipped that if Ludlum had written *Hamlet*, it would be called *The Elsinore Vacillation*).

Nowadays Ludlum is probably most famous for his Bourne books, which, with Matt Damon as Bourne, made excellent movies. But the Ludlum name is obviously still bankable, which explains why various up-and-coming thriller writers have been publishing books under the Ludlum aegis since the master's death. This, it turns out, is what happens to the bestselling writers of yesteryear: they don't die, they just evolve – or perhaps the word is sublime – into a brand.

The latest hireling to shoulder the Ludlum yoke is Douglas Corleone, who possesses an excellent surname for a thriller-writer but who also, unfortunately, possesses a prose style of the purest cardboard. Ludlum's own prose style never met an adjective it didn't like; the same went for adverbs. In this respect, if none other, Corleone does the master proud: 'Hammond, a tall man with slicked-back hair the colour of straw, directed Janson to an idling olive-green jeep driven by a private first class who couldn't possibly have been old enough to legally drink.' Even escapist fiction should at least aspire to clarity and elegance – how else to facilitate the daydream?

All thrillers, of course, are plot machines – they want to make you turn the pages. Corleone's feeble set-up tries its best. The son of US senator James Wyckoff wakes up in Seoul beside the body of his murdered girlfriend, and promptly does a runner. His father is understandably upset: 'If we don't clear Gregory's name in the next ninety-six hours, we may never be able to do so.' There's only one man for the job: ex-Navy SEAL Jason Bourne – sorry, I mean Paul Janson.

Janson is old-school tough. 'He didn't like to be asked personal questions.' Traumatized past? Check: 'He did not have a family – only the memory of one. Only the stabbing recollection of a pregnant wife and the dashed dreams of their unborn child, their future obliterated by a terrorist's bomb.' On top of it all, 'Janson's memories of working as a government-sanctioned killer refused to fade.' Well, we've all been there. But Janson isn't about to let any stabbing recollections stop him from getting the job done. 'This was what his post-Cons Ops life was all about: changing the world, one mission at a time.'

So, off Janson trots to Seoul, accompanied by his tough-but-sexy partner Jessica Kincaid ('Jessie could handle herself better than most soldiers on the planet'). On their quest to exonerate the senator's son, Janson and Kincaid must first hack their way through a jungle of undigested authorial research. They pause in the middle of deadly covert ops to note that Shanghai is 'the bustling, modern Chinese city of seventeen million people, home to some of the world's tallest and most architecturally breathtaking skyscrapers', or to remind themselves that a lynx is a 'wildcat common to northern and western parts of China, especially the Tibetan plateau'. You can practically hear Corleone clicking Wikipedia links between paragraphs.

So what exactly is the 'Janson Equation'? The publishers were presumably hoping for something like 'reliable brand plus hot new writer equals big success'. The bad news is, it's more like 'wonky plot plus dodgy prose equals major turkey'. Better luck next time, gang.

The Sunday Business Post, 2 August 2015

ARIANNA HUFFINGTON
The Sleep Revolution: Transforming Your Life, One Night at a Time

Arianna Huffington dedicates her new book to 'all those who are sick and tired of being sick and tired'. For such people, it seems, Arianna has the remedy. What she doesn't have, alas, is the remedy for anyone who is sick and tired of Arianna Huffington – an expert on nothing who has an opinion on everything.

Though perhaps that's a tiny bit unfair. Huffington is unquestionably an expert on at least one thing: she is a master of that uniquely contemporary fusion of hubris and entrepreneurial nous known as 'personal branding'. The Huffington brand, as we now know it, has been burnished over several decades of careful positioning. There have been upmarket celebrity biographies (she has published higher-trash accounts of Picasso and Maria Callas), brief forays into politics (she ran, unsuccessfully, for governor of California in 2003) and savvy investment strategies (her news-and-blog aggregator site, The Huffington Post, remains one of the world's top 1000 websites, despite a marked decrease in traffic since 2015). There has also been a tactfully handled political realignment: the quondam author of *The Female Woman* (an attack on feminism) and former supporter of Newt Gingrich and Bob Dole is now a hybrid-driving liberal in the millennial mould.

Huffington's rise to prominence has been viewed with scepticism in some quarters – one acquaintance has described her as 'the Sir Edmund Hillary of social climbing' – but in a sense Huffington's Kardashian-like success at transforming herself into her own most saleable product is one of the signal achievements of the twenty-first century. Like the Kardashians, Huffington understands that what a famous person does or says no longer matters – the point is to keep the brand alive, by whatever means necessary.

Huffington's latest self-promotional gimmick is *The Sleep Revolution*, a book whose entire meaning and purpose is summarized in its subtitle: *Transforming Your Life, One Night at a Time*. If you've read this subtitle and thought, *I bet she recommends getting a solid eight hours' sleep every night, avoiding pharmaceutical sleep-aids, and making time in your busy life to attend to your circadian rhythm*, then congratulations! You have already absorbed Huffington's latest message in its entirety, and there is no need for you to actually read the book. (You have also, incidentally, contributed to Huffington's quest for brand recognition, but there isn't much anyone can do about that.)

The Sleep Revolution bears all the hallmarks of a book assembled by a team of researchers (in her acknowledgments, Huffington thanks no less than five people 'for their skill and commitment in researching, organizing, and fact-checking every last detail – including the 1200 endnotes'). The style is briskly impersonal, and Huffington's argument is laid down amid a fusillade of statistics, interlarded with quotations from Professor Whom at the University of Wherever. Where the personal note obtrudes, it does so in the form of charming glimpses of an Arianna Huffington weighed down by the cares of a stressful book tour, the pressures of choosing the right Ivy League institution for her daughter.

It soon becomes clear that Huffington is out to slay a particular dragon. After collapsing 'from sleep deprivation, exhaustion, and burnout in April 2007', she has become a 'sleep evangelist', at war with the 'prevalent cultural norm of sleep deprivation as essential to achievement and success'. Must college students stay up all night, snorting Adderall, just to make the grade? Must truck drivers constantly push past the limits of tiredness – and endanger our lives while they're at it? Is sleep deprivation 'a specter haunting the industrialized world'.

Connoisseurs of left-wing discourse will enjoy this perhaps intentional reference to the opening line of *The Communist Manifesto*. But otherwise, all is banality. According to Huffington, sleep is 'one of humanity's great unifiers. It binds us to one another, to our ancestors, to our past, and to the future. No matter who we are or where we are in the world and in our lives, we share a common need for sleep'. This reminded me, inescapably, of the *Simpsons* episode in which Mr Burns remarks: 'Ah, sitting, the great leveller. From the mightiest pharaoh to the lowliest peasant, who doesn't enjoy a good sit?' Save your energy; skip *The Sleep Revolution*, and have a nap instead.

The Sunday Business Post, 26 June 2016

ANNIE PROULX
Barkskins

Annie Proulx's new novel apparently took five years to write. It takes about five years to read, too, clocking in at a wrist-straining 736 pages. Whether or not it's worth the effort is an open question. Long novels have a way of defusing serious criticism – the temptation is to just call it a 'masterpiece' and leave it at that. Well, *Barkskins* is no masterpiece. It contains several lengthy stretches of rich, vivid writing, but it is also shapeless, bloated and brimful of *longueurs*.

It doesn't help matters that this is less a novel than a dramatized polemic. *Barkskins*, it very rapidly becomes clear, is a *roman à thèse*. Proulx's hobbyhorse is deforestation: the annihilation of the North American wilderness through four centuries of colonialist greed. Proulx wants us to acknowledge the myriad fragile bonds that tie us to our ecosystem, and to consider the damage we have done to them. In her early pages, as she recounts the destruction of a virgin pine forest in 'New

France' (later New England), she writes: 'the vast invisible web of filaments that connected human life to animals, trees to flesh and bones to grass shivered as each tree fell and one by one the web strands snapped'.

The novel begins in 1693 with the story of René, a French settler who has signed on for three years' indentured servitude chopping down the trees of the freshly discovered North American continent. Here the French settlers seek 'to subdue this evil wilderness'. 'Men must change this land in order to live in it,' says Monsieur Trepagny, the overseer. 'To be a man is to clear the forest.' Monsieur Trepagny also says things like, 'All men must pay the debt of nature.' And just in case we haven't noticed that Monsieur Trepagny is a dubious sort of chap, Proulx gives us this: 'Thick brows couldn't shadow his glaring eyes, the whites so white and flashing they falsely indicated a vivacious nature.' Talk about a preachy book, as Homer Simpson once remarked of the Bible.

After 60 pages we bid goodbye to René (he winds up dead, scalped by the local Iroquois) and spend the next 100 pages with his former colleague, Duquet, who escapes from Monsieur Trepagny and sets himself up as a fur trader. This is one of the book's best bits, and Proulx generates real narrative momentum as Duquet expands his trade to China, taking passage on a Dutch ship and seeking an impossible audience with the emperor. Proulx's vivid historical sense, in these pages, breaks free of her undoubtedly copious research, and for a while the novel comes alive. But then – Duquet's story exhausted –we move on to the French missionary Louis-Joseph Crème, who has spent time with Mi'kmaq tribes: 'He saw that they were so tightly knitted into the natural world that their language could only reflect the union and that neither could be separated from the other.'

By now the reader will have twigged that *Barkskins* is one of those contemporary novels built out of several novellas bound together and ostensibly united by a common theme. Sometimes this works – as it does, debatably, in the novels of David Mitchell – but more often it makes for an unsatisfying aesthetic experience. No sooner has one story kicked off than another has arrived to take its place. Norman Mailer once remarked that 'the iron law of the conventional novel, the garden novel, is that the meaning of the action must grow on every page or else the book will wither'. Certainly Proulx's right-on environmentalist message 'grows on every page', but her characters – each abandoned in turn after his allotted span has ended – do not. This leaves *Barkskins* feeling even longer than it actually is – and it is already monstrously long.

Proulx has startling gifts as a nature writer: 'The heat of summer disappeared abruptly. Overnight a wedge of cold air brought a new scent – the smell of ice, of animal hair, of burning forest and the blood of the hunted.' But even regular flashes of this stuff aren't quite enough to redeem a novel that never adds up to more than an anthology of didactic fragments.

The Sunday Business Post, 3 July 2016

IAN McEWAN
Nutshell

In 1998, chatting with *The Paris Review*, Martin Amis discussed the value of the special-case narrator – the one-off point of view, the unique perspective. 'I did have the idea,' he said, 'of writing – I may yet, when it falls together – a short story narrated by a two-year-old.' Literary Theorists call this sort of thing *defamiliarization*. The benefits of scrutinizing the world from an unorthodox angle are clear: the hackneyed can once again seem strange, the stale can once again seem fresh. In his fifteenth novel, Ian McEwan has gone his old pal Mart one better. *Nutshell* is narrated by a child *in utero* – a special-case narrator if ever there was one.

'So here I am, upside down in a woman,' the novel begins, arrestingly. Our foetal protagonist – understandably nameless – is a boy, shortly to be born, and enjoying a special sort of consciousness. He has never seen anything – 'When I hear "blue", which I've never seen, I imagine some kind of mental event that's fairly close to "green" – which I've never seen.' The rhyme that mars this sentence – 'green' and 'seen' – rings troubling bells. It suggests that McEwan's ear for prose, usually tuned to an exquisite pitch (see the opening paragraphs of *Solar*, 2010), has gone a bit wonky. As it turns out, unintentional rhymes are the least of *Nutshell's* problems. This is in every way a terrible book: tone-deaf, arch, self-satisfied, unfunny and utterly – if you'll excuse the pun – misconceived. What went wrong?

Two things: the plot and the voice. Plot first: loitering in his mother's womb, McEwan's narrator has overheard 'the voices of conspirators in a vile enterprise'. His mother, Trudy, has deserted his father, John, and shacked up with his brother, Claude. Trudy and Claude are plotting to murder John so that they can inherit, and sell, his 'Georgian pile on boast-ful Hamilton Terrace' in London. But hang on a sec – what were those names? 'Trudy' and 'Claude'? As in 'Gertrude' and 'Claudius'? That's right: McEwan has trapped his unborn nar-rator in a ludicrous re-tread of *Hamlet*. Claude, in McEwan's version, is a property developer who's short of cash; Trudy is an amoral housewife who's grown sick of her publisher husband. Something is rotten in the state of Hampstead. The narrator, powerless to act, must listen as Trudy and Claude prepare a smoothie full of antifreeze and wait for John to knock it back.

The *Hamlet* parallels extend to frequent, unwise riffs on Shakespeare's language – which brings us to the problem of voice. 'Seems, mother? No, it *is*,' says the narrator on page two, and things get worse from there. At one point, Hamlet's 'I have of late, but wherefore I know not, lost all my mirth, forgone all custom of exercise' becomes 'But lately, don't ask why, I've no taste for comedy, no inclination to exercise.' It hardly seems necessary to point out that every time McEwan rewrites *Hamlet*, the results are banal to the point of mortification.

'Those admirable radio talks and bulletins, the excellent podcasts that moved me.'

That's right: podcasts. 'Oh god,' as the *Hamlet*-quoting epigraph has it, 'I could be bounded in a nutshell and count myself a king of infinite space, were it not that I have bad dreams.' The narrator's bad dreams – and his calamitous prose style – are indeed nourished by the radio shows and podcasts that Trudy listens to, as she drifts around the house, waiting for John's death to deliver her into a new life. He is capable of quoting Roland Barthes – not bad for someone who's never even seen a book. He also admires the audio version of *Ulysses* and muses on 'the condition of the modern foetus'. This is not, alas, merely further evidence of the by now near-total submission of Western bourgeois intellectuals to the tyranny of the podcast. It's also an index of where McEwan has gone wrong. Instead of emphasizing his narrator's valuably distinct perspective, he has made of him another typical McEwan protagonist – that is, a Western bourgeois intellectual.

He's even a wine buff – savouring, via his umbilical cord, various vintages that Trudy consumes:

> After a piercing white, a Pinot Noir is a mother's soothing hand. Oh, to be alive while such a grape exists! A blossom, a bouquet of peace and reason [...] The hint of violets and fine tannins suggest that lazy, clement summer of 2005, untainted by heatwaves, though a teasing, next-room aroma of mocha, as well as more proximal black-skinned banana, summon Jean Grivot's domaine in 2009.

McEwan might think that this is funny: a foetal wine bore! But it isn't funny. In fact, it's difficult to stress how not funny it is. It is also very badly written. But then, the whole book is badly written. 'Grant me all the agency the human frame can bear, retrieve my young panther-self of sculpted muscle and long cold stare, direct him to the most extreme measure – killing his uncle to save his father.' Again, the rhyme – 'bear' and 'stare' – is the least of it. Writing like this falls on the ear with a muffled thump. It aspires to ironized elegance; it achieves preciosity.

Something seems to happen to famous writers in late middle age – to famous male writers, in particular. They start to get wheezes – they fall for whacky notions. They can no longer tell the difference between good ideas and bad. Often, they go in for religiose kitsch – they write novels called *The Gospel According to the Son* (Norman Mailer) or *The Childhood of Jesus* (J.M. Coetzee) or *The Testament of Mary* (Colm Tóibín). Or they decide to muscle in on genre turf – they write alt-historical science fiction (Philip Roth's *The Plot Against America*) or nostalgic thrillers (John Banville's Benjamin Black novels). *Nutshell* nestles comfortably in this less-than-grand tradition. It is a folly – a half-bad idea executed with serene confidence and without a due sense of the ridiculousness of the enterprise. 'The rest is chaos,' goes the final line. The wiser course, as per *Hamlet*, might have been silence.

The Sunday Business Post, 16 October 2016

PAUL AUSTER
4321

'First thought, best thought,' wrote Jack Kerouac, offering perennial encouragement to the sort of writer who never has any
thoughts at all. Since anyone's first thought about anything is
likely to be a cliché, the business of literature should be to look
for the last thought – or, at the very least, to declare war on the
stock response.

Paul Auster is a first-thought writer who has somehow
acquired the reputation of being a deep-thought writer. Early
in his career – with the three arid metafictions that make up *The
New York Trilogy* (1985–6) – Auster adroitly surfed some of the
less gnarly waves of literary postmodernism. In thirteen further novels – most recently *Sunset Park* (2010) – he has riffed
repetitiously on a small handful of themes: existential dread, the
randomness of life (a 1990 novel is called *The Music of Chance*),
the burden of being a writer. Auster's novels are samey: a male
narrator, usually a writer or a writer-substitute, muses on the

accident or the crime (or the accidental crime) that knocked his life off course. Lately Auster's reputation has ebbed. In 2009 the *New Yorker* critic James Wood published an essay called 'Paul Auster's Shallowness', which parodied Auster's plots. 'He does nothing with cliché except use it,' Wood scoffed.

Now, after a seven-year hiatus, Auster is back with his longest and most ambitious book. *4 3 2 1* is a whopper: 866 densely packed pages. The governing conceit is not original – it was used by Kate Atkinson in her novel *Life After Life* (2013) and, to step Napoleonically from the sublime to the ridiculous, by the makers of the 1998 Gwyneth Paltrow movie *Sliding Doors*. *4 3 2 1* tells multiple versions of the same life story, demonstrating, not very interestingly, how every life is governed by random chance (or, you might say, by Austerity).

Wandering through Auster's mammoth maze of alternative histories is New Jersey-born Archie Ferguson. There are four versions of Archie, whom we meet in successive chapters titled '1.1', '1.2', '1.3' and so on. A prologue introduces us to Archie's parents, Stanley and Rose. Even in the novel's early pages, elephantiasis looms. Two obese paragraphs are devoted to listing Rose's reasons for marrying Stanley – there are eighteen, in case you're wondering. This prologue also clues us in to the scale of Auster's ambitions. We open on Ellis Island, with Stanley's father, a Russian Jew from Minsk, receiving his new American name (Ichabod Ferguson). Any book that opens with an Ellis Island baptism is plainly shooting for Great American Novel status. Twenty pages later, Rose reads Tolstoy. 'It was Tolstoy who […] understood all of life, it seemed to her, everything there was to know about the human heart and the human mind.' Stand back! Tolstoyan epic coming through!

The differences between Auster's alternate timelines don't add up to much – Archie Version 4, for example, doesn't find himself growing up in a world where Hitler won, or anything exciting like that. It's all minor stuff: one version of Archie falls out of a tree as a child and breaks his leg; another loses two fingers in a car accident. Toward the novel's end, Archie reflects that 'the torment of being alive in a single body was that at any given moment you had to be on one road only, even though you could have been on another, travelling toward an altogether different place'. If this is the upshot of your novel, then why not make your chosen alternatives more dramatic? – leaving aside, for now, the fact that this is a pretty banal conclusion for any saga to arrive at, after more than 800 pages.

Oscar Wilde's observation, in 'The Critic as Artist', that 'all bad poetry springs from genuine feeling' is quoted often; the sentence that follows it, almost never. 'To be natural,' Wilde wrote, 'is to be obvious, and to be obvious is to be inartistic.' Paul Auster is, in this sense, a natural writer. He is always obvious. He is almost always inartistic. Where a cliché will do, he uses a cliché. Where a cliché will not do, he uses a different cliché.

4 3 2 1 is, unsurprisingly, a factory farm of clichés. Archie's mother is a 'rock of composure'. A storm is 'a raging downpour'. Once 'Ferguson summoned up the courage to approach his mother,' 'she took the plunge'. After the death of their Uncle Lew, 'the Ferguson clan had been blown to bits'. Archie 'languishes' in bed with a broken leg, 'cooped up in his room', reflecting that 'there was no one to blame for this misfortune but himself'. His cousin Francie comes to visit, and 'the time he spent with her was always the most enjoyable part of the day'. Later, a conversation will 'hit Ferguson like a blow to the stomach'. 'They were the longest ten seconds of Ferguson's life.' And when his mother finds a location for her photography studio, 'her long search was finally over'.

Once again, there are 866 pages of this. Most mediocre novels have the decency to peter out after 200 pages – maybe after three or four hundred, in egregious instances (even mediocrity is tough to sustain over the long term). But *4 3 2 1* just keeps on rolling. It is mediocrity turned, *Spinal Tap*pishly, up to eleven. Meanwhile, a quick lesson in how to write: First thought, worst thought. Second thought, second-worst thought. And so on.

The Sunday Business Post, 26 February 2017

MOHSIN HAMID
Exit West

Keeping track of the many clichés sprinkled throughout Mohsin Hamid's new novel, I found myself assembling a sort of *Reader's Digest*-style condensed version of the whole: 'impressionable youth', 'going forward', 'in stark contrast', 'boggled the mind', 'Saeed steeled himself', 'there being a nip in the air tonight', 'Saeed's desperate entreaties', 'Neighbourhoods fell to the militants in startlingly quick succession', 'a thin column of smoke rising somewhere in the distance', 'Saeed's father saw the lemon tree and smiled for what seemed the first time in days', 'Vienna being no stranger, in the annals of history, to war', 'days passed like this, full of waiting and false hopes', 'insatiable brine', 'snatches of beautiful singing', 'jealousy did rear itself in their shanty from time to time', 'for time had done what time does'.

Every novelist publishes a bad book eventually. Even Harper Lee was not immune, in the end, to this iron law. With *Exit West*, Hamid publishes his bad novel. He has already had three good ones: *Moth Smoke* (2000), a noirish thriller about Lahore's idle rich; *The Reluctant Fundamentalist* (2007), a dry, despairing parable about Eastern ressentiment and Western complacency; and *How to Get Filthy Rich in Rising Asia* (2013), a witty satire of 21st-century gangster capitalism. What went wrong?

Part of the problem appears to be a lack of basic follow-through. *Exit West* is predicated on a potent *donnée*: all over the world, mysterious black doorways have appeared. Through these portals, individuals can travel magically from East to West – from war zones and refugee camps directly to Tokyo, London, Sydney. Naturally, in consequence, the global refugee crisis worsens by an order of magnitude. In the West, 'nativist' mobs spring up, threatening violence. The end of the present world order looms. A good contemporary science fiction writer – China Miéville, say – might have made of this notion something revelatory and strange. But Hamid, it appears, can scarcely be bothered to develop the larger implications of his conceit. Instead of guiding us through his own black doorway – instead of pointing us towards the iteration of some new, gnarled truth about the contemporary world – he is content, alas, to leave us with a limp and laboured love story.

The lovers are Saeed and Nadia, who live in an unnamed but certainly non-Western city. Saeed works for 'an agency that specialised in the placement of outdoor advertising'. Nadia works for an insurance company, 'handling executive auto policy renewals by phone'. War encroaches. Some central-casting militants invade the city. The situation deteriorates. Saeed and Nadia, having fallen rather boringly in love, resolve to flee. Via the black market, they purchase access to one of the mysterious doorways and make their escape to Mykonos, where they are held in a refugee camp. Finding the camp uncongenial, they slip through another doorway and land in a London mansion, on a street called Palace Gardens Terrace.

Having dawdled in London for a spell, awaiting a pogrom that never happens, they at last decamp to San Francisco, where they fall out of love. 'We are all migrants through time,' Hamid concludes, non-controversially.

Why do Saeed and Nadia fall out of love? They just sort of drift apart: 'each recognised it would be better to part now, ere worse came'. But hang on – did he say *ere worse came*? I'm afraid so. And here (or, forgive me, ere), we arrive at the other major problem with *Exit West*, which is its prose. Arch, periphrastic, stutteringly cod-archaic, often ungrammatical, Hamid's writing in this novel is a scandal. For instance:

> Nadia selected a record, an album sung by a long-dead woman who was once an icon of a style that in her American homeland was quite justifiably called soul, her so alive but no longer living voice conjuring up from the past a third presence in a room that presently contained only two, and asked Saeed if he would like a joint, to which he fortunately said yes, and which he offered to roll.

Setting aside the collision of 'presence' and 'presently', this sentence takes far too long simply to construe – you need to read it at least twice before you can figure out what it means, and that's before you've even wondered: why didn't he just write 'Nadia put on a soul record while Saeed rolled a joint'?

There are other examples. 'In times of violence, there is always that first acquaintance or intimate of ours, who, when they are touched, makes what had seemed like a bad dream suddenly, evisceratingly real.' Huh? 'This building had taken the same name as the cinema that preceded it: both once had the same owner, and the cinema had been so famous as to have become a byword for that locality.' I think I see what you're getting at. But I needn't go on. With its clichés, its rebarbative prose and its ineffectual protagonists, *Exit West* is unmistakably a misfire. As a novelist with a distinctively global purview, Hamid remains a valuable observer of the fault lines between East and West (and East and East, and West and West). The magical doorways that perforate the world of *Exit West* abolish those fault lines frictionlessly. The result is a novel that has very few interesting things to say and even fewer interesting ways in which to say them.

Literary Review, March 2017

JAMES WOOD
Upstate

Yes, that James Wood – as in, the critic James Wood. Chief book reviewer for *The New Yorker*. Professor of the Practice of Literary Criticism at Harvard. Author of *How Fiction Works* (2008). Coiner of the term 'hysterical realism' (to describe the information-glutted comedies of Jonathan Franzen and Zadie Smith). A famous critic, in an age when nobody is famous for criticism. And – though it may be contentious to say so – a great critic, in an age that desperately requires great criticism, and seldom gets it.

Asked about his critical method, T.S. Eliot once said: 'There is no method, except to be very intelligent.' In Wood's case, there is no method, except to have superb taste. Wood's taste isn't infallible: he was wrong when he faulted Jonathan Franzen's *The Corrections* for being fatally implicated in the social confusions it so brilliantly recreates. And his taste isn't particularly catholic, either: he has little to say about genres that deal with imagined futures or alternative worlds ('Since fiction is itself a kind of magic,' he once wrote, 'the novel should not be magical').

No: what Wood likes is realism. This is perhaps why many readers profess to find him narrow, or puritanical, or reactionary. The word 'realism' carries heavy freight: it makes you think of clunking great nineteenth-century novels, crammed full of wearisome detail about the lives of coal miners or provincial clerics. But what Wood admires is a realism that lets itself get mussed up by life – fiction that allows a disciplined prose to be torqued and 'fattened' (a favourite word of Wood's) by the textures of the given world. This is why he admires Saul Bellow above all others – Bellow, who writes, as Wood puts it, 'life-sown prose [...] logging impressions with broken speed'.

Wood's own fiction – a sparse stream: two novels in fifteen years – is, unsurprisingly, pretty Bellovian. His first novel, *The Book Against God* (2003), rather fussily attempts to anglicize Bellow's style. Narrated by Thomas Bunting, the immature son of a Durham clergyman, it is full of self-conscious 'noticings', as when Thomas observes 'streetlights going on all over town in amber hesitations'. For all its uncertainties (it feels a bit like a failed try at an old-fashioned British Comic Novel), *The Book Against God* does contain some exceptionally fine prose – enough to make you wonder if Wood should really have been spending so much time on criticism, when he was obviously so full of potential as a novelist.

Upstate, Wood's new novel, offers a chance to see what that potential was worth. The critical response so far has been snippy: Wood has stored up a lot of enemies in his reviewer's warehouse over the years. But it would be a shame to dismiss *Upstate* as just another critic's novel – like Edmund Wilson's *Memoirs of Hecate County* (1942) or Susan Sontag's *The Volcano Lover* – to be sniped at, or semi-respectfully ignored. *Upstate* is a thrillingly good book: moving, funny and superbly intelligent, it compresses a wealth of perception into its 240 immaculately crafted pages.

The protagonist is Alan Querry, a 68-year-old English property developer. The action of the book takes Alan from Northumberland to Saratoga Springs in upstate New York, where his middle-aged daughter Vanessa teaches philosophy. Vanessa has suffered all her life from depression. Now her new boyfriend, Josh, has summoned her family to help with a crisis. There are no showdowns or dramatic reversals – a car accident late in the book comes to nothing. There is only life – or as Wood might say, the real: 'the map over which all novelists thirst'.

Wood's prose is (to borrow his own term) 'life-sown'. He notices the 'bloated raspberry struggling to stay afloat' in a glass of champagne; the 'passive-aggressive' quality of a snowfall, 'insisting on its own white agenda': the 'freezing, martial spaces' of a decaying river town. His characters are permitted their mental digressions – their justifications, their self-descriptions, their passions and evasions. They feel enchantingly real.

A twilit afterlife tends to await the novels of great critics. Never widely read but never entirely forgotten, they bob along behind the larger reputation like tugboats behind a cruise ship. *Upstate* should sail under its own steam: it is a remarkable achievement by a remarkable novelist.

The Sunday Business Post, 6 May 2018

JAMES PATTERSON AND BILL CLINTON
The President Is Missing

James Patterson is the highest-paid fiction writer in the world (this is according to *Business Insider*, which would, presumably, know about such things). Bill Clinton is Bill Clinton: the former US president whose achievements include being impeached for perjury in 1998 and paving the way for the 2008 financial crisis by repealing the Glass-Steagall Act in 1999. Put them together and what do you get? A product that is less a book in the traditional sense and more the sort of mass-market commodity about which sales teams and PR moguls wistfully dream. Think of the brand recognition! Clinton and Patterson, together at last!

The President Is Missing: A Novel, says the cover. This is inaccurate in two senses. For one thing, the presidential hero of *The President Is Missing* doesn't actually go missing (he does, as the parlance has it, 'go rogue' for a while, but his Secret Service team knows exactly where he is at every second, which does spoil things a bit). And for another, *The President Is Missing* is only a novel in the sense that it has chapters and sentences and dialogue and things like that. It's actually just the sort of disposable flotsam you buy in the airport on your way to a beach holiday, like those miniature tubes of toothpaste or those inflatable pillows for the plane. Suntan lotion? Check! Gimmicky book? Check!

The Unique Selling Point of *The President Is Missing* is that it promises to disclose (testify, O blurb!) 'details only a President could know'. So, does our protagonist and narrator, manly war hero President Jonathan Lincoln Duncan, let us in on some juicy official secrets? Well, no, actually. Unless it thrills you to learn that the tunnel connecting the White House to the Treasury Building next door 'was designed in a zigzag pattern precisely to mitigate the impact of a bomb strike', you will come away from *The President Is Missing* disappointed. Things you might actually want to know – like, what's the protocol when the president needs the loo? Do Secret Service agents stand guard outside? – never crop up.

Instead, we get a by-the-numbers thriller (the plot, presumably, is Patterson's contribution) sprinkled with centrist rhetoric (Clinton's). Plot first. President Duncan – who is, like John McCain, a war vet (he was tortured in Iraq during the first Gulf War but 'some things you just don't talk about') – gets word of an apocalyptic cyberattack planned by one Suliman 'Suli' Cindoruk, who is, perhaps a shade unrealistically, a 'secular extreme nationalist' and 'the most dangerous and prolific cyberterrorist in the world'.

The good news is, some of Suli's former collaborators are willing to sell him out. Will President Duncan grow a beard, put on a baseball hat, and secretly leave the White House to meet these defectors? He will! Does the meeting go horribly wrong? It does! Is the president also suffering from an obscure disease (immune thrombocytopenia) that might put him out of action at any moment? He is! Is Russia somehow behind it all? Wait and see! Meanwhile, an international super-assassin code-named Bach does ominous things like stroke her favourite gun (a 'matte-black semi-automatic rifle' named Anna Magdalena) and visit Ford's Theatre ('site of the most daring presidential assassination in the nation's history').

Scattered throughout *The President Is Missing* are some heartwarming mini-lectures about American politics ('That's the permanent mission our Founding Fathers left us – moving toward the "more perfect union"'). That the import of these minilectures is an on-message plea for bipartisan consensus is as unsurprising as it is depressing. Less politically correct – and therefore less boring – are some peculiar bits of self-justification. Sneaking through Washington, DC, in disguise, Duncan spots two white cops beating up a Black man. 'I cross the street and head to my next destination,' Duncan says, before reflecting: 'speeches, words from my bully pulpit – these things can set the right tone, move us in the right direction'. Presidential lives matter.

More entertainingly, Clinton seems to have taken the chance afforded by *The President Is Missing* to rewrite some of the stickier bits of his own presidency. Will Duncan bomb a Middle Eastern target to distract the country from his political troubles – the way Clinton was alleged to have bombed a Sudanese pharmaceutical factory to appear (as Christopher Hitchens put it) 'presidential for a day'? 'No. The answer is no.' Good on you, President Clinton! Uh, I mean, President Duncan! Of course, if *The President Is Missing* really is a bit of Clintonian wishfulfilment in thriller form, I wonder what we should make of the fact that Duncan's wife is conveniently dead?

Absurdly plotted and utterly lacking in irony or ambiguity of any kind, *The President Is Missing* is complete nonsense from start to finish. I enjoyed it enormously.

The Sunday Business Post, 17 June 2018

MARLON JAMES
Black Leopard, Red Wolf

Winning the Man Booker Prize is like winning the lottery: it falls on the deserving and the undeserving alike. Marlon James's *A Brief History of Seven Killings*, which won the prize in 2015, was a deserving winner. It had ambition – more than 700 pages' worth of ambition. Spinning an elaborate alternative history from the nucleus of a real event – the shooting of Bob Marley in Kingston in 1976 – *A Brief History* was rich, dense, lurid. It was a national epic recounted in a furious, highly charged blend of Jamaican patois and jolting prose-poetry. It was much too long. But you can't have everything.

Now James has followed it up with another megalith. *Black Leopard, Red Wolf* is a 640-page fantasy epic set in an imagined precolonial Africa. Here the natural and the magical coexist in slippery and indeterminate ways. The narrator is Tracker, an outcast tribesman with a mystically acute sense of smell – he can find anyone based on their scent, no matter how far away they are. As the novel begins, Tracker has been imprisoned, possibly because he has been responsible for the death of a child (it's hard to tell). The substance of *Black Leopard, Red Wolf* is Tracker's account of his life, spoken to an unidentified 'Inquisitor'.

There is a sense in which *Black Leopard, Red Wolf* is fundamentally unreadable. Take this, from the novel's cryptic opening paragraphs:

> No, I did not kill him. Though I may have wanted him dead
> [...] Oh, to draw a bow and fire it through his black heart
> and watch it explode black blood, and to watch his eyes for
> when they stop blinking, when they look but stop seeing
> [...] Yes, I glut at the conceit of it. But no, I did not kill him.

Violent imagery unspooling in a vacuum is no way to begin a 640-page novel. For half a dozen pages, the reader flails around, trying to deduce basic things like where and when the story takes place, who's speaking, and so on. Clarification arrives, eventually. But James's actual plot – which involves Tracker being recruited by a shape-changing leopard-man to find a missing child for unclear reasons – takes another 115 pages to even begin.

Long before we get there, a sense of readerly disquiet has taken hold. James is inviting us to inhabit the world of myth, with its primary colours and posturing types. Characters make grandiose gestures and say grandiose things: 'I threw the King's blood in the air. "Now both of our fates are mixed," I said.' He has crammed his book with marvels – in the first ten pages, he gives us a wall of vertical river water and a journey to the kingdom of the dead, where Tracker sees 'men who were blue, and women who were green, and children who were yellow, with red eyes and gills in the neck'.

This is inventive. But it's something like the zero degree of inventiveness: daubs of colour standing in for real imaginative detail. The other problem is that when everything is a marvel, nothing is truly marvellous. There's a reason *The Lord of the Rings* begins with a birthday party in a rural village. Plunged into the mythic cosmos of *Black Leopard, Red Wolf*, the reader finds nothing ordinary to light the way.

There's also the prose, which sounds like this:

> I kept walking until I came to an old woman by a river with a tall stick sitting at the banks [...] The stories say she rises each morning youthful and beautiful, blooms full and comely by midday, ages to a crone by nightfall, and dies at midnight to be born again the next hour.

The way to achieve mythic grandeur is not, I would suggest, to make your book sound like a modern translation of *Gilgamesh*.

Black Leopard, Red Wolf has been extravagantly praised by genre stars like Neil Gaiman and Jeff Vandermeer. But in an important sense it fails to do what great fantasy fiction should: i.e. make incontrovertibly real a wholly imagined world. Like an ambitious and energetic tyro's first draft, it's massively over-long and massively underwritten. It's the first volume of a trilogy. God help us all.

The Sunday Business Post, 17 February 2019

MICHEL HOUELLEBECQ
Serotonin

By page seventy of Michel Houellebecq's new novel, the narrator, Florent-Claude, has stepped out of his life and become 'voluntarily missing'. He abandons his expensive Paris apartment, his Japanese girlfriend, Yuzu, and his job (he is 'a contractual worker within the Ministry of Agriculture'). He doesn't go far: he moves into a hotel in the 13th arrondissement. Here he smokes and takes a new antidepressant, Captorix, which works by 'increasing the secretion of serotonin', the neurotransmitter associated with happiness.

Florent-Claude is, of course, the narrator of a Michel Houellebecq novel, which means that leaving his life behind is easy: he doesn't have much to live for. His parents have committed suicide together ('They had taken the pills in the early evening on the day of their fortieth wedding anniversary'). His job is a bureaucratic nothing. Digging around on Yuzu's computer, he has found a video of her having sex with two dogs for the delectation of a room of strange men. His past love affairs have ended in spectacular acts of self-destruction ('I don't feel anything for that girl, I'd been drinking').

As a 'voluntarily missing' person, Florent-Claude is free to wander self-indulgently through his past. He relives his disastrous love affairs. He goes to visit his friend Aymeric, an aristocrat who has tried to make a living as a traditional dairy farmer in Normandy. Everywhere he goes, Florent-Claude encounters despair, emptiness, the void: all the morbid symptoms of the decline of Western social democracy. If this makes *Serotonin* sound like a parody of a Michel Houellebecq novel, well, *Serotonin* very much reads like a parody of a Michel Houellebecq novel. A sad middle-aged man drifts through a meaningless world of make-work jobs, failed love and explicitly described transgressive sex (at one point, we're treated to a repellent two-page description of a 'paedophile video' that has zero bearing on the plot).

There's a standard move that critics (let's be honest: male critics) make when talking about Houellebecq's work. Yes, they say, his work appears to be grimy with misogyny and white male anger – but actually Houellebecq is a very clever analyst of the terminal years of Western culture and his misogyny and hatred should not be taken at face value. He isn't a misogynist, these critics say: he is merely parodying the exhaustion of traditional patriarchal values.

It seems reasonable to wonder about this. Isn't it more sensible to point out that Houellebecq sets out his comic stall in the grey zone where misanthropy is imagined to stand as a sufficient excuse for misogyny? And that the 'comedy' he's selling gets less funny with each book? Take Yuzu, Florent-Claude's Japanese girlfriend. We learn that 'her sexual skills were of a very high level, particularly [in] the crucial area of the blowjob' and that she is 'exceptionally gifted at anal'. We also learn that she likes shopping and 'gangbangs'. And that's all we learn. Yuzu isn't a character: she's an empty object of hatred and desire.

Or take Claire, one of Florent-Claude's other unfortunate exes. When he meets her, after ten years apart, he notes that 'she had swollen up horribly, there was fat poking out more or less everywhere and her face was frankly covered with blotches'. Florent-Claude is depressed: he will not get to have sex with Claire again. You could read this as a grim satire on male shallowness. Or you could read it as male shallowness, undiluted. Certain (male) critics tend to meet Houellebecq more than halfway on this question. But there's something about *Serotonin* – the strange sense of exhaustion and hatred rising unmistakably from its pages, perhaps – that repels critical sympathy.

In the second half of *Serotonin*, Florent-Claude finds himself apathetically involved in a *gilet jaune*-style protest: Aymeric and his fellow farmers (all men), disenfranchised by EU regulations, load their shotguns and stand up for themselves. Aymeric himself reads like another parody of white male rage, and Houellebecq has been praised for anticipating the recent mood of French workers (as he supposedly anticipated the Charlie Hebdo attacks in his last novel, 2015's *Submission*). By this point in the book it is difficult to care, either about the nihilistic characters or about Houellebecq's diagnoses of their ills. 'All of a sudden,' Florent-Claude thinks at one point, 'I felt like a drifting pile of misery.' But it is *Serotonin* itself that is the drifting pile of misery: a plotless book about a depressed man who hates women even more than he hates himself.

In this book the Houellebecq aesthetic – so edgy! so funny! so dark! – stands revealed as nothing but a spent gimmick. Running along the same old track since *Whatever* (1994), Houellebecq's fiction has at last come to embody the very exhaustion it claims to satirize. The end of the West? More like the end of Monsieur H. *Quelle horreur!*

The Sunday Business Post, 3 November 2019

NEW YORK TIMES EDITORS
The Decameron Project

The Covid-19 pandemic is, to understate the case, not over yet. Is it too soon to write about it? Absolutely, if what you're looking for is the definitive fictional take. What is true of the individual life is also true of literature: traumatic experiences need time to percolate, and sometimes it's better to look at them obliquely, rather than directly. The definitive Covid novel or story, if it ever arrives, probably won't even mention Covid, or lockdowns, or Wuhan, or masks, or 5G conspiracy theories – just as the definitive novel about 9/11, Cormac McCarthy's *The Road* (2006), never mentions the World Trade Center attacks at all. Good art tends to work at a remove. It is anti-febrile medication, administered to treat the raging fever of Now.

Which isn't to say that fiction about the pandemic, written right in the heart of the crisis, doesn't have its value. Fiction is one of the most important ways in which we think about the world around us; rapid-response fiction can be just as useful for this purpose as can a carefully considered masterpiece. This was the assumption behind *The Decameron Project*, a concept proposed by the novelist Rivka Galchen in March 2020 and taken up by the editors of *The New York Times Magazine*. Galchen's inspiration was Boccaccio's *Decameron* (1351), the famous anthology of tales told by escapees from the Florentine Black Death. What if, Galchen wondered, the *Times* asked contemporary writers to contribute tales to a Covid-inspired *Decameron*? It's not the worst idea anyone has ever had; though perhaps it's not the best idea, either.

The results appeared in the *Times Magazine* on 12 July 2020; now the stories, or twenty-nine of them at least, appear in book form. Contributors include Colm Tóibín, Margaret Atwood, Kamila Shamsie, Tommy Orange, Etgar Keret, Andrew O'Hagan, Rachel Kushner, Téa Obreht, Charles Yu and David Mitchell – some big names, as they say in the marketing department.

The *NYT* journalist Caitlin Roper contributes a foreword in which she makes some large claims: 'We hadn't expected the degree to which [these writers] would be able to turn the horror of our current moment into something so powerful. It was a reminder that the best fiction can both transport you far away from yourself but also, somehow, help you understand exactly where you are.'

Editorial puffery aside, there is something to be said for the idea that fiction can help us to understand exactly where we are. Usually this occurs with some subtlety – as, for instance, a reading of *The Road* teaches you something about how 9/11 plunged us all into a world of apocalyptic omens and errors. But it can happen in a more straightforward fashion, too. The stories assembled in *The Decameron Project*, taken together, convey a strange feeling of reassurance. If you had to put this feeling into words, you would probably say this: *Whatever I'm going through, in this pandemic, literally everybody else on earth is going through it, too.* Perhaps because it depends on a kind of empathetic leap – the imaginative entry into other minds and other hearts – it turns out that fiction can do this in a way that no amount of journalistic hot takes can manage.

The individual stories are, of course, hopelessly variable in quality. The most sensible of the writers included here work by parable; the less sensible, by direct address. Margaret Atwood contributes a science-fictional squib about octopoidal aliens who have arrived to take care of us during a time of plague; one of their number, who calls itself 'a mere entertainer' retells the fairy tale of Patient Griselda in such a way as to suggest that its human charges will very soon be turned into food.

Rachel Kushner's 'The Girl with the Big Red Suitcase' is probably the best piece in the book. Framed, like the *Decameron* itself, as a story told in a villa during a time of plague – in this case, an artist's retreat – it's a beautifully devious bit of old-fashioned storytelling, about a Norwegian writer and the tale of how he met his wife. Charles Yu's 'Systems', on the other hand, is no better than its dud premise: it's narrated, in alternate paragraphs, by Google and Covid-19, and it is exactly as bad as it sounds.

Colm Tóibín's 'Tales from the L.A. River' takes the form of a diary kept by a middle-aged writer marooned by lockdown in LA and keeping fit, with his boyfriend, by cycling. In summary, it's banal; in execution, typically graceful and moving. David Mitchell's 'If Wishes Was Horses' is a ghost story so transparent you see the twist coming from the first page (what happened to the author of *Cloud Atlas*?). On the other hand, Karen Russell's 'Line 19 Woodstock/Glisan' manages to find a powerful analogy for the Covid experience: a bus driver, Valerie, finds her bus and all of its passengers frozen in a moment of magically distended time, just before it hits an ambulance; in this moment of suspension, they must work together to change things, or they will all die. Thus, everyone, as Covid rages.

So: a mixed bag. But how could it be otherwise? More to the point: these are fevered stories, written in a fevered time. Will the fever break? And when it does, what stories will we tell about it? *The Decameron Project*, I'm afraid, leaves us where we started: awaiting stronger medicine.

Irish Independent, 29 November 2020

ROISIN KIBERD
The Disconnect: A Personal Journey
Through the Internet

Generationally speaking, the internet is a millennial: born in the late 80s, and now entering its uncertain thirties. On the world-historical scale, though, the internet remains the *enfant terrible* of communications technologies. By comparison, the printed codex has been with us for six centuries; TV is tuning up for its first centenary (in 2027); commercial radio is doddering towards its 121st birthday this year. All of these established technologies are now boringly regulated, declared largely safe for daily use (barring the occasional panic about, say, the crassness of reality television). But the internet hasn't yet been tamed, or even, perhaps, properly understood.

Now millennials themselves – the people who have grown up alongside (or maybe just on) the internet – are beginning to ask what the new technologies mean, and to write searching books about their online lives. 'I was born in Dublin,' writes the journalist and essayist Roisin Kiberd, 'the same month and year as the internet as we know it' – that is, in March 1989, when Tim Berners-Lee submitted his proposal for a 'World Wide Web' to his employers at CERN. From this fateful conjuncture, Kiberd has spun a dark, funny, unsettling and in some ways problematically limited 'personal history' of our extremely online world.

'I am an emotional cyborg,' Kiberd writes her preface. 'I outsource my opinions, my memories and my identity to the internet, and I have spent more time with my laptop than with any living being on earth.' For Kiberd, and for other members of her generation, 'the internet and mental health' are 'closely intertwined'. Promised a technological utopia, internet users have instead been 'led into fixed identities, each person given a biography, a Timeline, and a filter bubble of their own'. The result, for Kiberd at least, has been 'a slow depersonalisation' in which she has found herself 'cut off from reality, from sincerity and sensation'. In 2016, she attempted suicide. 'It took a while to realise that the internet had eaten my life. It took even longer to realise that I was experiencing a breakdown, because so much of the internet feels like a breakdown already.'

The essays collected in *The Disconnect* – which range beyond the codes and cultures of the web to tackle other hypercapitalist grotesqueries (energy drinks, 24-hour gyms, sleep hotels) – were written, Kiberd says, 'during and about a process of recovery, but not withdrawal, from the internet. They are an attempt to make sense of what we've lost, and to consider the lonely dystopia in front of us'.

As a sequence of subjective reports from the heart of the lonely dystopia, *The Disconnect* is superbly choreographed. The prose is sometimes witty and aphoristic ('The history of the internet is a history of girls in their bedrooms, waiting for someone's message or call'); sometimes lyrical (drinking

Monster Energy: 'Starry-eyed, shaky, my mind becomes a hive of bees, my heartbeat an ill-mannered rattle'); sometimes scathing (the Dublin docklands, transformed by Big Tech, are now 'an enclave of a new and stratified Ireland', a place 'designed to be seen from a boardroom: tall buildings, surrounded by other tall buildings, air-conditioned and clinical and gleaming').

The two best pieces in the book are 'The Night Gym', in which Kiberd ruminates on the phenomenon of the 24-hour gym and its CEO-worshipping culture of 'luxurious abstention', and 'Bland God: Notes on Mark Zuckerberg', a reflection on the Facebook founder as 'a model of millennial blamelessness', a 'cybernetic black hole'. In these essays, ideas crowd the pages. There is a coldness to Kiberd's perceptions that serves her, and her readers, extremely well, as she maps with an unblinking gaze the smooth and sinister territories where money, tech and culture intersect, the world of 'unicorns, blitzscaling and vaporwave'.

Slightly less satisfying are the essays about energy drinks, online dating and the capitalist colonization of sleep. These pieces offer a volatile synthesis of raw confessional essay, quasi-Marxist cultural criticism and opinionated reportage that is reminiscent of – and suffers from some of the same flaws as – quite a lot of recent writing by millennials about 'late capitalism' and the internet. Take 'Monstrous Energy', a witty reflection on Kiberd's addiction to caffeinated energy drinks. Products like Monster Energy, Hype Energy and Red Bull, she argues, tell us important things about the culture of work in the twenty-first century: 'Where once energy drinks were geared towards recovery and wellness, now they are about performance enhancement in the capitalist hellscape.'

The glibness of that last phrase is indicative of a larger problem with *The Disconnect* (and, I would suggest, with a great deal of contemporary cultural criticism). In these essays, the experience of personal crisis (depression, anxiety) is used to guarantee the authenticity of the cultural analysis, and cultural analysis appears not as rigorous critique, but as the aphoristic outgrowth of personal crisis.

What this means is that *The Disconnect* tends to portray 'the capitalist hellscape' as the sole cause of personal crisis, and personal crisis as illustrative of all that is wrong with the capitalist hellscape. It's a hall of mirrors: capitalism, in this view of things, ends up looking a lot like depression, and depression ends up looking a lot like capitalism. 'The internet today is boring,' Kiberd says in her preface. It's a startling insight, and one that feels true: with most of human knowledge in your pocket, it's amazing how quickly, these days, you can run out of interesting things to do online. (Shop. Scroll. Text. Post. Like. Repeat.) But Kiberd doesn't chase down the implication: that a boring technology is one that has already lost some of its power to shape our minds, and that there might be more to the future than an endlessly unfurling 'capitalist hellscape'.

Until then, of course, we are in urgent need of lucid reports from the hellscape's digital heart. We should count ourselves lucky, therefore, to have Roisin Kiberd, sending us these glittering, provocative notes from the frontiers of the lonely dystopia.

The Irish Times, 6 March 2021

SALLY ROONEY
Beautiful World, Where Are You

It isn't a millennial love story. It's two millennial love stories. Alice, a writer, falls in love with Felix, who works in a shipping warehouse. Meanwhile Eileen, a literary editor, falls for Simon, an older parliamentary adviser. The couples flirt. They sleep together. They have minor crises. They find out who they are.

Rooney territory, obviously. But if the emotional temperature of *Conversations with Friends* and *Normal People* was medium-cool, the emotional temperature of *Beautiful World, Where Are You* tracks closer to zero degree, at least for the first three-quarters of the book. (In the last quarter, things warm up emotionally and the book collapses.)

The novel alternates between chapters composed in a chilly third-person objective mode and chapter-length emails between Alice and Eileen, who became intimate friends in college and who are doing their best to carry that intimacy into their uncertain late twenties. The third-person chapters subject the characters' vicissitudes to a deadpan gaze. The emails – by far the best bits of the book – allow Alice and Eileen to talk about ideas. What does it mean to believe in God? Is our civilization about to collapse? What is sex for? Has the literary novel become irrelevant?

Both methods – the distant third person and the emails – invite the suspension of judgement. We see these characters from the outside; and, in the case of Eileen and Alice, we read their unedited self-presentations. The author tactfully withdraws, leaving the business of analysis to us.

To Sally Rooney's enormous credit, she has not bothered to pretend that she is not Sally Rooney (Sally Rooney!), or that her third novel is not Sally Rooney's Third Novel. Rooney, famously, is a Marxist. Appropriately, therefore, *Beautiful World, Where Are You* exists in a dialectical relationship to Rooney's first two books. Alice and Felix recapitulate Marianne and Connell from *Normal People* (class difference; emotional misunderstandings). Eileen and Simon recapitulate Frances and Nick from *Conversations with Friends* (age difference; emotional misunderstandings). But the low-temperature prose, and the resolutely limited point of view, are designed to frustrate the sort of easy identification with character that the earlier novels invited.

Even more to the point, Alice has published two gigantically successful novels about relationships while still in her twenties, and has found herself (as she puts it) 'a widely despised celebrity novelist'. Alice's success has alienated her, not just from Eileen, but from life itself. When the novel begins, she has escaped, alone, to a house in a Mayo village (this is where she meets Felix). To Eileen, she writes: 'I can't believe I have to tolerate these things – having articles written about me, and seeing my photograph on the internet, and reading comments about myself.' Her own fame, she suggests, is a symptom of a 'disfiguring social disease'.

Interestingly, the novel doesn't really reconcile Alice to her celebrity. At the end, she is still complaining to Eileen about the online response to her public image. Her complaints about her success are, of course, simultaneously an accurate perception of reality and the sort of thing a depressed person might harp on – just as, when she pops out to Spar for lunch, she cannot help but think about the exploited workers whose labour stocks the shelves. Thus Rooney provides cover for her critiques of capitalism and of her own success: Alice, of course, is depressed; this is how she would feel.

If, as Rooney herself has said, her first two books echo the classic nineteenth-century novels of love and marriage (Connell in *Normal People*, of course, is moved by Jane Austen's *Emma*), then *Beautiful World, Where Are You* toys with other inheritances. Alice and Eileen's emails hark back both to eighteenth-century epistolary fiction (Samuel Richardson's *Pamela*, Choderlos de Laclos's *Les Liaisons Dangereuses*) and to the novel of ideas, in which characters become mouthpieces for particular intellectual positions (Aldous Huxley's *Crome Yellow*, Thomas Love Peacock's *Headlong Hall*). The third-person chapters are reminiscent of the 1950s French nouveau roman, with its precise, robotic descriptions of surfaces and empty rooms.

To attempt to combine these disparate traditions in a single novel is evidence of enormous intellectual ambition. To say that Rooney only partly succeeds in synthesizing all of this stuff effectively is really to cavil, since the intellectual richness of the book is one of the most impressive things about it.

It's also probably cavilling to point out that the novel states its Big Themes (climate change, civilizational collapse, inequality, the possibility of religious belief) but doesn't really dramatize them. Alice and Eileen – privileged, profoundly intelligent – discuss these concepts eloquently. Their emails are vastly pleasurable to read. But the ideas they discuss don't especially impinge on the book's central drama, which is about (that ancient theme) the relationship between self-knowledge and love.

There is a fascinating undercurrent of hostility towards the reader in this novel. It wants both to satisfy and to alienate its audience: both to scare off the plain folk who wept over Connell and Marianne and to create equally vivid characters in the frame of an equally moving love story. Among the topics debated by Alice and Eileen is the worth of literary fiction. 'Who can care,' Alice asks, 'what happens to the novel's protagonists, when it's happening in the context of an increasingly fast, increasingly brutal exploitation of a majority of the human species? [...] My own work is, it goes without saying, the worst culprit in this regard.'

Alice's argument might make us feel abashed for reading, and enjoying, a novel about privileged young women falling in love. Or perhaps we might wonder why, if this is a genuine concern of Rooney's (as opposed simply to the voice of Alice's depression), no one in the novel changes their life in response to this brutal exploitation. In Benjamin Kunkel's *Indecision* (2005), the hapless narrator gives up his Western privilege to become a Marxist activist. Rooney's characters do not do this. They enjoy their privilege anxiously, but they do not reject it or seek to change the world. They have their cake and eat it, too. Sometimes you find yourself wondering if this is also what Rooney is attempting. She wants to write a successful novel that declares novels irrelevant. She wants to critique her fame while also courting it. It's a tricky path to travel. But Rooney is gifted in many ways. She shouldn't be underestimated.

What's good about *Beautiful World, Where Are You*? Many things. Alice and Eileen are convincingly real. Rooney writes about sex superbly well. The book is full of interesting ideas.

Its various unreconciled aesthetic elements (the soapy ending; the fact that Felix and Simon are wish-fulfilment figures rather than believable characters), jostle fascinatingly alongside the richness of its ideas, the stray pleasures of its prose, and the complexities of its ambition. The faults of gifted writers are often more instructive than the competencies of bad ones. Accordingly, *Beautiful World, Where Are You* is not just worth reading. It's worth thinking about.

The Irish Independent, 2 September 2021

COLSON WHITEHEAD
Harlem Shuffle

Mr Realism himself, James Wood, has never actually reviewed a Colson Whitehead novel. But he has, over the years, shot a few casual arrows Whitehead's way. Writing about Jonathan Lethem for *The New Republic* in 2003, Wood complained that both Lethem and Whitehead are 'fond of rampantly dangling sentences'. And assessing David Foster Wallace for the *London Review of Books* in 2004, Wood remarked in an aside that 'Colson Whitehead's prose frequently seems unaware of its own illiteracy'.

Hardly surprising that Wood, who proposed in *How Fiction Works* (2008) that realism is not a genre but rather 'the origin' – 'what allows magical realism, hysterical realism, fantasy, science fiction, even thrillers, to exist' – should scorn Whitehead, a playfully belated practitioner of genre pastiche. But interesting that Wood should go out of his way to demote Whitehead's talents as a prose stylist, because, like any good pasticheur, Whitehead is really something of a prose virtuoso. His books are dense with densely worked phrases. His control over assonance and his feeling for the internal structure of a paragraph bespeak both a finely tuned literary ear and a profound self-consciousness about the technical aspects of writing: imagery, pacing, telling detail. Admire me! his sentence say. And they are often easy to admire. Perhaps, actually, a bit too easy.

I can't be the only reader who finds Whitehead's self-consciousness to be peculiarly contagious. In other words, you tend to become aware of yourself in the act of admiring his sentences. 'What a fabulous sentence,' you say to yourself, as you read. It doesn't make for easy involvement in the story. Plenty of writers want to stun you into admiration, of course, and don't especially care about the story. And there are sound aesthetic reasons to write the sort of prose that enforces critical distance from the story being told – this, really, is both Modernism 101 and Postmodernism 101.

But this isn't quite what Whitehead is doing. His stories are *meant* to involve you. They're meant to evoke pathos and narrative tension, to create memorable characters. But his books don't really do pathos; they do 'pathos' (more marvellous sentences). They don't really do narrative tension; they do 'narrative tension'. And they don't really do memorable characters; they do 'memorable characters'.

Whitehead's breakthrough hit, *The Underground Railroad* (2016), offers a case in point. Page by page, the prose is beautifully engineered. The central conceit is one of those ideas so good it seems blindingly obvious in retrospect: what if the Underground Railroad conducting escaped slave northward had been an actual underground railroad? But Whitehead, hobbled by self-consciousness, handles this conceit with tweezers: it remains, for all of the passion and care with which he sets it forth, not so much a brilliant conceit as 'a brilliant conceit'. *Zone One* (2011) is a zombie novel done with high literary production values – again, a slam-bang, why-didn't-I-think-of-that? idea. But in execution it reads as simply that: *Dawn of the Dead* with brilliant prose and some witty gags (the military clean-up crew receiving their marching orders in an empty Chinese dumpling joint: clever, yes; more than that? Not so much).

Harlem Shuffle, Whitehead's eighth novel, is another pastiche, this time of the 1950s noir thrillers of (mostly) Chester Himes and (a little bit) Raymond Chandler. Ray Carney operates his own furniture store on 125th street in Harlem. Occasionally he fences stolen goods, in a don't-ask-don't-tell sort of way, for his no-goodnik cousin Freddie. Ray's father was a low-end gangster; now Ray is (mostly) going straight. When the novel begins, the year is 1959: a period when it is necessary for a Black businessmen to sell mostly to Black customers; when, if a Black person wants to travel south, they need to know 'the safe routes around the sundown towns and cracker territories where you might not make it out alive'.

Freddie (who is, along with Ray, Miami Joe and Pepper, a half-vivified cliché) has sucked Ray into a big-time heist at the Hotel Theresa, 'the Waldorf of Harlem'. In the aftermath, things, of course, go wrong. Arthur winds up dead. Ray has a daughter and a pregnant wife. He has been 'a wall between the criminal world and the straight world, necessary, bearing the load'. Will he be able to bear the load much longer? Will the repercussions of Ray's actions play out over the years that follow?

Whitehead plays things straight – that is to say, he plays them 'straight'. The noir lingo is precisely marshalled: 'they thumped up the stairs, these mean-eyed rogues with flashy style and smiles as counterfeit as the twenties in their hip pockets'. Sometimes a wonky lyricism: the city is 'that rustling,

keening thing of people and concrete'. Also occasional jolts of
the real thing: 'Or the city did exist but he stood with it heaving
against him.'

It all spools by, feeling twice-belated: carefully done, often
dazzling; overall, oddly willed and unconvincing. Take those
'mean-eyed rogues'. We see the language. We don't see the eyes,
or the rogues themselves. This being the whole problem. The
idea, I suppose, is to bring those high literary production values
to bear on another marginal genre. The production values are
there, all right. But the screen feels strangely empty.

Literary Review, October 2021

Envoi

CLIVE JAMES (1939–2019)

He called his first book *The Metropolitan Critic*, and metropolitan is what he thought every critic should be: urban and urbane, scorning the ivory tower for the café and the pub, filing copy to deadline like any other professional, and turning the critical eye on anything that wasn't nailed down. But by metropolitan he also meant cosmopolitan, in the old-fashioned liberal-humanist sense of the word. His model was Edmund Wilson, the twentieth century's exemplary critic-without-portfolio, and 'The Metropolitan Critic', that first book's title essay, is both a portrait of Wilson and a self-portrait of Clive James himself in 1972 – or perhaps it's a portrait of what James knew he would one day become:

> He is the ideal of the metropolitan critic, who understood from the beginning that the intelligence of the metropolis is in a certain relation to the intelligence of the academy, and went on understanding this even when the intelligence of the academy ceased to understand its relation to

the intelligence of the metropolis. When Wilson called the Modern Language Association to order, he performed the most important academic act of the post-war years – he reminded the scholars that their duty was to literature.

The metropolis is not the academy: this was the point. Clive James knew that the literary essay, the book review, the *feuilleton* (whatever you want to call it: the occasional piece written to enlighten and amuse) was not just where culture happened, but where art could happen, too, especially if you believed that 'literary journalism ought to be written from deep personal commitment and to the highest standards of cogency the writer could attain'. As James saw it, neither culture nor art stood much chance of happening in theory-besotted university departments. Here he is, in *Cultural Amnesia* (2007), on Walter Benjamin:

> Part of his sad fate has been to have his name bandied about the intellectual world without very many of its inhabitants being quite sure why, apart from the vague idea that he was a literary critic who somehow got beyond literary criticism: he got up into the realm of theory, where critics rank as philosophers if they are hard enough to read.

Which is, or should be, the final word on a whole generation of 'theorists' and their academic epigones. But James knew that it would not be the final word, and that 'an unintelligent intelligentsia is a permanent feature of human history'. He knew that the hard-to-read would go on being worshipped, and that writers who were merely funny, informed and scrupulously honest would have to find their way as best they could.

Merely funny: as if being funny wasn't the best thing a writer could be, and as if being funny wasn't an aspect of being sane – maybe the defining aspect ('a sense of humour', he wrote, late in life, 'is just common sense dancing'). James enjoyed one great advantage over his hero Edmund Wilson: he was funny. Of course, being funnier than Edmund Wilson isn't exactly a major accomplishment. But James was funnier than everyone else, too. His TV columns for the *Observer*, collected in *Visions Before Midnight* (1977), *The Crystal Bucket* (1981) and *Glued to the Box* (1983), remain readable when every trace of the programmes he reviewed has vanished from the collective memory: because they're funny. 'Mary and Plunket were both insistent that work should be enjoyed, but never got around to tackling the problem posed by the millions of people who are well aware of this, but still don't enjoy their work.' You don't have to know who Mary and Plunket were to get the gag. And his books are full of sentences like that one. No, not just full: replete. Open any book to any page and there it is: a sentence so good that most of us would be happy to have written nothing else that year, or that decade, or that lifetime. On Judith Krantz's sex-and-shopping opus *Princess Daisy*: 'As a work of art it has the same status as a long conversation between two not very bright drunks, but as bestsellers go it argues for a reassuringly robust connection between fiction and the reading public.'

He could do this stuff at will. Everyone knows his description of Arnold Schwarzenegger: 'a brown condom filled with walnuts'. But everyone *should* know his description of the Sydney Opera House: 'a typewriter full of oyster shells'. Or his retitling of a TV programme featuring Jonathan Miller in conversation with Susan Sontag: 'Captain Eclectic Meets Thinkwoman.' Or his assertion that *Moby-Dick* is 'one of those books you can't get started with even after you've finished it'. Or his crushing summary of the career of Colin Wilson, author of the 1956 pop-philosophy hit *The Outsider*: 'His reputation ebbed away to the peripheral bedsits of the barely employable not-quite-bright, where it lined itself up along brick-and-pine bookshelves in a row of paperbacks from progressively less prestigious publishers.' The Wilson piece was so devastating that, when it was collected in *The Metropolitan Critic*, James felt moved to apologize for it: 'This is a textbook example of how not to write an article.' Of course, it isn't any such thing. What James meant was that obliterating Wilson was too easy – that Wilson himself was such a clodhopping literalist that setting Clive James on him was like dropping a nuclear warhead on a water pistol. The brilliant are as susceptible to temptation as the rest of us. He could do it; so he did it.

To borrow a gag from Martin Amis's *The Information*, when Clive James reviewed a book, it stayed reviewed. Once a year or so I reread his assessment of John Le Carré's *The Honourable Schoolboy* (collected in *From the Land of Shadows*, 1982):

> To start with, the prose style is overblown. Incompatible metaphors fight for living space in the same sentence. 'Now at first Smiley tested the water with Sam – and Sam, who liked a poker hand himself, tested the water with Smiley.' Are they playing cards in the bath? Such would-be taciturnity is just garrulousness run short of breath.

Unimprovable. Sometimes he overdid it, of course. Writing about the sex life of Ford Madox Ford (the piece appears in *The Metropolitan Critic*), he couldn't stop himself: 'The Grade A crumpet came at him like kamikazes, crashing through his upper decks in gaudy cataracts of fire.' To say that you wouldn't get away with that nowadays is to ignore the fact that James barely got away with it then. The least of it was that he was mocked for engaging in 'stunt writing', and it's fair to say that he never managed entirely to dispel the whiff of attention-seeking that wafted from his fancier phrases. But stunts, by definition, are memorable – maybe especially when they don't come off. 'Kamikaze crumpet' is a permanent fixture of my mental concordance of Clive James one-liners. It doesn't really work, but it only fails according to the highest standards of taste (although I do cringe at 'Grade A crumpet' – you wouldn't get way with that nowadays because you *shouldn't* get away with it). Lesser writers don't even fail this interestingly. The danger with stunt writing, I suppose, is that it will lapse into spectacle. But spectacles are – what else? – spectacular. Even a failed spectacle is worth the price of admission.

The glittering, omniscient style was there from the beginning, though he always spoke of himself as a slow learner. On Keats: 'Given all the qualities at a young age, it would have been large of Keats to envy the plodders who acquire them, if at all, only over time.' Implicitly, James aligns himself with the plodders. But in his early essays (the Edmund Wilson piece, done anonymously for the *TLS*, was his first big hit), the voice is already there: the big square paragraphs (solid blocks of thought, with every corner sealed up tight); every rift loaded with ore; the sentences that hinged on neat reversals, or reversed themselves neatly on hinges smoothly oiled by extended metaphors (tricky to do, as you can see; he made it look easy).

Several generations of writers have now tinkered with the Clive James formula: not just TV critics (Charlie Brooker equals Clive James plus misanthropy) but restaurant critics (A.A. Gill equals Clive James plus snobbery), theatre critics, movie critics (Anthony Lane equals Clive James plus archness). But there is no substitute for the real thing. And he never stopped producing the real thing. The voice that comes through the pages of *Latest Readings*, a short collection of literary essays published in 2015, when James was already gravely ill with leukaemia and COPD, is still the voice of the metropolitan critic: 'How did literary theory get started? Because the theorists couldn't write.'

He could write. And he had read everything, and he made you want to read everything, too, even if it was always tempting simply to read more of him instead: how could the classic writers he praised (Montale, Hazlitt, Benedetto Croce) possibly be as entertaining as he was? *Cultural Amnesia* – 876 pages in my Picador hardback edition – would be endlessly re-readable even if it was twice as long and included twice as many essays on writers I had never heard of before I read it and still have not gotten around to reading even now (Marcel Reich-Ranicki? Alfred Polgar? Leszek Kolakowski?).

Cultural Amnesia is the book for which he hoped to be remembered, even if his title satirized his ambition before the first page was turned. Alphabetically arranged and subtitled *Notes in the Margin of My Time*, *Cultural Amnesia* is a kaleidoscope of *feuilletons*: essays of startling brilliance on writers from Anna Akhmatova to Stefan Zweig, though really, as James says in his introduction, it is a single digressive essay about 'philosophy, history, politics, and the arts all at once, and about what happened to those things during the course of the multiple catastrophes into whose second principle outburst (World War I was the first) I had been born in 1939'.

In other words, *Cultural Amnesia* is a kind of *summa theologica* of the politically sceptical, passionately literary strain of twentieth-century liberal humanism. This was what the metropolitan critic represented and embodied, and in *Cultural Amnesia* we meet the metropolitan critic in full cosmopolitan flight. In writing it, James knew that he was fighting a rearguard action ('a competent writer would look twice at "rearguard action" to make sure that he means to evoke a losing battle' – from the essay on Georg Christoph Lichtenberg). Of the twenty-first century – which grew from the twentieth century, he said, 'as a column of black smoke grows from an oil fire' – James observed that 'the arts and their attendant scholarship are everywhere [...] they have a glamour unprecedented in history – but humanism is hard to find'.